A GEORGE ELIOT COMPANION

A GEORGE ELIOT COMPANION

Literary Achievement and Modern Significance

F. B. PINION

Barnes & Noble
Totowa, New Jersey

First published 1981 by
THE MACMILLAN PRESS LTD
London and Basingstoke
Companies and representatives
throughout the world

First published 1981 in the USA by
BARNES & NOBLE BOOKS
81 Adams Drive
Totowa, New Jersey, 07512

MACMILLAN ISBN 0 333 25594 1
BARNES & NOBLE ISBN 0 389 20208 8

Typeset in Great Britain by
Scarborough Typesetting Services
and printed in Hong Kong

Contents

Contents

List of Maps and Plates

Reference Abbreviations

Fiction

(small roman numerals indicate chapters; ep. = epigraph)

AB	*Adam Bede*	R	*Romola*
DD	*Daniel Deronda*	SCL1	'Amos Barton'
FH	*Felix Holt*	SCL2	'Mr Gilfil's Love-Story'
M	*Middlemarch*	SCL3	'Janet's Repentance'
MF	*The Mill on the Floss*	SM	*Silas Marner*

TS	*Impressions of Theophrastus Such*
WR	*The Westminster Review*

Letters

Most of the extracts are taken from *George Eliot's Life* by J. W. Cross, and, as dates provide the only form of ready access to the letters in that work, they have been preferred for reference. With hardly an exception, all extracts will be found in Gordon S. Haight's *The George Eliot Letters*, the text of which has been followed by kind permission of Yale University Press and the editor.

Acknowledgments

My greatest obligation is to Professor Gordon S. Haight. His well-known biography of George Eliot and his magnificent edition of her correspondence have been my major reference books, and I have welcomed his assurances on a number of points, mainly connected with the brief visit paid by the Leweses to Gainsborough. I wish to thank him and Yale University Press for permission to quote from *The George Eliot Letters*, and also to use the text of that edition for extracts from the letters and journals in J. W. Cross's *George Eliot's Life*. Most of the passages quoted from her reviews and earlier essays are taken from Thomas Pinney (ed.), *Essays of George Eliot*, Routledge & Kegan Paul, 1963.

I am most grateful to the Warwickshire County Library, Nuneaton, for generous assistance at all times; also to the City of Coventry Libraries Arts and Museums Department, and Miss V. Gilbert in particular; the President of the George Eliot Fellowship, Tenniel Evans; and its most helpful Secretary, Mrs Kathleen Adams.

I am especially indebted to Dr Clyde Binfield for checking the chapter on relevant historical background, and for adding precision to some of the more complicated issues. One section of this survey owes much to John Prest, *The Industrial Revolution in Coventry*, Oxford University Press, 1960; a few details derive from the more historical portions of Marcella M. Carver, *A Positivist Life*, Brookside Press, 1976.

Mrs Elsie Bellamy very kindly sent me an interesting collection of George Eliot material when this work was begun, and Professor Colin Beattie and Dr James Oakden have provided helpful information on medical and dialectal questions.

Illustrations have entailed many obligations: to Mr P. R. Morley and his staff at the University of Sheffield for photographic assistance; Mr David Fletcher, on behalf of William Blackwood and

Sons, Ltd (plates 1 below, 9 above and below, 15 above and below, 16–17 above and below, 18–20, 23 above and below, 24 right); the Warwickshire County Library, Nuneaton (1 above, 2 above, 3 above and below, 5 above, 6 below, 7 below, 12 above and below, 13 all three); the City of Coventry Libraries Arts and Museums Department (7 above, 8 above, 8 below left and right, 10 left, 11 left, 14 below left); Hodder and Stoughton, Ltd (5 below, 6 above, from a centenary article in *The Bookman*, November 1919); and the Sheffield Central Library (14 below right, from *A Selection of Views in the County of Lincoln*, 1805). Plates 10 right and 24 left are reproduced by courtesy of Mrs Susan Womersley and the Lady Reigate respectively; 22 has been supplied by the National Portrait Gallery; 2 below is the author's. Plate 21 is from *The Cornhill Magazine*; 4 above, from William Mottram, *The True Story of George Eliot*, Fisher Unwin, 1905; 4 below, from Charles S. Olcott, *George Eliot, Scenes and People in her Novels*, Cassell, 1911; 14 above, from Herbert Spencer, *An Autobiography*, Williams and Norgate, 1904; and 11 right, from *Chambers's Cyclopaedia of English Literature*, W. and R. Chambers, 1906.

Finally I wish to thank Mr T. M. Farmiloe, Miss Julia Tame, and Mrs Ann Marangos for their co-operation on behalf of the publishers; above all, my wife, for her assiduity in helping to check and clarify the text at important stages in its development.

Chronology

1773   Birth of Robert Evans
1789   *Outbreak of the French Revolution*
1793   *England at war with France*
1801   Robert Evans' first marriage. *Negotiations for peace with France*
1802   *Peace of Amiens*
1803   *War with France resumed*
1806   Robert Evans takes over the management of the Arbury estate
1813   His second marriage
1815   *End of the war with Napoleon*
1819   Mary Anne Evans born at South Farm, Arbury (22 November), a few months before her family moves to the farm at Griff
1824   After attending the dame school across the road from Griff House, she joins her sister Christiana as a boarding-school pupil at Attleborough
1828   Sent to a boarding school at Nuneaton where the evangelical Maria Lewis is the principal teacher
1829   *Catholic Emancipation Act*
1832   *First Reform Bill. Election riot at Nuneaton.* Mary Evans transferred to the Franklin sisters' school at Coventry
1836   After the death of her mother (3 February) she shares the management of affairs at home with her sister; reads Walter Scott to her father in the evenings
1837   In charge at home after the marriage of Christiana in May
1839   Visited by her Methodist aunt Mrs Samuel Evans
1840   Travels with her father to her aunt's at Wirksworth, and to other relatives in Staffordshire (June). *The penny post instituted*

1

1841   They move to Foleshill, near Coventry, leaving her brother Isaac in charge at Griff

1842   Buys Charles Hennell's *An Inquiry into the Origins of Christianity*, and asserts her religious independence (January)

1843   Stays at Devizes with Dr and Mrs Brabant (November–December)

1844   Agrees to continue the translation of Strauss's *Das Leben Jesu* which Miss Brabant had begun (published in 1846)

1845   Rejects a marriage proposal. Visits Scotland (October)

1849   Begins her translation of Spinoza's *Tractatus Theologico-Politicus*. Death of her father. European holiday with the Brays. Remains at Geneva from July to March 1850

1850   Reviews Mackay's *The Progress of the Intellect* at the request of its publisher John Chapman

1851   Lives in the Chapman ménage (January–March). *The Great Exhibition opened at the Crystal Palace, Hyde Park, 1 May.* Returns in September to undertake the editing of *The Westminster Review*, which Chapman (the nominal editor) purchases

1852   The first number under its new editorship appears in January. Friendship with Herbert Spencer

1853   Growing friendship with George Henry Lewes. Translation of Feuerbach's *The Essence of Christianity* begun (published in 1854). Lewes's *Comte's Philosophy of the Sciences* (September) and Harriet Martineau's *The Positive Philosophy of Auguste Comte* (November) published

1854   *The re-erected Crystal Palace, Sydenham, opened (June).* 'Marian' Evans leaves England for Weimar with Lewes (July). They meet Liszt. She begins the translation of Spinoza's *Ethics* in Berlin

1855   Return to England (March). They settle at Richmond (October)

1856   'Naturalizing' at Ilfracombe and Tenby. Begins 'Amos Barton' in September, and 'Mr Gilfil's Love-Story' on Christmas Eve

1857   Lewes's *Seaside Studies* continued in the Scillies and Jersey, where 'Janet's Repentance' is concluded. *Adam Bede* begun (October)

1858   Continued in Europe (April–August) and finished in November

1859   Move to Holly Lodge, Wandsworth (February). 'The Lifted

Veil' written, and *The Mill on the Floss* resumed. Wales, Weymouth, and Gainsborough (August–September)

1860   *The Mill on the Floss* completed (March). Italy (March–June). 'Brother Jacob' written, and *Silas Marner* begun. Move to 16 Blandford Square in December

1861   *Silas Marner* finished (March). *Outbreak of the American Civil War.* Second visit to Florence. Preparation in London for *Romola*, which George Eliot begins in October

1862   Starts *Romola* afresh. Publication begins in *The Cornhill* (July)

1863   The novel completed (June). Move to the Priory, Regent's Park, in November

1864   Visit to Italy. First version of *The Spanish Gypsy* abandoned

1865   *Felix Holt* begun (March). *End of the American Civil War*

1866   The novel completed, and work on *The Spanish Gypsy* resumed

1867   In Spain (January–March). *The Second Reform Bill passed*

1868   *The Spanish Gypsy* completed (April). Germany (June–July)

1869   Fourth visit to Italy (March–May). *Middlemarch* begun (August). Death of Thornton Lewes (October)

1870   *Forster's Education Act passed, to provide primary education for all*

1872   All but the finale of *Middlemarch* completed by September. Homburg, Stuttgart, and Karlsruhe

1873   Preparations for *Daniel Deronda*

1874   First sketches of the novel (January–February). *The Legend of Jubal and Other Poems* published (May)

1876   *Daniel Deronda* finished in June

1878   Essays written at Witley (published as *Impressions of Theophrastus Such* in 1879). Death of Lewes on 30 November

1879   Death of John Blackwood, George Eliot's publisher (29 October)

1880   She marries J. W. Cross (May). Dies at 4 Cheyne Walk, Chelsea, on 22 December

1885   *George Eliot's Life* by J. W. Cross published

George Eliot's Life

The most critical turning-point in the life of Mary Anne Evans came when she decided to live with George Henry Lewes. But for this she might not have been a novelist, and would never have been known as 'George Eliot'. She chose 'George' for her *nom de plume* because it was her husband's name, and 'Eliot' because it was 'a good mouth-filling, easily-pronounced word'.

The most important event in the genesis of the novelist George Eliot took place much earlier, in June 1840, when Mary Ann (as she wrote her name at the time; later it was 'Marian') drove at the age of twenty with her widowed father Robert Evans on family visits, first to Wirksworth in Derbyshire, then on to Ellastone, Staffordshire. After staying overnight and much of the next day with Samuel and Elizabeth Evans at Wirksworth, they spent three days at Ellastone. Aunt Elizabeth had been a guest at Griff House the previous year, and the story of her life had made a deep spiritual impression on Mary Ann; one episode in it was the germ of *Adam Bede*, and Ellastone and its surroundings, with some of her father's recollections, were to form one of the main inspirations of the novel. The journey included memorable visits to Ashbourne Church, Alton Gardens near Ellastone, and Lichfield Cathedral.

Robert Evans was a man of great physical and moral strength, who showed unusual competence, versatility, and industry. Born in a small cottage at Roston Common near Ellastone and Norbury (where he sang in the church choir), he began working for his father, the local carpenter. Like Adam Bede's, the master who kept the 'night-school' which he attended not far from his home was named Bartle Massey. Orthography plagued Robert for the rest of his life, but his intelligence, excellent craftsmanship, and sense of responsibility soon selected him for recognition. Francis Parker of Wootton Hall (where Rousseau began his *Confessions* in

1766) engaged him, first as forester and then as bailiff of his estate. Harriet Poynton was on the domestic staff at the time; her home was at Ellastone, where she and Robert were married in May 1801. The following year they moved to Kirk Hallam near Ilkeston, where Robert had taken a farm, his main responsibility being the management of the property his master had inherited at West Hallam. The most famous of the Newdigate-Newdegates, Sir Roger, founder of the Newdigate Prize for poetry at Oxford, lived at Arbury Hall near Nuneaton, Warwickshire. When he died in 1806, his estate passed to Francis Parker, who promptly invited Robert Evans to manage it. Robert's place at West Hallam was taken by the brother who had succeeded him at Wootton, where the resulting vacancy was filled by another of Robert's brothers, who had developed a thriving carpentry and building business at Ellastone.

Robert Evans moved with his wife and two children to Arbury Farm (later called South Farm). Mrs Evans died in 1809, after giving birth to a child who did not long survive her. As a memorial tablet in Astley Church testifies, she had been 'for many years the faithful friend and servant' of the Newdigate family. When Robert Evans married again, in 1813, he had deservedly acquired respect and social status. His wife Christiana was the youngest daughter of Isaac Pearson, a farmer of yeoman descent at Astley, where he was churchwarden; her brother Isaac had a profitable farm at Fillongley, and her three sisters (from whom the Dodsons of *The Mill on the Floss* derive some of their features) had made good marriages, all living within a few miles, Mary (Mrs Evarard) at Attleborough, Ann (Mrs Garner) at Sole End, and Elizabeth (Mrs Johnson) at Marston Jabbett. Three children were born to the Evans at Arbury Farm: Christiana (1814), Isaac Pearson (1816), and Mary Anne (on St Cecilia's Day, 22 November, 1819). At the end of March 1820 (on or about Lady Day) they moved into the large red-brick farmhouse facing the Coventry coach-road near its junction with Arbury Lane. This was Griff House, the home which meant so much in retrospect to George Eliot. Soon after the removal, Robert and Frances Lucy, the children of the first marriage, returned to their former home at Kirk Hallam, Robert to act as his father's sub-agent, and Frances to keep house for her brother.

Robert Evans' estate duties were not limited to forestry and the maintenance of farms; he was responsible for the improvement and building of roads, the mining of coal, and its transportation

by tramway and canal. Other landowners, including Lord Ayles-
ford of Packington, engaged his services. He was, George Eliot tells
us, *unique* among land-agents for the width of his knowledge and
experience, and particularly because he saved landowners the
payment of large fees to more professionally qualified advisers
(30.ix.59). He could have been rich, but his greatest reward was in
work well done regardless of time.

The French Revolution and its imperialistic aftermath made Mr
Evans and the majority of English people apprehensive of re-
formers and radical ideas. In his work he could see the widespread
benefits of enlightened order and progress. Fear of rioting and
extremism stiffened his conservatism both in politics and religion.
Near the end of her life, in the essay 'Looking Back' (TS), George
Eliot recalled his prepossessions:

> Nor can I be sorry, though myself given to meditative if not
> active innovation, that my father was a Tory who had not
> exactly a dislike to innovators and dissenters, but a slight
> opinion of them as persons of ill-founded self-confidence. . . .
> To my father's mind the noisy teachers of revolutionary doctrine
> were, to speak mildly, a variable mixture of the fool and the
> scoundrel; the welfare of the nation lay in a strong Government
> which could maintain order; and I was accustomed to hear him
> utter the word 'Government' in a tone that charged it with awe,
> and made it part of my effective religion, in contrast with the
> word 'rebel', which seemed to carry the stamp of evil in its
> syllables, and, lit by the fact that Satan was the first rebel, made
> an argument dispensing with more detailed inquiry. . . . Alto-
> gether, my father's England seemed to me lovable, laudable,
> full of good men, and having good rulers, from Mr Pitt on to the
> Duke of Wellington, until he was for emancipating the Catho-
> lics . . .

Mrs Evans was a shrewd, industrious farmer's wife 'with a considerable dash of the Mrs Poyser vein in her'. Unfortunately her
health declined after the birth of twins, who died when they were
ten days old. Christiana was sent to a boarding-school at Attleborough; Isaac and Mary Anne played indoors and out, much like
Tom and Maggie Tulliver, and attended the dame-school across
the road. Griff House and its surroundings afforded ample room
for adventure. In front there was a spacious garden with lawns,

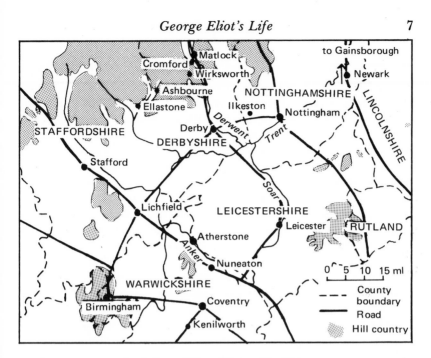

1 A General Map of George Eliot Places

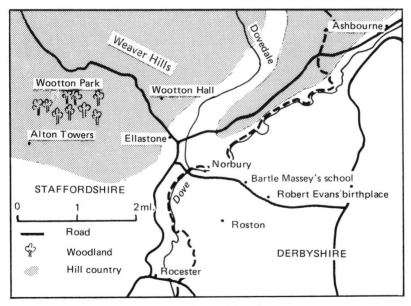

2 The 'Adam Bede' Country

a large yew tree and, on each side of the main entrance, a tall Norwegian fir. The passing of the mail-coach, from Birmingham in the morning, or from Stamford in the afternoon, was often an exciting occasion. In *The Mill on the Floss* George Eliot recalls 'the great attic that ran under the old high-pitched roof', her 'favourite retreat on a wet day' or when she was driven to fret out her ill-humour. A photograph of the house from her niece, Isaac's daughter, when he no longer communicated with her, revived the sensation of the air through the attic window from which she often looked when she was a small girl towards the 'College' or work-house at Chilvers Coton (9.v.74). At the back of the house, to the right of the farmyard, was a large fruit and vegetable garden like that described in *Adam Bede*. Not far away, a pond and a rookery exerted their varying attractions. Mrs Evans doubtlessly preferred to know that her two younger children were on this side of the house, for on the other, not too far beyond the main road, ran the Coventry Canal; further north this was joined by the colliery canal which ran through Griff Hollows. The 'Brother and Sister' sonnets record memories of these haunts, particularly of the stroke of fortune which excited Isaac's admiration after Mary Anne had sat in a day-dream while fishing in the canal, unaware of her catch and of the oncoming barge that threatened the line until he awoke her attention. Intensely affectionate by nature, she followed him with 'puppy-like' devotion, and was vexed or grief-stricken when he showed indifference or ill-temper.

She craved attention, and as an instance of this yearning told Lewes how, when she was four, she played on the piano, not knowing a single note, 'in order to impress the servant with a proper notion of her acquirements and generally distinguished position'. She remembered Sunday services at Chilvers Coton church, the instrumental music particularly, and the personalities of parishioners they usually met. Mary Anne was her father's favourite; he loved to take his 'little wench' with him in his gig, leaving her sometimes with the servants in the kitchen at Astley Castle or with the housekeeper at Arbury Hall. In *Middlemarch* (xii) she recalls landscape features which became familiar to her on these outings. She could remember riding with her parents during her childhood on a visit to uncle William, a rich builder in Staffordshire, but she had no recollection of their visit to Aunt Elizabeth's en route (7.x.59).

When Isaac was eight he was sent to school at Foleshill near

Coventry; at the age of five Mary Anne joined her sister as a weekly boarder at Attleborough. Her abiding memories of the school were unpleasant, although the older girls made a pet of her; in winter they sat so close round the fire that she was rarely near enough to keep warm, and at night she began to be haunted with fears to which she remained long a prey. In 1828 she was sent to Mrs Wallington's school at Nuneaton, where the principal governess Miss Maria Lewis, a devout Evangelical and admirer of Mr Jones, the original of Mr Tryan in 'Janet's Repentance', took great interest in her. Miss Lewis's affection awakened a deep response, and her spiritual hold on her pupil lasted several years. Mary Anne was plain, shy, and awkward. Apparently she had been a slow learner; under Miss Lewis her progress was remarkable.

Her astonishing gifts may be seen in her reading. Although a rather late beginner, she was only seven when she began to read Scott (9.viii.71); her sister had borrowed *Waverley*, and, not having had time to read it fully, Mary Anne began to write the story, as she records with a fictional slant in *Middlemarch* (ep.lvii). *Aesop's Fables*, *The Pilgrim's Progress*, and *The Vicar of Wakefield* were favourite books at home; *Rasselas* proved to be another; she also enjoyed the less conventional *History of the Devil* by Defoe, *Joe Miller's Jest Book*, and some of *The Essays of Elia*.

At the end of 1832, when she had outgrown Mrs Wallington's school, Mr Evans acted on good advice and transferred her to a flourishing school run by Mary and Rebecca Franklin in Coventry. Miss Rebecca, who had spent a year in Paris, was 'remarkable for her elegance in writing and conversation'. Under her, Mary Anne developed a musical voice, became highly proficient in English composition, and studied the English poets. She learnt French and German from visiting masters. The organist of St Michael's was her music tutor, but soon discovered that he had no more to teach her. Her excellence at the piano was such that on special occasions she was persuaded to play for the entertainment of visitors, though she dreaded the performance, and sometimes wept with nervous exhaustion when she subsequently retired to her room. She won the first-year prize, and was awarded a copy of Pascal's *Pensées*. A notebook, signed 'Marianne Evans', includes an essay on affectation and conceit, and an original story set anachronistically in the Cromwellian period. On Sundays the pupils attended the Baptist chapel where Mr Franklin preached. Rufus Lyon in *Felix Holt* originated from him; and he and his daughter are innocently associated with an electioneering riot similar to that which occurred at Nuneaton in December 1832, near the completion of Mary Evans' final term at Mrs Wallington's.

Three years later she left the Miss Franklins' school, knowing that her mother had short time to live. In the summer Mrs Evans had been too ill to be driven in the gig, and her husband had taken her out in his 'little 4 wheel carriage'. Shortly after Mary Anne's return, he was smitten with a severe attack of kidney stone, which recurred several times. Mr Bucknill, a Nuneaton surgeon, stayed with him day and night, bled him, and applied numerous leeches. Then Mrs Evans' feet became paralysed, and he was called in again; she suffered increasing pain, and died at the beginning of February. Mary Anne helped her sister 'Chrissey' as much as she could; she supervised the servants, mended her father's clothes, and read Sir Walter Scott to him in the evenings, a practice she continued at various times during his last years. On Christmas Day 1836 the two sisters accompanied him to the morning Communion service at Chilvers Coton, Mary Anne receiving the sacrament for the first time. Her domestic responsibilities increased when Chrissey married Edward Clarke, a surgeon at Meriden near Coventry, the following May; but it would be wrong to assume that she had to undertake heavy menial duties in the home or dairy. She probably lent a hand in times of stress; she made mince pies, damson cheese, and currant jelly; and she had much to do in preparation for harvest suppers like that described in *Adam Bede*, though she flinched at any licence in the jollifications that followed.

Her reading continued, its trend being religious. Shakespeare and Milton still commanded attention, but Young's *Night Thoughts* was her favourite work, and she was drawn increasingly to the poetry of Cowper. During her visit to London with Isaac in 1838 she attended St Bride's to hear the Reverend Thomas Dale (whose poetry she admired), observed lack of reverence in a service at St Paul's, and refused to attend the theatre; her chief purchase was Josephus's *History of the Jews*. Isaac had developed High Church leanings, whereas his sister's Evangelicalism had become more Calvinistic. Writing to her former mistress, the exemplary Miss Lewis, now a governess in Northamptonshire, may have induced some bias in substance and expression, but the tenor of a letter written twelve weeks after rejoicing in the birth of a hand-some boy to Chrissey is consistent with subsequent epistles to her

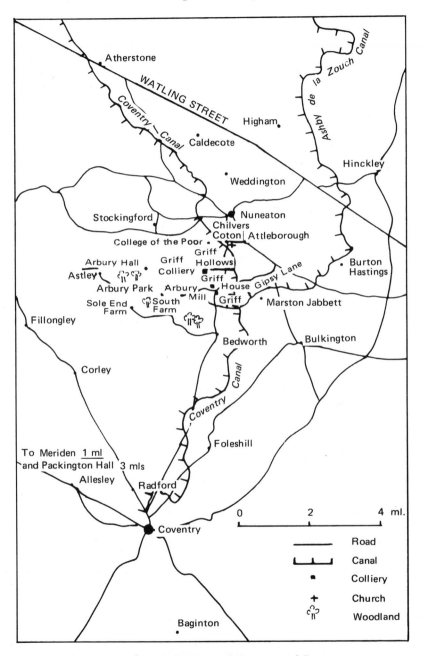

3   George Eliot Country around Nuneaton and Coventry

spiritual tutor, and suggests that any such bias was slight. 'For my part,' she affirms, 'when I hear of the marrying and giving in marriage . . . I can only sigh for those who are multiplying earthly ties . . . I must believe that those are happiest who are not fermenting themselves by engaging in projects for earthly bliss, who are considering this life merely a pilgrimage.' She was not one of the many 'who can warmly love the creature, and yet be careful that the Creator maintains His supremity in their hearts'. Like Dr Johnson with wine, she found 'total abstinence much easier than moderation'. She had enjoyed Hannah More's letters immensely, and thought 'the contemplation of so blessed a character as hers . . . very salutary'. The scriptural admonition 'That ye be not slothful' meant much to her; we are 'generally too low in our aims', she added, wishing with Young that 'we could live only for Eternity' (18.viii.38). After hearing an oratorio in Coventry, where she was disgusted that a solemn passage of Scripture should serve to display a singer's talent, she felt she would have no regret 'if the only music heard in our land were that of strict worship'.

Mary Evans had a strong social conscience. There was considerable poverty in the neighbourhood, especially in the families of cottage weavers, for whom she organized a clothing club and other charities. To raise funds for the new church at Attleborough, she worked six months on the compilation of a chart of ecclesiastical history, before discovering that such a diagrammatic compendium had already been published. For this, and in the pursuit of other interests, she was allowed to borrow books from the library at Arbury Hall. To counteract her Evangelicalism, the squire of Chilvers Coton lent her some of the Oxford *Tracts for the Times*. After applying rigorous inquisition to her reading of literature, she defended standard works 'whose contents are a matter of constant reference' (including Scott and the poetical romances of Byron; Shakespeare had a higher claim). One had to be exposed to malign influences, as in life, but she admitted the dangerous lure of fiction, and recalled her transport when she was alone in her early years, the chief actress of her imaginary world. In her first published poem 'Knowing that shortly I must put off this tabernacle', she bade farewell to all books except the Bible:

> Books that have been to me as chests of gold,
> Which, miser like, I secretly have told,
> And for them love, health, friendship, peace have sold.

She corresponded with her aunt, Mrs Samuel Evans of Wirksworth. Early in 1839 this zealous Methodist accepted her brother-in-law's invitation to stay at Griff House. Mary Ann was delighted to have the company of this tiny, black-eyed sexagenarian, whose mother had died when she (Elizabeth Tomlinson) was about one year old. Elizabeth left home at fourteen, to become a lace-mender in Nottingham. Well-paid for her technical skill, she went to 'the giddy dance, sometimes to card-playing' before being converted to Wesleyanism in 1797. When Mary Voce was condemned to death at the 1802 assizes for the murder of her child, Elizabeth was one of two women appointed to pray with the prisoner the night before her execution. The girl confessed her crime, and the next morning Elizabeth accompanied her in the cart that made its way up to Gallows Hill on Mansfield Road. Samuel Evans heard her preach at Ashbourne, and they were married at St Mary's, Nottingham, in 1804. In 1807 they moved to Derby; seven years later he and two partners set up a tape factory at Wirksworth. Both the Evanses were preachers, but the withdrawal of women from the circuit caused Elizabeth to secede from the Wesleyans and set up a more independent, locally-controlled, Arminian Methodist church. When she came to Griff she had retired from preaching. She had many discussions with her niece, and disagreed with her Calvinistic views. At the time Mary Ann was not pleased; later she thought her aunt's faith 'beautiful' (7.x.59).

In November 1839 Robert Evans joined Mr Charles Newdigate Newdegate and his tenantry to meet Queen Adelaide at Griff and escort her on her way through Nuneaton, where her entry was greeted with church bells and the singing of the national anthem in the market-place by massed choirs of school-children. Had he been allowed to ride less rapidly, the ageing Mr Evans might have found the festive occasion more enjoyable. Preparations for the Queen's reception had been made by Mrs Buchanan, daughter of Mrs Wallington. She died at Margate the following July, about the time her husband, driving to Coventry, was severely injured when one of his carriage wheels came off, and he was run over in his attempt to dismount. Mary Evans described this disaster as a scourging from God, and later turned it to good account in 'Janet's Repentance'.

Taking stock of her intellectual pursuits and position, she assessed her multifarious knowledge no higher than:

an assemblage of disjointed specimens of history, ancient and modern, scraps of poetry picked up from Shakspeare, Cowper, Wordsworth, and Milton, newspaper topics, morsels of Addison and Bacon, Latin verbs, geometry, entomology and chemistry, reviews and metaphysics, all arrested and petrified and smothered by the fast thickening every day accession of actual events, relative anxieties, and household cares and vexations.

She told Miss Lewis that her self-indulgence had extended to the purchase of 'Wordsworth at full length' (Moxon's edition of his poetical works in six volumes, three of which she had read); no other writer expressed so many of her feelings to her complete satisfaction. Later she found 'sweet poetry' in Keble's *The Christian Year*. Hearing *The Messiah* one morning in Birmingham, and selections of other oratorios the next day, prompted her, while she was drowsy after 'standing sentinel over damson cheese and a warm stove', to recommend Wordsworth's 'On the Power of Sound' to Miss Lewis. Joseph Brezzi came from Coventry each week to teach her German and Italian, and she made rapid progress with both, but found a greater kinship with the former. There seemed to be no limit to her appetite for knowledge and self-improvement.

Isaac meantime was preparing to succeed his father, the daughter of one of whose old friends, a Birmingham leather merchant, he married in June 1841; she was ten years his senior, and they lived at Griff House for the remainder of their lives. Three months earlier Mary Evans and her father had moved to Bird Grove, a dignified semi-detached house at Foleshill near industrial Coventry.

*   *   *

Mr Evans and his daughter attended Trinity church, Coventry. They were friendly with their immediate neighbours, Mr and Mrs Pears. (Mr Pears was a ribbon manufacturer, who became Mayor of Coventry the following year.) Mary Ann loved to have Chrissey's children with her at Bird Grove, and she kept in touch with her half-sister Frances, now Mrs Houghton, who lived at Baginton, south of the city. Through Rebecca Franklin, she became acquainted with the minister of the Independent Chapel in Vicar Lane, John Sibree, whose daughter Mary soon became her ardent admirer. She continued her German and Italian with Mr Brezzi, and received lessons in Latin and Greek from Thomas Sheepshanks, head of Coventry Free Grammar School. Yet she felt lonely, longed for the country, and particularly to be active in good works. She read very seriously; *Sartor Resartus* and books on astronomy and geology provided much for religious thought. Dissatisfied with all that fell short of moral perfection, she yearned for the beauty of holiness. She was shocked by frequent sights of poverty in Coventry, where, with the help of Mrs Pears, she organized a clothing club:

> The prevalence of misery and want in this boasted nation of prosperity and glory is appalling, and really seems to call us away from mental luxury. O to be doing some little toward the regeneration of this groaning travailing creation! I am supine and stupid, overfed with favours, while the haggard looks and piercing glance of want and conscious hopelessness are to be seen in the streets.

So she wrote to Miss Lewis, with whom she was shortly to adopt a lighter, less strained and affected, more adult style than she had been accustomed to practise. It was time to give up addressing each other sentimentally in floral terms, Maria Lewis as 'Veronica' and herself as 'Clematis' (Martha Jackson also, a friend she had made at the Miss Franklins' school, as 'Ivy'). Still 'a solitary, though near a city', she wished Miss Lewis to come at Christmas, and wondered whether there was 'any *conceivable* alteration' in herself to prevent it. She was growing up.

Eleven days previously she had met Charles Bray at Rosehill, his home on the Radford road. Like his brother-in-law Mr Pears, he was a prosperous ribbon manufacturer; he was also a free-thinker, author of *The Philosophy of Necessity*, a writer on education, and a keen student of phrenology. His wife Caroline was the sister of Charles Hennell, who, in *An Inquiry into the Origins of Christianity* (1838), had independently reached conclusions similar to those reached in the German historical criticism which undermined everything miraculous and supernatural in the Gospels. It is said that Mrs Pears introduced Miss Evans to the Brays in the hope that her Evangelicalism would counteract the heterodoxy of her brother and sister-in-law. The result was far otherwise; Mary Ann bought Hennell's book, now in its second edition, and inscribed her name in it on 2 January 1842. The next day her father attended Trinity Church and stayed for Holy Communion, not with her but with Miss Lewis.

Two weeks later he went alone. He had felt the shock and

disgrace deeply, and was no longer on speaking terms with his daughter. At the end of February she wrote him a long letter, telling him that her love remained unchanged, that she would be happy ministering to his comfort in his cottage at Packington or anywhere else if he chose to move, but that she could not modify her views. She admired the teaching of Jesus, but regarded the Scriptures as histories which mingled truth with fiction. Even if she forfeited what he had intended to bequeath her, she could not play the hypocrite by joining in public worship against her principles. In his *Nineteenth Century Studies* Basil Willey pictures the effect of Hennell's 'intoxicating draught' on 'our ardent young "wrestler for the truth", our Theresa of the Midland flats' who only a few years before 'had been fain to diet herself on the husks of Hannah More and Wilberforce'; he describes it as 'a dreadful exhilaration, like that of Eve after eating the forbidden fruit'. The domestic peripeteia may have been dramatic, and one wonders how much of it was witnessed by Miss Lewis, who now had her own school at Nuneaton and did not leave Foleshill until 14 January. Mary Ann's decision could not have come suddenly; she had been shocked by the low moral sense of Methodists she visited, and Hennell illuminated what she had increasingly suspected. Rebecca Franklin persuaded a learned Baptist minister to remonstrate with her; after the interview, he told John Sibree, 'That young lady must have had the devil at her elbow to suggest her doubts, for there was not a book that I recommended to her in support of Christian evidences that she had not read.' Years later she told her friend Mrs Congreve that her first sceptical thoughts had come from reading Walter Scott.

At Meriden with Chrissey, Mary Ann was visited by Isaac, who argued that persistence in heterodoxy would make her less eligible for marriage. She thought of teaching at Leamington, but could not bear to leave her father. Isaac grew more sympathetic, and invited her to stay with him and his wife Sarah. When, after she had been at Griff House a month, he persuaded his father to relent, she returned to Bird Grove, ready to compromise and observe outward forms, following the counsel of Fanny Houghton, who had read Hennell and privately accepted his conclusions. Mary Ann consented to attend church with her father, experience having begun to teach her that kinship of feeling and common interests transcend the divisiveness of creeds. For intellectual friendship she still turned to the Brays. When Sara Hennell,

Mrs Bray's sister, came to Rosehill in the summer, and heard the story of her fight for religious independence, she was anxious to meet her. In little time their kinship was established. Sara had been a governess for ten years; she was interested in literature, art, music, theology, and philosophy, and read German. As Mary Ann's chief correspondent for a number of years she succeeded Miss Lewis; unlike Miss Lewis, she had a sense of humour.

Elizabeth Brabant came to Rosehill in the autumn. Known as Rufa from her reddish hair, she had been engaged to Charles Hennell, and at his suggestion had undertaken the translation of Strauss's *Das Leben Jesu*. Her father Dr Brabant, who could boast of Samuel Taylor Coleridge and Thomas Moore among his patients, had found Charles's lungs unsound, and opposed the engagement for that reason. Charles followed Rufa to Rosehill, and Mary Ann spent musical evenings with them. In May 1843 she accompanied the Brays and Charles and Sara Hennell to Malvern and Worcester; in July she travelled with the Hennells and Rufa to South Wales, where the engagement with Charles was renewed. After attending their Unitarian wedding at Finsbury as bridesmaid, she accepted, against the Brays' advice, Dr Brabant's invitation to stay at his home in Devizes; she was to be his second daughter, his Deutera, he said. Responding with almost neophytic adoration to the attentions and 'pretty speeches' of this fussy sexagenarian, she was in 'a little heaven', and he was 'its archangel'. He had met Strauss, and studied German to keep abreast with the 'higher criticism' or historical analysis of the Scriptures. She read German to him; they studied Greek, and walked together; and Mary Ann wrote to her father, requesting further leave of absence. Mrs Brabant was blind but, acting on her sister-in-law's reports and suspicions, she took rigorous measures; her culpable husband cowered, and a susceptible young woman found herself on the train for Coventry ten days sooner than she expected. Eliza Lynn, who visited Dr Brabant in 1847, described the 'epoch-making' work he had in mind as 'something like Penelope's web'; he was so critically fastidious that he never got beyond the introductory chapter of the book which was to be 'the final destroyer of superstition and theological dogma'.

Soon after her marriage Rufa lost interest in translating Strauss, and Mary Ann agreed to continue the work, with the advice and assistance of Sara Hennell at critical points. After two years of this formidable task she was 'Strauss-sick'; Mrs Bray told Sara that 'it made her ill dissecting the beautiful story of the crucifixion'. A cast of Thorvaldsen's *Risen Christ* and a copy of Delaroche's engraving *Christ* helped to sustain her through this crisis at Foleshill. The last hundred pages proved to be intolerably dull. Her main reward lay in contributing to the cause of truth; when *The Life of Jesus* appeared in June 1846 without the translator's name, Mary Ann received £20 for a translation which Strauss praised for its accuracy and clarity.

Half-way through her task, she had become weary of coping with 'a great book of 1500 pages'; she suffered 'dreadful head-aches', felt she was too old for twenty-five, but counted idleness a disease and the exhortation 'Work while it is day' her most salutary cure. She had declined a marriage proposal from a young artist, a picture-restorer, whom she met and admired at Baginton. She had not fallen in love, but her decision not to accept an engagement was made with much emotional reluctance and not without subsequent regret. Relief came at intervals, and she enjoyed giving Mary Sibree weekly German lessons at Bird Grove. In April 1845 Harriet Martineau was a guest at Atherstone Hall; Mary Ann dined with her, and found her charming, full of the marvels of mesmerism. After visiting London with Charles Bray to meet Mrs Bray and Sara Hennell, she went with the Brays to see Macready as Brutus in *Julius Caesar* at Birmingham. In July she spent a holiday with them by Windermere; in October she accompanied them to Scotland, where she was in ecstasies to find herself amid scenes dear to her imagination from the novels of Scott. On hearing that her father had broken his leg the day she left home, she would have returned immediately but was persuaded to take another day for a visit to Melrose and Abbotsford.

After completing her Strauss translation, Mary Ann spent some time with Sara Hennell, her *fidus Achates*, in London. She took her ageing father to the seaside for his health: to Dover in the summer of 1846, to the Isle of Wight the following year, and to St Leonards at the end of May 1848. She read much more widely. One of her greatest discoveries was Richardson's *Sir Charles Grandison*. She found much more to admire in Hennell's *Inquiry* than she had done about five years earlier (16.ix.47). Disraeli made her impatient: 'The man hath good veins, as Bacon would say, but there is not enough blood in them', she wrote of *Sybil*; *Tancred* seemed very 'thin'. More surprising than the volte-face occasioned by Hannah Moore, who now appeared in both her books and letters as 'that most disagreeable of all monsters, a blue stocking', is the violent antipathy aroused in her by *Jane Eyre* (11.vi.48); however 'diabolical' the law by which its central conflict is resolved to satisfy the demands of Victorian morality, there is a nobility in the heroine's 'self-sacrifice' to which the more mature George Eliot would not have remained blind. Mary Ann described a comment she made on 'a glorious production' of Mendelssohn's *Elijah* in Exeter Hall, the composer himself conducting, as the kind of impiety that could be expected of a lady who, to use the impertinent expression of Disraeli, had been *guanoing* her mind with French novels. She was transported by George Sand; in six of her pages she found passion and moral discrimination quite beyond the usual range of experience. The genius of Rousseau awakened new intellectual and moral perceptions, and affected her like an electric thrill (9.ii.49).

Miss Evans had contributed some reviews and articles to the local newspaper which Charles Bray had bought to promote a progressive outlook. Her lively letters to Mary Sibree's brother John (who had helped her in the reading of Greek) indicate that she still found religious inspiration in the pantheism of Spinoza and some of Wordsworth's poetry: 'The ocean and the sky and the everlasting hills are spirit to me, and they will never be robbed of their sublimity'; 'Is not the universe itself a perpetual utterance of the one Being?' She was enthusiastic about the 1848 'French Revolution', and thought the English too selfish and unenlightened to follow suit; they were 'slow crawlers', less endurable than the Queen, 'little humbug' though she was, for she evoked a spirit of chivalry. Soon after her return from St Leonards, Mary Ann met Emerson at Rosehill; he was the first *man* she had ever seen. Struck by her conversation, he asked what had first stimulated her to think deeply. She replied, 'Rousseau's *Confessions*', and he told her that it had had the same effect on Carlyle. Writing to Sara Hennell, her *cara sposa* whom she addressed with 'a husband's privileges', Mary Ann said that her life was 'a perpetual nightmare'; she was always haunted by a sense of what needed to be done. During her father's illnesses she found consolation in Thomas à Kempis. Just before his death at the end of May 1849, she wondered how she would manage without his 'purifying restraining influence'; it was as if she were losing part of her moral nature. He left her £2,000 which had to be held in trust; with the share she inherited from her aunt Mary's estate, her income would be about £100 a year.

The Brays, who had planned a continental tour, kindly invited Mary Ann to join them. From Paris they travelled by coach to Lyons, by boat down the Rhone to Avignon, then on to Marseilles and Genoa. After a week there, they moved on via Milan to Lake Como and Lake Maggiore, before riding on mules over the Simplon Pass. Sunburnt and exhausted, they reached Geneva, where Mary Ann decided to prolong her stay. In the pension by the lake where she lived several weeks, she met some interesting guests, including a marquise who dressed her hair and got rid of her curls; she made headway with her translation of Spinoza's *Tractatus-Theologico-Politicus*. As winter approached, she obtained good accommodation in the city with the D'Albert Durades. Monsieur was a hump-backed painter who stood no more than four feet high; his wife was an excellent cook; and they did much to create one of the happiest periods in Mary Ann's life. With friends they provided a musical evening each week; she hired a piano, translated, read, studied mathematics, and attended lectures on experimental physics. After a severe winter, she suffered from headaches, but recovered with the approach of spring. She returned to England regretfully in March, accompanied as far as London by M. D'Albert. Staying at Griff with her brother, she thought everything dismal — the weather, the country, and the people. It was as if an envious demon had driven her across the Jura to a place where she was no longer wanted.

She found Chrissey the kindest of her family, but was relieved that she was not needed. More than ever she thought Melchizedek the only happy person. She thought of living in London, but stayed at Rosehill several months. M. D'Albert Durade came up for three days, and visited Stratford, Warwick, and Kenilworth with her. John Chapman arrived in October with R. W. Mackay, whose book *The Progress of the Intellect* he had published. As Mackay's views on the mythical origin of much in the Bible coincided with Strauss's, Mary Ann was invited by Chapman to write an article on the book for *The Westminster Review*. Her essay shows critical independence, a firm command of the subject, faith in 'positive truth' based on the reconciliation of religion and science or philosophy, and recognition of the 'inexorable law of consequences' in both the physical and moral worlds. She no longer derived comfort from pantheistic creeds. Taking her script to London in November, she stayed two weeks with the Chapmans at 142 Strand, near Somerset House, and met the writer Eliza Lynn at one of their soirées. Invited to return to the Chapmans' in January, Mary Ann decided to make London her home, and live by her pen.

Tall, handsome, and attractive, John Chapman lived with his wife and three children on the first floor above his business premises; Elizabeth Tilley, governess and general assistant in the home, was his mistress. They let rooms to guests, and Mary Ann's was a comfortable one at the end of a long passage; she hired a piano, and the amorous young publisher came to hear her play Mozart, then to learn German or Latin. With little reviewing in prospect, she began an analytical catalogue of his publications; she attended lectures, theatres, concerts, an exhibition of Turner water-colours, and *Lucia di Lammermoor*. His dependence on her excited continual scenes, especially with Elizabeth; eventually wife and mistress united in jealous opposition against her, and on 24 March 1851 the susceptible, affection-hungry Miss Evans found herself on a train for Coventry, in circumstances which inevitably recalled her precipitate departure from Dr Brabant's.

Soon afterwards Chapman agreed to purchase *The Westminster Review* and become its nominal editor. He knew, however, that he needed Marian (as she now signed herself) to manage it, and came to Rosehill to see her. By Kenilworth Castle he discussed the mysterious nature of beauty, and Marian, too conscious of her lack of it, wept bitterly. They vowed solemnly to do only what was right. She read Thomas à Kempis, and lent him her copy, finished his prospectus for the *Review*, and promised to write an article on foreign literature for each number. Still hoping to reconcile his wife and mistress to her return, he arranged that she should visit the Great Exhibition at the Crystal Palace with the Brays. He had no solution to report when he met her, and visited Rosehill in August and September for editorial consultation. Somehow his domestic conflict was resolved and, after requesting the restoration of the piano to the room she had previously occupied, Marian returned to the Strand in November. She had dissuaded him from contributing to the *Review*, and it was clear that she was in command of the editing business and of her place in the Chapman ménage.

After much negotiation and preparation, the first number in the new series of *The Westminster Review* appeared in January 1852. Marian remained its virtual editor, without any remuneration; she received board and lodging, but the work, though heavy and exhausting at times, brought its own reward. 'I am half ashamed of being in such clover both spiritually and materially while some of my friends are on the dusty highways without a tuft of grass or a flower to cheer them', she wrote to Sara Hennell (16.vii.52). She met Europeans such as Karl Marx, Mazzini, and Louis Blanc; Horace Greeley, editor of *The New York Tribune*, and William Cullen Bryant from the States; Thomas Carlyle, J. A. Froude, Sir David Brewster, T. H. Huxley, and Joseph Parkes, who had subsidized the publication of her Strauss translation and whose daughter Bessie (later Mrs Belloc, mother of Hilaire Belloc) became one of her best friends. William Hale White, a shy young lodger at 142 Strand, who was employed by Chapman after expulsion from theological college, noticed her remarkable personality, responded to her sympathetic encouragement, and recalled years later her delight in music, particularly one evening when she played Beethoven to him alone. Herbert Spencer was attracted by her intellect; he thought her 'the most admirable woman, mentally' he ever met. He took her to plays and operas, and she always felt 'better for being with him'. By the Thames, when it was sunny and warm, they walked and talked on Somerset House terrace, to which Chapman had a key. Spencer had warned her that their intimacy could not pass beyond friendship, but Marian fell in love with him, and made a virtual proposal by letter. After bitter disappointment, she accepted his rejection philosophically, and they remained on good terms, though Spencer was relieved when she became friendly with George Henry Lewes.

One May evening in 1852 Marian witnessed a very successful meeting of authors and publishers which Chapman organized for the removal of trade restrictions on the sale of books. Dickens presided, and at midnight when all the others had left except Herbert Spencer she saluted Chapman on the piano with 'See the Conquering Hero Comes'. The Brays joined her when she was on holiday at Broadstairs. Harriet Martineau and the phrenologist George Combe, both of whom she had met in Warwickshire, called at 142 Strand. The hospitality of the Combes in Edinburgh made Marian think she enjoyed *le meilleur des mondes possibles*; she stayed two weeks in October, and then travelled by coach to Ambleside, where she was welcomed by Harriet and found her 'charming in her own home'. She looked at the model cottages Miss Martineau was building, and took advantage of one fine day to visit Borrowdale. The London fog depressed her when she returned;

she was overworked, and suffered repeatedly from headaches. Her brother-in-law Edward Clarke died just before Christmas. Marian attended the funeral, and wondered how she could help Chrissey and her six children. 'Heaven help us! said the old religion; the new one, from its very lack of that faith, will teach us all the more to help one another', she wrote in the New Year.

Her comment on *Ruth* at this time casts a forward glance towards her own fiction; she felt that Mrs Gaskell was charming with her graphic touches and scenes, but 'constantly misled' by love of sharp contrasts or 'dramatic' effects. 'She is not contented with the subdued colouring − the half tints of real life'; 'she agitates one for the moment, but she does not secure one's lasting sympathy'. After reading *Villette* and finding it more wonderful than *Jane Eyre*, she discussed Charlotte Brontë with Lewes and, hearing his description of her, could not help contrasting the plain, sickly appearance of this small provincial old maid with the fire and passion of her novels. 'Quite as much as in George Sand, only the clothing is less voluptuous', she wrote, after stating that Lewes had been 'as always, genial and amusing. He has quite won my liking, in spite of myself.' A little later (16.iv.53) she writes: 'People are very good to me. Mr Lewes especially is kind and attentive and has quite won my regard after having had a good deal of my vituperation.'

Lewes had been introduced to her by Spencer in 1851. Though unprepossessing in appearance (she described him as 'a sort of miniature Mirabeau'), he could be most attractive; he was lively, gesticulative, anecdotal, an excellent mimic, and good company. His versatility was amazing; he had been on the stage, had written a tragedy, two novels, a life of Robespierre, and a popular history of philosophy in four volumes; he was working on Comte, and was to show wider interests, particularly in science and psychology. A frequent contributor to periodicals, he had written several articles for *The Westminster Review*; his subjects included Goethe, French literature, and English women novelists including Charlotte Brontë and Mrs Gaskell. Marian had sometimes criticized the form in which his essays had been presented, but she respected his literary judgment; later, as an over-diffident writer of fiction, she depended on it. He was also a gifted dramatic critic. In 1850 he and Thornton Hunt (son of Leigh Hunt) had founded *The Leader*, a weekly newspaper. Lewes's wife was beautiful and accomplished, and they had been very happy. He had travelled extensively to meet people or pursue research in Germany and France, and as an actor and lecturer at home. They held Shelleyan views on love and marriage. The youngest of their four children (all boys) died in March 1850. Shortly afterwards Mrs Lewes gave birth to a son, eighteen months later to a daughter, both the off-spring of Thornton Hunt. Unfortunately, by registering the son as his, Lewes had condoned adultery and thereby made it impossible to secure divorce. When he became acquainted with Marian, his home was irretrievably broken up, and he was completely dis-illusioned with free love. Her outlook and sympathy revived his hope; 'to know her was to love her', he wrote in his journal.

Largely as a result of Marian's high standards and industry, *The Westminster Review* had recovered much of the prestige it enjoyed as a liberal periodical under John Stuart Mill; but Chapman's lack of business acumen, his inability to reward her financially, and overwork contributed to Marian's discontent early in 1853. When she returned from a holiday at St Leonards in September, she chose lodgings in Cambridge Street, Hyde Park Square. Here, with a landlady and servants, she had less to do and more personal freedom. She had frequent guests. Harriet Martineau was one of the first to call, promising a copy of her translation and abridg-ment of Comte. When Marian introduced her to Lewes she showed displeasure, prompted not so much by rivalry (his book on Comte having appeared a few weeks before hers) as by the recollec-tion of his attack on her previous work. Bessie Parkes was a frequent visitor, sometimes with her friend Barbara Leigh Smith, an artist who lent Marian some of her water-colours to brighten her room. George Lewes, it is thought, came more and more often. Two books by Marian had been announced by Chapman, *The Idea of a Future Life* and Ludwig Feuerbach's *The Essence of Christianity*, a translation. Not having time to study for the first, she began the second. Chapman's business was in such a precarious state that she had to insist on his fulfilling his 'engage-ment' to the public; better to publish without paying her than pay her without publishing. He had offered little more than £30. Feuerbach's apotheosis of human love added warmth to the intel-lectual altruism of Comte, which formed the basis of the new religion for J. S. Mill and other Positivists. The translation appeared in July 1854, the only work by Marian Evans with her name on the title-page. Lewes had been ill, and she had helped him with articles for *The Leader*. After careful thought, and against the Brays' advice, she had decided to brave public opinion (which judged harshly by the letter of the law) and live with him. She knew that Lewes's wife did not oppose such a course, but she did not realize what the cumulative weight of British ostracism could be. On 27 June she and George went to see *Sunshine through the Clouds*, a play he had adapted from the French. On 20 July they left together for Germany.

*   *   *

From London they sailed by steamer to Antwerp; thence they proceeded to Brussels (mindful of *Villette*) and on to Cologne, where they met Dr Brabant with Strauss. For three months they stayed at Weimar, George collecting material on Goethe. One of the most friendly of the many people who welcomed them was Liszt. For the first time in her life, Marian saw real inspiration as she watched him play one of his own compositions; he had that *laideur divinisée* which was her 'favourite kind of physique'. She was very happy, and soon recovered her energy and zest for knowledge. Her reading then, and for months to come, was assiduous, mainly in German literature and Shakespeare. In Berlin she helped Lewes by translating much from the German for the biography of Goethe which he was completing; her own principal work was the translation of Spinoza's *Ethics*, which she had almost finished when they returned to England in March 1855.

While George searched for lodgings in London, and took steps to ensure that his legal wife Agnes and her children did not lack financial support (in addition to Lewes's three boys, she now had three children by Thornton Hunt), Marian remained at Dover. Fortunately Chapman, who had great respect for her critical sagacity, invited her to take charge of the *belles-lettres* section of *The Westminster Review* at £50 a year, and this led to the writing of reviews and essays which were of great importance in her literary development. While she and Lewes were living at East Sheen, near Richmond Park, Chapman sought her advice on an article he had written. It was trenchant; she had a hawk-like eye for imprecision and the otiose, and sent her observations with the unceremoniousness of 'the old days', confident that he would appreciate her frankness (25.vi.55). She had lost most of her old friends. Miss Martineau never forgave her, but Bessie Parkes was loyal, though a source of embarrassment when she directed her letters to 'Miss

Evans'. Sara Hennell ultimately plucked up courage and called, only to find that Marian and Lewes were out on one of those delightful walks for which East Sheen had been chosen. George had been ill, and she had read *Old Mortality* and *The Fair Maid of Perth* to him, the one 'beneficent' result of preparations to write an article on Scott which had to be abandoned. After a holiday at Worthing, they rented rooms at 8 Park Shot, Richmond, which remained their home for more than three years. Both worked hard to support not only themselves but Lewes's children and their mother, and there were harassing times when 'the scraping of another pen' in their only sitting-room drove Marian almost wild. She spent Christmas with Chrissey and her family (now living at Attleborough), and returned to read Meredith's *The Shaving of Shagpat* one day and write a review of it the next.

Social ostracism had its rewards, for it enabled Marian to renew the reading of Greek, a practice to which she returned several times during the remainder of her life. At East Sheen, George had turned his attention to biological studies; both were happy, 'writing hard, walking hard, reading Homer and science and rearing tadpoles'. At Richmond she read many of the Greek plays; she stated, when she was famous, that she had been influenced most by Sophocles. The revised text of Spinoza's *Ethics* was delivered to the publishers, with false expectations; interest had been lost, satisfactory terms could not be reached, and the translation remains unpublished.

In May 1856 the indefatigable pair left to further George's marine studies at Ilfracombe and Tenby. On the way they had time to walk round Windsor Castle; at Bristol, to visit 'the grand old church' of St Mary Redcliffe and remember Chatterton, 'the sleepless Soul that perished in his pride'. At Ilfracombe the Revd George Tugwell, author of a manual on sea-anemones, stimulated George's biologizing. Barbara Leigh Smith travelled to Tenby to sketch and renew Marian's acquaintance; she looked older and sadder. The previous year she had expressed her intention to live with Chapman, but her father had speedily put an end to the affair. The Leweses spent three months from home, and Marian never felt fitter in mind and body than she did towards the end of this period. She had written one of her finest articles, on Riehl; more important, she had thought of the story that became 'The Sad Fortunes of the Rev. Amos Barton'. It was at Tenby that the career of George Eliot really began.

Marian had written an introductory chapter to a novel, 'describing a Staffordshire village and the life of the neighbouring farm houses', but, convinced that she lacked dramatic skill in both construction and dialogue, she had given up hope in this as in everything else relating to her future. Repeatedly, from the time she read this introduction to him in Berlin, Lewes had encouraged her to turn to fiction; Herbert Spencer and others had told him she should write a novel, but at Tenby he urged her to begin with a story. She was anxious to do so, but first, while he took his two older boys, Charles and Thornton, to Hofwyl, a school near Berne founded on Pestalozzian principles, she began the article 'Silly Novels by Lady Novelists'; when it was finished she spent the next week reviewing twenty-seven books for the *belles lettres* and history sections of *The Westminster Review*. She began her story on 22 September and finished it on 5 November; the next day Lewes sent it to John Blackwood, who had published his first series of *Seaside Studies*. Blackwood accepted it, and invited a second, which was begun on Christmas Day, after Marian had completed another long stint of reviewing and her essay on Young. She had now finished her work for Chapman, and was filled with new vigour. Among the books she read during December and January were Sophocles' *Ajax*, Harriet Martineau's *History of the Peace*, Carlyle's *The French Revolution*, Burke's *Reflections on the French Revolution*, and *Mansfield Park*. When Blackwood sent her a February copy of his magazine ('Maga') containing the second half of 'Amos Barton', he addressed his letter 'My Dear Amos'. In her reply Marian expressed her resolve to preserve her incognito, and signed herself 'George Eliot' for the first time.

Lewes continued his seaside studies, and Marian her fiction, in the Scillies and Jersey during the spring of 1857. She read more Sophocles, Shakespeare, and Jane Austen, in addition to *Cranford* and *The Life of Charlotte Brontë* (with no illusions about Branwell). 'Mr Gilfil's Love-Story' was finished one sunny morning on Fortification Hill in the Scillies, where 'Janet's Repentance' was begun ten days later. Marian asked Isaac to deduct £15 from her half-year interest to enable Chrissey and her children, who had been ill, to have 'a change of air'. No reply came, and she wrote telling him her position, with a request that the income due to her be paid to the banking account of Mr G. H. Lewes. Isaac's family solicitor replied, asking for further particulars. Marian admitted that her marriage was not legal, and immediately she was excommunicated by her brother and sisters, even by Chrissey. Visitors at 8 Park Shot that summer included Sara Hennell, Barbara Leigh Smith and her French husband (she had met Dr Bodichon in Algiers and married him in London, despite the opposition of her family), and Herbert Spencer. Rufa Hennell (now Mrs Call, after a widowhood of seven years) invited the Leweses to dinner. George had taken his youngest son Herbert to join his brothers, who were flourishing at Hofwyl.

John Blackwood was a discerning, intuitive reader but, as a magazine editor, he had continually to bear in mind the exacting tastes of rigidly conventional readers. He was taken aback by the realism of 'Janet's Repentance', referring with scant concern for differences of authorial tone and intention to its 'harsher Thackerayan view of human nature'. Marian agreed that she resembled Thackeray in not excluding 'disagreeable truths' from her presentations of life, but was not 'conscious of being in any way a disciple of his, unless it constitute discipleship to think him, as I suppose the majority of people with any intellect do, on the whole the most powerful of living novelists'. Blackwood's criticism in no way weakened her determination to present 'mixed human beings' rather than characters of irreproachable behaviour. Lewes hinted that it would be wiser not to be critical unless there were serious objections, lest George Eliot lose heart altogether. Blackwood, who did not 'fall in with George Eliots every day', was quick to respond and praise, but Marian decided to close the series (*Scenes of Clerical Life*) sooner than she had planned. With growing confidence in her creative ability, she wished 'to take a large canvas' and write a novel; she had not forgotten the dramatic story told her by her aunt Elizabeth, and had thought of merging it with the main features of the Staffordshire novel she had in mind when she wrote her 'introductory chapter'.

On 22 October Marian began *Adam Bede*, but her reading was not discontinued. 'There is so much to read and the days are so short! I get more hungry for knowledge every day, and less able to satisfy my hunger', she wrote in December. John Blackwood's brother, Major William, called, and was soon in no doubt about the identity of George Eliot. On the last day of 1857 she wrote in her journal:

My life has deepened unspeakably during the last year: I feel a greater capacity for moral and intellectual enjoyment; a more acute sense of my deficiencies in the past; a more solemn desire to be faithful to coming duties than I remember at any former period of my life. And my happiness has deepened too: the blessedness of a perfect love and union grows daily. I have had some severe suffering this year from anxiety about my sister, and what will probably be a final separation from her – there has been no other trouble. Few women, I fear, have had such reason as I have to think the long sad years of youth were worth living for the sake of middle age. Our prospects are very bright too. I am writing my new novel. G. is full of his 'Physiology of Common Life'. . . . we have both encouragement to think that our books just coming out, 'Sea-side Studies' and 'Scenes of Clerical Life', will be well received.

Scenes of Clerical Life appeared in January, and created considerable interest. John Blackwood called on the Leweses, and after talking about the book asked if he was to meet George Eliot. Lewes consulted Marian, and she decided to dissemble no further. Blackwood came again, looked at the opening chapters of *Adam Bede*, and was pleased with them; not only his wife but Thackeray and the novelist Mrs Oliphant had assured him that the *Scenes* had not been written by a woman. Some of the letters written in acknowledgment of presentation copies are of special interest on this head: Dickens, shrewdly observant of feminine touches, had little doubt that George Eliot was a woman; J. A. Froude wondered whether he was addressing an old or young man, a clergyman or a layman; Mrs Carlyle found the book very *human*, 'written out of the heart of a live man' whom she imagined 'of middle age, with a wife from whom he has got those beautiful *feminine* touches', not a clergyman, but 'brother or first cousin to a clergyman'. People in Nuneaton and its neighbourhood soon recognised not only scenes but several of the characters, and rumour had it that the author was Mr Liggins of Attleborough. He encouraged such claims, and Marian likened the Warwickshire worthies who supported them to the wise men of Gotham. Controversy was heightened by the publication of *Adam Bede*. Correspondence in *The Times* led to Marian's intervention, and the identity of George Eliot (spotted by Barbara Bodichon in Algiers solely on the evidence of reviews) had to be made public in the summer of 1859. Grundyan disapproval of 'Mrs Lewes' undoubtedly affected the sale of her books, and some critics were quick to find moral taint and godlessness in them. Liggins died in the workhouse at Chilvers Coton, the 'College' of 'Amos Barton', in 1872.

When Blackwood read the first of the three projected volumes of *Adam Bede* in March 1858 he must have had qualms about the development of the Arthur—Hetty relationship, for he circumspectly requested an outline of the sequel before deciding on serialization. Marian refused to supply one, on the grounds that it could not be judged apart from presentation or treatment, 'which alone determines the moral quality of art'; in such circumstances as hers, she argued, a skeleton of *The Heart of Midlothian* would have proved highly objectionable. Together with her consequent decision not to serialize, which Blackwood wisely accepted, this refusal was perhaps the most judicious and momentous in George Eliot's literary career, for it gave her greater freedom and control at a critical period. Soon afterwards she and her husband were in Munich, where they were never short of intellectual company, partly by reason of George's scientific pursuits, partly in consequence of his prestige as a Goethe scholar. Dutch paintings gave Marian far more pleasure than modern German art, with results that are patent in *Adam Bede*, on which she continued to work as much as she could. From Munich they travelled via the Tyrol to Salzburg, Vienna, and Prague, where they visisted the Jewish burial-ground and the old synagogue described in 'The Lifted Veil'. At Dresden they concentrated on work, rising at six and writing for hours in the morning. They visited the art gallery, studying more Dutch pictures; a Madonna by Holbein and *The Tribute Money* by Titian were especially fascinating, but the 'sublimest' of all the paintings, and the one to which they returned again and again, was Raphael's *Sistine Madonna*. They found time also for the theatre, open-air concerts, and country walks. When they returned to Richmond at the end of August, two-thirds of *Adam Bede* had been completed. The novel was finished on 16 November; '*Jubilate*', Marian wrote in her journal, though she was sad to part with Mrs Poyser and some of her other characters. Blackwood had already read most of the manuscript, and offered £800 for a four-year copyright. The book was published on 1 February 1859, and was a tremendous success, a second edition of two impressions, and a third of four impressions, appearing before the end of the year.

Evidently the planning of *The Mill on the Floss* began soon after the completion of *Adam Bede*, for Marian and George went 'into town' on 12 January 1859 and examined *The Annual Register* to find 'cases of *inundation*'. Three weeks later they moved to Holly

Lodge, Wandsworth, not a house after their heart's desire, but tall, three-storeyed, with rooms for the boys when they left Hofwyl. Once again there were 'glorious breezy walks' in the neighbourhood. They had not been there many days when a letter from Chrissey 'ploughed up' Marian's heart: she was dying of consumption, regretted that she had not kept in touch with one who had always been kind to her and her family, and asked Marian to write again. She did so, and would have gone to see her if invited; but no invitation came and, by the middle of March, Chrissey had died. '*Non omnis moriar*', Marian read a day later, about the time her publisher was writing to inform her that a second edition of *Adam Bede* was a certainty.

In order to be near the Crystal Palace, one of the centres of all that was 'high in Art', Charles Bray, who had retired during the depression of 1856, and sold Rosehill to Mary Sibree's husband John Cash, a wealthy ribbon-manufacturer, had built a house at Lawrie Park, Sydenham. He had let it for a short period, as he hoped to do each year, but in June he came up with his wife for the Handel Festival. After hearing *The Messiah* at the Palace, the Leweses dined with them at their lodgings, and Marian was moved, after a separation of five years, to reveal that she was 'the author of "Adam Bede" and "Clerical Scenes" '. Sara Hennell was present, and three days later they all dined at Holly Lodge, the Leweses having read the manuscript of Sara's *Thoughts in Aid of Faith*, and found that they could not accept her views. Marian reflected sorrowfully on egoistic blunderings which thwart the current of sympathy and outgoing interest, making it difficult to re-establish communication between friends who meet after a long interval. Mindful of the needless suffering caused by belief and opinion in the world, she wrote to Charles Bray (5.vii.59):

If Art does not enlarge men's sympathies, it does nothing morally. I have had heart-cutting experience that opinions are a poor cement between human souls; and the only effect I ardently long to produce by my writings, is that those who read them should be better able to *imagine* and to *feel* the pains and the joys of those who differ from themselves in everything but the broad fact of being struggling erring human creatures.

Foremost in her mind when she wrote this must have been the inhumanity that passed for religion in those of her family and old friends who had severed all relations with her in strict, pious conformity to the conventionally moral.

A short visit to Switzerland brought a welcome change. At Lucerne the Leweses met their new neighbours, the Congreves. George travelled to Hofwyl; when he told his boys about his new domestic circumstances they were delighted to hear about Marian, who, on returning to Wandsworth, wrote to Charles, telling him how much she looked forward to playing duets with him. After completing 'The Lifted Veil' in response to Blackwood's request for another story, she resumed her Tulliver novel. She was unsettled, however, partly as a result of anxiety induced by the thought of public expectation after the great success of *Adam Bede*. After a holiday in North Wales, where it turned cold and wet, she and George moved to Weymouth, staying *en route* at the Swan, Lichfield, which Marian remembered visiting with her father. Her main purpose in Lichfield was to see Chrissey's daughters, and do all she could to ensure that they were happy at school. At Weymouth her novel was not forgotten; she and Lewes examined two mills in the Radipole district, and rambled in the meadows by the Frome near Dorchester, hoping to find a suitable setting. It was to provide scenes in the novels and poems of Thomas Hardy, but time and chance made it impossible for the Leweses to know they were exploring country viewed almost daily by a young man whose development as a novelist was to owe more than a little to George Eliot. Less than three weeks later they were rowing, with the 'eagre' in mind, down the Trent to the confluence of the Idle, along which they walked before returning to Gainsborough on foot. Marian had found the locale for her second novel.

She wanted a more attractive home than Holly Lodge, and there can be no doubt that, as business partners, she and Lewes had an eye to the main chance. Equally it is clear that but for him Marian would never have been deeply involved in commercial calculations; he was the 'clever' one. George Smith the publisher called to interest him in his new venture, *The Cornhill Magazine*, not without hope that he might secure George Eliot one day. Dickens dined with them, anxious to serialize Marian's new novel in *All the Year Round*; and Lewes, prospecting for better terms, approached another editor. In all the business transactions which preoccupied the Leweses from time to time, it is John Blackwood whose integrity remains undimmed. He had promised a gratuity of £800 on the success of *Adam Bede*, and knew the way the wind was blowing from hints in Lewes's letters. The restraint in George Eliot's reference to his generosity did not pass unnoticed, and he ultimately told her that he would not stand in her way. Explanations of a sort followed; he dined at Holly Lodge, and favourable terms were reached for the publication of *Maggie*. His good opinion of the author was restored; reading the penultimate chapters in manuscript, he could not resist telling his brother what a wonderful woman she was. He proposed 'The Mill on the Floss' for the title; and it remained, despite its inaccuracy, the mill being on a tributary of the Floss. Hardly had the final chapter been completed when the Leweses left England to be in Rome for Holy Week. *The Mill on the Floss* was greeted rather less enthusiastically than *Adam Bede*, but 5,600 copies were sold within a month of its publication on 4 April 1860.

They travelled by train via Paris, and by starlight in mule-sledges over the Mont Cenis Pass, then by train to Turin (where they caught sight of Count Cavour) and Genoa, on to Civitavecchia by steamboat. The crowds in Rome made walking difficult; while separated from George, Marian knelt down to receive the Pope's blessing; there were times when she saw a madonna and child at every third or fourth upper window. She regretted, however, spending so much time watching hollow, wearisome ceremonies. They explored the sites and memorials of ancient Rome, visited the graves of Keats and Shelley, saw the statues in the Vatican Museum by torchlight, and were exhilarated by the illumination of St Peter's. After visiting Naples, Pompeii (which was unforgettable), Paestum, Amalfi, and Sorrento, they went by steamboat from Naples to Florence, where they found a quiet hotel. During their busy stay, Marian was 'fired' by the prospect of a historical romance relative to the life and times of Savonarola, and much of their sight-seeing was directed by this ambitious project. From Bologna they travelled to Padua, Venice (which Marian found enchanting), Verona, and Milan, after which they crossed Lake Como and passed through glorious and sometimes forbidding Alpine scenery into Switzerland. They called at Hofwyl, and Charles returned with them to England at the end of June, after they had visited the D'Albert Durades in Geneva.

Marian and Charles played Beethoven duets, and home was 'doubly cheery' for his presence. 'It is very sweet as one gets old to have some young life about one', she wrote (when she was forty). At the end of August she informed Blackwood that, although she had planned a historical romance, and Lewes had encouraged her to persevere in this project, she wished first to write another English novel. From this, however, she was diverted by *Silas Marner*, which she began after completing 'Brother Jacob'. Through the influence of Anthony Trollope, Charles was able to enter an examination for a Post Office vacancy; he passed well ahead of all his competitors, and became a supplementary clerk in August. Thornton was transferred to the High School, Edinburgh, at the end of September, to give him better preparation for his Civil Service examination; he was placed with a family recommended by Blackwood. In the meantime, since Holly Lodge was too far from the city for Charles, the Leweses took a furnished flat near Regent's Park until they found a home in Blandford Square, which they rented for three years. *Adam Bede* appeared in a French edition, the first of the George Eliot translations by M. D'Albert Durade. Removals, physical tiredness, and depression hampered Marian's literary work during the second half of 1860, at the end of which she received £3,685 for *The Mill on the Floss* alone. Popular concerts at St James's Hall provided the Leweses' 'easiest and cheapest pleasures', but their greatest joy was in having Charles with them. Marian had chosen to have no children of her own, and *Silas Marner* is rooted deep in her emotional experience.

She disliked the city and its thick fog, but two days of rambling and driving in the country around Dorking made her feel 'a new creature'. She made good progress with *Silas Marner*, and finished it early in March. Eight weeks later she was in Florence, after a delightful journey from Paris. The historian had taken command over the novelist, and George was continually required to help with her researches in the Magliabecchian Library. A curious mixture of tiredness and determination characterizes the note written in her journal soon after returning home on 14 June:

> This morning for the first time I feel myself quietly settled at home. I am in excellent health, and long to work steadily and effectively. If it were possible that I should produce *better* work than I have yet done! At least there is a possibility that I may make greater efforts against indolence and the despondency that comes from too egoistic a dread of failure.

Preparatory work continued. She read numerous histories and

books on Florence, did research in the British Museum, and gradually became more depressed. George encouraged her as they took their daily walk in Regent's Park or the Zoological Gardens. They bought a grand piano and had a Beethoven evening. The next day she began *Romola*, but she was soon buried in 'musty old antiquities' again, and more despondent than ever. She finished a summary of the plot in December, and began *Romola* again on New Year's Day, 1862.

George Smith came to see Lewes on the publication of his 'Studies in Animal Life', which had appeared in the first numbers of *The Cornhill*, and made 'a magnificent offer' for Marian's next novel. 'This made me think about money — but it is better for me not to be rich', she wrote. A month later he proposed £10,000 for its appearance in *The Cornhill* and the entire copyright. She was disinclined to accept the offer, not out of regard for John Blackwood, but from a sense of her own unworthiness. Her health had suffered; her work robbed her of joy, and she doubted if she had ever felt 'so chilled and oppressed'. When Thackeray resigned his editorship of *The Cornhill*, Lewes consented to act as consulting editor at £600 per annum, and this new relationship may have weighed with the Leweses when they reached agreement with George Smith. Marian read several chapters of *Romola* to him one evening; she could not agree to the original offer of serialization in sixteen parts, and a compromise to publish in twelve was accepted, with complete copyright for seven years, at £7,000. John Blackwood was informed; he was justifiably hurt, especially at not being consulted, but behaved with impeccable politeness and restraint.

Marian was happier in the country, and she wrote much of *Romola* at various times in Surrey and Sussex, at Dorking particularly. Only three parts had been written when publication began in July 1862. Concerts provided her chief recreation in town. Mrs Congreve and Bessie Parkes called occasionally, and Mrs Bodichon almost daily whenever she was staying with her father. Robert Browning paid his first visit one evening in December, and the next day Marian felt 'extremely spiritless, dead, and hopeless' about her writing. She put 'the last stroke' to *Romola* on 9 June 1863. Years later she told J. W. Cross 'how cruelly she had suffered at Dorking from working under a leaden weight . . . The writing of "Romola" ploughed into her more than any of her other books . . . marking a well-defined transition in her life. In her own words, "I began it a young woman, — I finished it an old woman."'

*   *   *

Almost immediately she and George set off for the Isle of Wight, where they had a delightful holiday; with Charles at home, they were not yet free to travel abroad. She read Renan's *Vie de Jésus* with admiration, so 'eminently tender and reverent' did she find him 'towards the forms in which the religious sentiment has incarnated itself'. After hearing *The Messiah* on the previous Christmas Eve, she had written:

> What pitiable people those are who feel no poetry in Christianity! Surely the acme of poetry hitherto is the conception of the suffering Messiah − and the final triumph 'He shall reign for ever and ever.' The prometheus is a very imperfect foreshadowing of that symbol wrought out in the long history of the Jewish and Christian ages.

In July George brought Herbert home from Hofwyl. The Priory, a secluded house in grounds by the Regent's Canal, was bought in August, and its decoration and furnishing were left entirely to the art decorator Owen Jones. To Marian, who had been 'swimming in Comte and Euripides and Latin Christianity', the 'fringing away of precious life, in thinking of carpets and tables', was an affliction. George, who had taken care to keep the most critical reviews of *Romola* from her notice, was pleased, despite the expense. After hearing Barbara Bodichon on the excitement of shooting big game out there, Thornton Lewes, who had lost interest in the Indian Civil Service and failed his final examination, had embarked for Natal. Herbert had begun to learn farming in Scotland. A housewarming was given at the Priory on 24 November to celebrate Charles's coming of age, and Marian had to appear 'splendid in a grey moire antique' to please Owen Jones.

She felt better for playing the piano with gusto, and having lessons in accompaniment from the violinist Leopold Jansa. In March 1864, after Lewes had suggested that she should write a play he had sketched for the actress Helen Faucit, they travelled to Glasgow to see her in Shakespearian roles, before going to see how Bertie was faring in his apprenticeship on a Lanarkshire farm. In May they set out for Italy, and the idea of *The Spanish Gypsy* occurred to her in Venice. She read much Spanish history, and began her play, her first serious attempt in blank verse. Illness compelled George to relinquish his work for *The Cornhill*, but visits for 'water cure' to Harrogate and Scarborough, and later to Malvern, proved beneficial. On Christmas Day, Marian read him the third act of her drama, and he praised it highly. So depressed did she become over its resolution, he took her to Paris for ten days, but its continuation made her so ill he was compelled to remove the work. Five weeks later, near the end of March 1865, she began *Felix Holt*. Charles had married Gertrude, sister of Octavia Hill; and George was busy again, as adviser to George Smith on *The Pall Mall Gazette* (a lucrative position for more than a year) and as editor of *The Fortnightly Review*, a new periodical, the management of which restored his annual £600.

Marian's reading about this time included Aeschylus, Aristotle's *Poetics* (read again with 'great admiration'), J. S. Mill (including an article on Comte), much history, and novels by Anthony Trollope. After a month with George in Normandy and Brittany, she returned to *Felix Holt*, but found the legalities of its sub-plot so complex that she lost faith in her ability to solve them without expert advice. On 9 January, Professors Huxley and Beesly (a leading Positivist), Frederic Burton (the artist), and Herbert Spencer dined at the Priory; Frederic Harrison, an eminent lawyer and Positivist, was invited for the evening, in the hope, it seems, that he would come to Marian's assistance. He agreed, read the manuscript with admiration, worked out possibilities at considerable length, and provided the assurance she needed to prosecute her work. George Smith, who had not done well with *Romola*, and attributed the decline in the sales of *The Cornhill* to its inclusion, decided not to publish *Felix Holt* when Lewes informed him that George Eliot expected £5,000 for the copyright. Within two days of receiving the manuscript of the first two volumes, Blackwood offered the same sum for a five-year contract. A week later, at the end of May, the novel was finished. Frederic Harrison, who had already read it three or four times, read it again on its publication, and asked whether the poetry which suffused it was wasted, suggesting that no writer was more artistically endowed than George Eliot to impart Comtian idealism to imaginative pictures of life.

On returning from the 'health-seeking journey' which took her and George to Schwalbach and Schlangenbad, after a fortnight in Belgium and Holland, Marian found much comfort in Harrison's letter, and reflected on his proposal. In her reply (15.viii.66) she stressed the 'tenfold arduousness' of the kind of work he had in mind by referring to her difficulties in *Romola*, where she felt that 'the necessary idealization could only be obtained by adopting the clothing of the past'. The problem was to make ideas 'incarnate' without becoming didactic and 'offensive': 'consider the sort of agonizing labour to an English-fed imagination to make art a sufficiently real background for the desired picture, to get breathing, individual forms, and group them in the needful relations, so that the presentation will lay hold on the emotions as human experience − will, as you say, "flash" conviction on the world by means of aroused sympathy.'

George and Marian were now accepted by many distinguished men and women, and Sunday afternoon gatherings at the Priory were becoming the mode. Lewes, 'a mercurial little showman' in the eyes of Meredith, loved to mix with society, and wanted Marian to be recognised. Her interests lay deeper. Almost at the end of 1866 she wrote: 'Science, history, poetry − I don't know which draws me most. . . . I learned Spanish last year but one, and see new vistas everywhere. That makes me think of time thrown away when I was young − time that I should be so glad of now. I could enjoy everything, from arithmetic to antiquarianism, if I had large spaces of life before me.' She travelled with George to Spain at the beginning of 1867, preparatory to the resumption of work on *The Spanish Gypsy*, now conceived as a dramatic poem. Progress was again slow and interrupted, with holidays in Germany, first in August, and then at the end of the year, when Lewes wished to consult specialists in Bonn and Heidelberg on theories relative to his new psychological studies. Marian had realized what 'illumination' she owed to Comte, and attended lectures given by Dr Congreve; she wrote the lines 'O May I Join the Choir Invisible' during her visit to Germany in August. *The Spanish Gypsy* was published soon after its completion at the end of April 1868, and *The Spectator* rated it 'the greatest poem of any wide scope and on a plan of any magnitude' ever written by a woman, and 'far superior' to Mrs Browning's *Aurora Leigh*. It sold well and was so favourably received that George Eliot was encouraged to write poems at various periods during the next six years.

Some time in August, after Lewes had met him at the annual conference of the British Medical Association, Marian was introduced to Dr Clifford Allbutt, physician at Leeds General Infirmary, whose choice of medicine as a career had been influenced by Comte's Positivism. Their conversation made her ask whether the low moral requirements of society indicated that the highest possible religion had been evolved. She wanted a creed that was human and practical, and not uncompromisingly related to the unknown. She and George visited his hospital in Leeds (and the great art exhibition held for its benefit), and travelled north again to see a 'stupendous' iron-works at Sheffield; afterwards, 'for a variety', they made Matlock their centre, and on one outing passed through Cromford, where Marian recognised cottages and the Arkwrights' house from the visit she had made with her father when they were staying at Wirksworth nearly thirty years previously.

At Cambridge early in 1869, in the rooms of the public orator W. G. Clark, she sat next to Oscar Browning, and talked earnestly 'about the duties of life, about the shallow immorality of believing that all things would turn out for the best, and the danger of fixing our attention too much on the life to come, as likely to distract us from doing our duty in this world'. Among the tasks she set herself at the opening of the year were several poems and *Middlemarch*, but soon came an alarming letter from Thornton in Natal (where Bertie had assisted for more than two years on his farm of 3,000 acres) which caused his father to send £250 with an urgent summons to return at once for an operation. Before his arrival on 8 May, long before he was expected, the Leweses were absent on a nine weeks' tour, mainly in Italy. In Rome they met J. W. Cross, who had been working as a New York broker in his family business, and was about to enter the London office. Marian's health was poor throughout most of the holiday, and she and George were shocked to see Thornton so thin and worn three days after their return. Next day he was writhing in agony on the floor when a young American, Henry James, arrived and was soon on his way by cab to call in James Paget, the Queen's surgeon. Thornton was afflicted with spinal tuberculosis, and his suffering made it impossible for Marian to concentrate long on her writing. Barbara Bodichon came twice a week to talk to the patient, who was wonderfully sweet-tempered. After completing her 'Brother and Sister' sonnets, Marian ventured to begin *Middlemarch*. A week later Thornton was paralysed below the waist; he died peacefully on 19 December.

Some comfort came from living three weeks with 'nice people in an old-fashioned farm house' at Limpsfield, Surrey. Marian turned to poetry, continuing 'The Legend of Jubal'. Neither she nor George could settle to their principal work. In March they went to Germany, where they met many eminent people; Lewes visited hospitals and discussed psychiatry; neither cared for the Wagnerian operas they heard. From Berlin they travelled to Prague, Vienna, Salzburg, and Munich. Marian suffered from a severe cold and ulcerated throat, and they were weary of travelling when they reached the Priory. Sunday afternoon receptions and outside engagements were continued. Marian consented at length to dine at Lord Houghton's, with exhausting effects. The following week they were the guests of the Mark Pattisons at Lincoln College, Oxford. Cromer, Harrogate, and Whitby were tried, chiefly for George's health. Returning to Limpsfield in August for another three weeks, they found renovation in rural quietude; and Marian wrote most of 'Armgart' in this 'favourite Surrey retreat'. The Franco-Prussian war distressed her. 'What novices in wickedness were Milton's devils!' she reflected as she thought of the autumn sunshine on the hideous guns being hauled to Paris. She began the 'Miss Brooke' story in November, and spent Christmas with Barbara Bodichon on the Isle of Wight.

Middlemarch was Marian's main preoccupation in 1871. So much remained to be done that she decided ultimately not to attend the Scott centenary celebrations in Edinburgh lest she should 'break down and die without finishing it'. With the inclusion of 'Miss Brooke' she had an unusual amount of material. At Shottermill near Haslemere real progress was made from May to September, while extensions and improvements were being effected at the Priory. During this period the Leweses had few visitors, and were glad to escape the 'oppression of peeresses, poets, philosophers, and indiscriminate Christians' who had made Sundays so exhausting; they met the Tennysons two or three times, and heard the Poet Laureate read some of his poems. Soon after returning to London, Marian was seriously ill. Christmas was brightened by the arrival of a gift from an admirer, Alexander Main; it was a copy of his *Wise, Witty, and Tender Sayings, in Prose and Verse, Selected from the Works of George Eliot*, an anthology which was to be expanded, to include selections from her subsequent publications. New Year's Day was spent with the Crosses at Weybridge. Not until she took refuge at Redhill for three months in the summer of 1872 was Marian able to make steady headway with *Middlemarch*. Except for the finale, it was completed by the second week of September. Lewes, who was dubbed the 'von Moltke' of strategy by Blackwood's manager Simpson, had made arrangements for its publication in the United States, Europe, and Australia. Its reception at home was even more enthusiastic than that of *Adam Bede*; reviews were almost unanimous in praise; and soon George Eliot was sought after by the élite of London society.

The finale of *Middlemarch* was written at Homburg, where the Leweses became acquainted with Lady Castledown, her two daughters, and a number of their friends. Despite bad weather and headaches, they enjoyed the waters and baths; the Kursaal, where they watched the gambling, provided the germ for *Daniel Deronda*. After a rest at Stuttgart and Karlsruhe, they returned to the Priory and Sunday afternoon receptions, which were more popular and exhausting than ever. As the social level of their guests became more elevated, the Leweses had to conform more to their standards. Marian showed greater interest in dress, and George bought her jewellery; but, as J. W. Cross testifies, 'She took things too seriously, and seldom found the effort of entertaining compensated by the gain.' Her talk was 'always most enjoyable *à deux*. It was not produced for effect . . . but welled up from a heart and mind intent on the one person with whom she happened to be speaking.' In May 1873 she and George were guests at Trinity College, Cambridge; F. W. H. Myers remembered her conversation in the Fellows' Garden on God, immortality, and duty; and her pronouncement that the first was inconceivable, the second unbelievable, the third peremptory and absolute. A visit to Balliol College, Oxford, followed in June, after which they travelled in France and Germany again. In the autumn a restful period was spent at Blackbrook, Bickley, Kent, a house they had thought of leasing for a year. Attending one of the Priory receptions in November, John Fiske, assistant librarian at Harvard, found Lewes utterly fascinating, and nothing masculine in George Eliot save her mind. She did not talk like a bluestocking; Spencer thought her 'the female Shakespeare, so to speak', and Fiske imagined he was not far wrong.

Marian had read much on the Jews in preparation for *Daniel Deronda*; her espousal of Zionism had been fostered by the memory of Emanuel Deutsch, a scholarly cataloguer at the British Museum who had given her lessons in Hebrew, and who had died recently of cancer in Alexandria. From early June almost to the end of September she and George lived near Redhill, and it was here that she wrote most, if not all, of the earliest chapters. Much time was taken up in the search for a country home. Then, after a visit to Paris and Brussels, they travelled to Salisbury, Devizes, Bowood, Lacock Abbey, and Corsham Court in search of background for *Daniel Deronda* scenes. Next year Lewes took a house at Rickmansworth where Marian could write more easily in the summer months. The book was not finished until June 1876. Its progress had been hampered by frequent depression and illness; towards the end, Marian accepted few invitations, and annoyed Lord Houghton by refusing to meet the King of Belgium. As soon as she was free, she set off with George for Switzerland.

George Eliot and her works inspired the devotion of a number of women in her later years, among them Mrs Congreve and Elma Stuart, a widow who regarded Marian as her spiritual mother, sent her gift upon gift, including specimens of her wood-carving, and chose to be buried next to her grave. The most helplessly in love of these worshippers was Edith Simcox; her passion was lesbian, and she was happy to kiss the feet of her 'goddess'. Lewes and George Eliot indulged the pathetic infatuation of this hypersensitive and importunate intellectual, whose climactic reward came when her 'darling', after expressing her preference for men and telling her she was silly, complied with her request for a kiss.

The Leweses had bought a fashionable carriage in 1873, and one of Edmund Gosse's memories was of a strange pair in their victoria as he walked towards Whitehall from north-west London in 1876 and later. Although clearly unsympathetic, written for effect, and misleading at one point (Marian was not large in person), the impression he gives has vivid pictorial features which are based on genuine recollection:

> The man, prematurely ageing, was hirsute, rugged, satyr-like, gazing vivaciously to left and right; this was George Henry Lewes. His companion was a large, thickset sybil, dreamy and immobile, whose massive features, somewhat grim when seen in profile, were incongruously bordered by a hat, always in the height of the Paris fashion, which in those days commonly included an immense ostrich feather; this was George Eliot. The contrast between the solemnity of the face and the frivolity of the headgear had something pathetic and provincial about it.

Her contemporary fame was 'a portentous thing', he adds. Serious thinkers, who despised novels, regarded her writings as 'contributions to philosophical literature'. 'While she lived, critics compared her with Goethe', to the latter's disadvantage.

George Eliot was now accepted as the great novelist of the post-Dickensian period; she had admirers all over the world. By example and encouragement, she and Lewes had stimulated each other to strenuous endeavour and high aims. Her thirst for knowledge was still unquenchable, but they were now content with a quieter life. As their social engagements declined, one visitor (whom Edith Simcox regarded with a jealous eye) came more frequently. This was J. W. Cross, their financial adviser. He took them to see the Heights at Witley near Haslemere. It was the country house they desired, and it was secured for them just before Christmas 1876, which they spent with the Crosses at Weybridge.

There was some thought of giving up the Priory, but this did not happen. Extensive alterations and improvements were necessary at the Heights. Tennyson lived near at Blackdown, and they met him several times in London. On Good Friday evening a large party assembled at the Priory to hear him read *Maud* and, for good measure, the two dialect versions of 'Northern Farmer'. Important social engagements followed. Liszt's daughter, Mme Wagner, arrived, and the Leweses had to attend the Wagner Festival; Princess Louise was introduced to them at a dinner given in her honour; and once again they were guests of Jowett at Balliol. Five days of 'uninterrupted excitement' followed with the Sidgwicks at Cambridge, where they visited Girton and Newnham colleges. (Girton had been founded in response to the efforts of Barbara Bodichon and others, and Marian, though never an ardent feminist, was one of its benefactors.) At the Heights, the Leweses were cordially received by the neighbours, including Lady Holland. They stayed from June to October, enjoying walks and drives in their beautiful surroundings. Jowett was a guest of the Hollands, and they met him several times; their visitors included John Blackwood, the Congreves, Spencer, Frederic Harrison, Charles Lewes and, most of all, 'Johnnie' Cross, who persuaded them to take up lawn tennis; later he sent them equipment for badminton, which they played in the Priory drawing-room.

At the end of February they were guests at the wedding of Lionel Tennyson in Westminster Abbey. Invitations led to several meetings with Tennyson in town that spring. Attending concerts at St James's Hall, as they had done for years, George Eliot and Lewes excited much interest, even from members of the Royal Family. In the summer, at Witley, Marian worked on her *Impressions of Theophrastus Such*. George suffered from sudden bouts of severe cramping pains, but Cross could remember how once, between two attacks, 'he sang through, with great *brio*, though without much voice, the greater portion of the tenor part in the "Barber of Seville" – George Eliot playing his accompaniment, and both of them thoroughly enjoying the fun'. Once again, for a few days in October, they were guests of Cross's brother-in-law at Six Mile Bottom. Another guest was Turgenev; Marian found him most congenial company, and sat next to him at the Newmarket races. Shortly after their return to the Priory from the Heights, Lewes was taken very ill and died (at the age of sixty-one). Not many days later, John Cross's mother died.

For several weeks Marian received no one except Charles Lewes and visitors on necessary business. 'Here I and sorrow sit', she wrote in her diary on 1 January 1879. She did not drive in her carriage until early February, or agree to see Johnnie until three weeks later. Much of her time was spent in the laborious task of revising manuscripts for the fourth volume of George's *Problems of Life and Mind*. In memory of him she wished to create a studentship in physiology, held initially at the University of Cambridge. It was 'a great stay' for her to discuss the terms of its institution, and she transferred £5,000 to its trustees. With Cross's assistance, her bank account, her two houses, and her securities (over £30,000), which had all been in Lewes's name, were made over to her. Cross came more often, and she was delighted to be his tutor in Dante; together during the next year they made a close study of the *Inferno* and *Purgatorio*. 'The divine poet took us into a new world. It was a renovation of life', he wrote. On 27 May, at the Heights, he persuaded her to play the piano for the first time after her husband's death. During the summer she prepared the final volume of *Problems of Life and Mind* for the press. On 16 October she began a letter to Johnnie, 'Best loved and loving one', and signed it 'Beatrice'. Then came the sad news of John Blackwood's death. Generous to the end, he had sent her a bonus for *Impressions of Theophrastus Such*, after the sale of more than 6,000 copies.

The following April she summoned Sir James Paget, informed

him that John Cross had asked her hand in marriage for the third time, and, thinking principally of her twenty years' seniority, sought his advice. In the evening she consented to marry her 'nephew', who took her to view his house in Cheyne Walk; it over-looked 'a very picturesque bit' of the Thames, and became their London home. They were married on 6 May at St George's, Hanover Square. News of this sanctified union astonished friends, but enabled her self-righteous brother to break 'the long silence' with great pleasure, offer his sincere congratulations, and sign himself affectionately.

The couple proceeded to Venice for their honeymoon, travelling via Paris, Grenoble, and the Mont Cenis Tunnel, with a visit to the Grande Chartreuse. They spent a week in Milan, and enjoyed many gondola excursions and much sight-seeing in Venice, before Cross, under the stress of some mental affliction, jumped into the Grand Canal from his balcony at the Hôtel de l'Europe. He was rescued by gondoliers; leading specialists were summoned, chloral administered, and an urgent telegram sent to William Cross, who reached his brother from England without loss of time. They left Venice, to return by easy stages. In *George Eliot's Life* Cross attributes his illness (of which he gives no details) to the heat, lack of exercise, and the fetid air of drains. In 'the pure sweet mountain air' of Innsbruck, where they stayed a week, he soon recovered; the attack, however, remained a source of deep anxiety to his wife.

They spent the summer at Witley, meeting friends and visiting Cross's relatives. At the end of September they went to Brighton for the sake of Marian's health. Two months later, when she had made a slight recovery, they moved from Witley into a London hotel, before taking up residence in Cheyne Walk on 3 December. The next day they attended a Popular Concert at St James's Hall. On 17 December Marian was at St George's Hall, following a performance by Oxford students of Aeschylus's *Agamemnon* in Greek. Two days later she had a sore throat, and told Edith Simcox that she believed she had caught a chill while watching the play. She grew worse, with laryngitis and a recurrence of the kidney trouble from which she had suffered acutely in June 1879 and at Brighton. Dr Andrew Clark found that her heart was affected, and that little resistance was left. 'Tell them I have great pain in the left side', she whispered to her husband just before she lost consciousness. She died that evening, 22 December 1880. Many thought it fitting that she should be buried in Westminster Abbey, but it was soon realized that her views were too heterodox to find favour with the Church. For her interment, Cross chose unconsecrated ground in Highgate Cemetery, where it touched one corner of Lewes's grave. Among the countless mourners who assembled in wind, sleet, and rain to witness her burial were William Blackwood, Browning, Spencer, Congreve, Beesly, Harrison, Burton, Sir Henry Thompson, T. H. Huxley, Edmund Gurney, Lionel Tennyson, John Morley, Leslie Stephen, Oscar Browning, Isaac Evans, and his son, the rector of Bedworth. For many the memorial climax to an impressive service in the crowded chapel came when the Unitarian minister concluded his address with lines from 'O May I Join the Choir Invisible'.

In both life and thought George Eliot was a woman of the highest integrity. As a writer, she fulfilled the ideal she expressed when she wrote with Carlyle in mind: he 'awakes men from their indifference to the right and the wrong'; he 'nerves their energies to seek for the truth and live up to it at whatever cost'; 'he inspires their souls with courage and sends a strong will into their muscles'. If truth is hard to recognise, it is because the prejudices of faction and self-interest are stronger. George Eliot's humanitarian philosophy is basic and penetrating; it looks beyond the general practice of her own age, and of our own. Whether it constitutes a religion or a morality, it must be a key to the wholeness and welfare of any civilization.

The moral stigma attached to George Eliot's union with Lewes has almost wholly vanished, but qualified approbation based on 'conforming falsities' still casts a fitful shadow, so much does orthodoxy frown on any heterodoxy, however progressive. On the centenary of her birth, George Sampson could observe astringently, with reference to her early Evangelical bigotry, that 'the scorner of connubial happiness lived to enjoy that happiness without the respectable sanction of a ceremony'. Belated honour was paid to her greatness in 1975 when the Dean and Chapter of Westminster Abbey gave permission for the unveiling of a memorial to her in Poets' Corner, on the centenary of her death. A wider, active, and more crucial recognition of the values in life for which she consistently stood will be more difficult to achieve.

Relevant History

George Eliot's ultimate subject is humanity and its welfare, 'the growing good of the world' which is dependent on 'unhistoric' as well as historic acts. Having seen some of the worst effects of industrialization in Britain, she could not but reflect that people deserved the benefits of a religion which affected the whole of life. Most of the historical references in her fiction, from the end of the eighteenth century to the years almost immediately preceding the publication of her last novel, are a reflection of her interest in social developments and related causes. This interest in public morality grew not only from contemporary movements and events but from her father's recollections. She liked 'to mark the time, and connect the course of individual lives with the historic stream' (DD.viii). As a novelist, she thought Gwendolen Harleth a subject of the highest moment; as a philosophical historian, she knew that, in the pride of youth, she was a most 'insignificant thread in human history', at a time when 'the universal kinship was declaring itself fiercely', as Lancashire cotton operatives demonstrated by supporting the anti-slavery campaign during the American Civil War, even though it led to their own unemployment and starvation (DD.xi). 'Any one watching keenly the stealthy convergence of human lots, sees a slow preparation of effects from one life on another which tells like a calculated irony on the indifference or frozen stare with which we look at our unintroduced neighbour. Destiny stands by sarcastic with our *dramatis personae* folded in her hand', she writes, thinking of the changes in and around Coventry about 1830, when 'the old stocking gave way to the savings-bank, and the worship of the solar guinea became extinct; while squires and baronets, and even lords who had once lived blamelessly afar from the civic mind, gathered the faultiness of close acquaintanceship'. She finds 'much the same sort of movement and mixture' in this 'old England' as in older Herodotus' (M.xi).

Beginning with the period of *Adam Bede* and *Silas Marner*, the sketch which follows is restricted to historical features most relevant to George Eliot's fiction. The French Revolution led to an intensification of radical agitation, and to strong countermeasures by the British government. *The Rights of Man*, Tom Paine's reply to Burke's *Reflections on the French Revolution*, was banned, and the Habeas Corpus Act suspended. The building of barracks enabled troops to be used more effectively throughout the country to suppress any disorder, and they were reinforced by the yeomanry, a new mounted force drawn from the upper and middle classes. The prevailing opinion was, however, conservative; Tom Paine's effigy was burned by Durham miners. As England normally imported corn from Continental Europe, the ensuing Napoleonic wars combined with a series of poor harvests at home to cause a steep rise in the cost of bread. While farmers became richer, their labourers became poorer. A temporary peace which was negotiated in 1802 was not wholly welcome to the former. War profited the landowners, for rents were increased, while rectors benefited from increased tithes. The ancient practice whereby tenant-farmers paid a tenth of their produce to the Church as 'God's portion' (and parsons' income) continued to strain parish relations; dissenters objected on principle, and a *modus vivendi* (FH.vi) sometimes obtained which made money or some other form of payment acceptable. To meet these objections, rent charges, based on the average price of corn over the previous five years, were substituted by the Tithe Commutation Act of 1836: the Society of Friends, however, remained opposed even to this solution until 1873.

The brief picture drawn by Marian Evans in her essay on Riehl on family life about 1806 in the home of an English tenant-farmer or small farming proprietor is probably based on her mother's reminiscences:

> . . . when the master helped to milk his own cows, and the daughters got up at one o'clock in the morning to brew, − when the family dined in the kitchen with the servants, and sat with them round the kitchen fire in the evening. In those days, the quarried parlour was innocent of a carpet, and its only specimens of art were a framed sampler and the best tea-board; the daughters even of substantial farmers had often no greater accomplishment in writing and spelling than they could procure

at a dame-school; and, instead of carrying on sentimental correspondence, they were spinning their future table-linen, and looking after every saving in butter and eggs that might enable them to add to the little stock of plate and china which they were laying in against their marriage.

Martin Poyser does not frequent public houses, but likes 'a friendly chat over his own home-brewed'; after being complimented by Adam Bede on the new tap (the last brew), Mrs Poyser discusses the secrets of good brewing, and emphasizes 'the folly of stinginess in "hopping", and the doubtful economy of a farmer's making his own malt'. Spinning-wheels hummed busily in farm-houses, linen being spun from flaxen threads before being woven by weavers such as Silas Marner. The housemaid Molly, who is keen to learn spinning, spoils too much flax to please Mrs Poyser, who, after reprimanding her unreasonably and at length, asks why she stands there instead of getting the wheel out. She has had linen spun and stored, thinking it will make sheets for Hetty when she is married. Her checkered tablecloth is no 'bleached "shop-rag"', but a good whitey-brown homespun that will last for two generations. Mrs Tulliver recalls all the cloths she spun, and how Job Haxey, who wove them, brought a piece home on his back before she thought of marrying Mr Tulliver, and how she chose a pattern and sewed it herself (MF.III.ii). Nancy Lammeter's hands bear traces of butter-making, cheese-crunching, and still coarser work; though a rich farmer's daughter, she seems vulgar to the Miss Gunns because she says 'mate' for 'meat', 'appen' for 'perhaps', and 'oss' for 'horse' (SM.xi). Quick to take offence, Mrs Jerome tells her husband he is always finding fault with her china because she bought it before she was married (SCL3.viii).

Many cottagers, like Silas Marner, did their cooking over the open hearth. Those who could afford it had their best meals cooked at the village bakehouse, especially on Sundays or at Christmas (SM.x), but more people among the lower classes were copying the practice of the rich, and having brick ovens installed at home (AB.i). Apart from public houses for men, the parish church afforded the main social centre in rural areas. Traditional festivities such as May Day, Harvest Home, and Christmas were the main occasions for communal merrymaking. Farm-labourers continued to wear smock-frocks until the second half of the nineteenth century.

Apart from farming and quarrying, the main local industries which George Eliot remembered from her youth were coal-mining and the weaving of silk rather than of linen. By the end of the eighteenth century, Sir Roger Newdigate had completed a railway-canal system for the transport of coal on the Arbury estate. One horse could draw a number of linked waggons along a railway to one of two canals which joined the Coventry Canal. When Robert Evans was overseer of the estate it is probable that only one of these private canals (the one running through Griff Hollows) was operative (cf. FH.xi, where the railways are called 'tram-roads'), but coal-production increased through the nineteenth century, and George Eliot remembered a flat, ugly district, the roads 'black with coal-dust', and brick houses 'dingy with smoke' (SCL1.ii).

The prohibition of foreign ribbons (1768—1826), followed by a protective tariff, led to rapid industrial growth in Coventry, and on a smaller scale in Nuneaton, Bedworth, and villages familiar to Mary Evans. Imported silk was sent from London and Manchester to Coventry manufacturers who had it dyed (cf. M.xiii); it was then distributed by 'undertakers', who returned the ribbons to the manufacturers. By 1838 there were 7,000 single handlooms in country districts around Coventry and Nuneaton; in Coventry and Foleshill most handlooms had been superseded by engine looms (manually worked, not power-driven) which wove two or more ribbons simultaneously; there were over 300 of these in Bedworth, and 200 in Nuneaton. Only owners of engine looms, assisted by their families, could afford butchers' meat. Weavers were afraid of putting money into savings banks lest employers got to know and reduced wages; instead, and as a measure of insurance against illness, they joined provident societies and 'benefit clubs', which were often organized by public houses (cf. M.xlv) and increasingly by dissenting churches, especially as the temperance movement gained strength. Silk-weaving was unhealthy; windows usually had to be closed to keep damp out of the silk, and most operatives had to work without a fire because smoke was damaging to the product. In the district Mary Evans knew best, the majority of the weavers were wives of miners or quarrymen; even children of eight or nine were employed, working from 7 a.m. to 8 p.m. for 1/6d per week. Adults averaged less than 5/- a week over the year; they had to live mainly on bread, potatoes, a little tea, and occasional scraps of the cheapest bacon. Girl weavers knew little about domestic economy;

most had to marry at the age of 16 or 17, and their husbands, with rare exceptions, sought the company of friends in gin-shops where much of the family earnings was spent. 'Every other cottage had a loom at its window, where you might see a pale, sickly-looking man or woman pressing a narrow chest against a board, and doing a sort of treadmill work with legs and arms' (SCL1.ii). Mr Vincy is described by Mrs Cadwallader as 'one of those who suck the lives out of the wretched handloom weavers in Tipton and Freshitt' (M.xxxiv).

The rapid continuation of land enclosure for farming added to the plight of the poor. Around Coventry, however, a very large area remained unenclosed (cf. FH.ep.iii), because the grazing rights belonged to artisans who, as freemen of the city (for which status they qualified after serving seven years of unbroken apprenticeship), had the right to vote for their parliamentary representatives. The general effect of enclosure was to deprive cottagers of their livelihood on the land, forcing many of them to join the migrants who sought employment in the new industrial areas. In 1815, at the end of the war with Napoleon, prices fell, but the landowners caused great distress by having a bill passed to maintain the price of corn. Deflationary policies, including a return to the gold standard in 1819 and the subsequent 'cessation of one-pound notes' (FH.iii), reduced living standards. The Corn Law, which was not repealed until 1846, ruined many tenant-farmers; by maintaining high prices for bread, especially when harvests were bad, it antagonized not only the working-classes but townspeople generally, and in so doing promoted the demand for parliamentary reforms.

Paupers in workhouses were trained for industry, and thousands were sent to become cotton operatives in Lancashire. The destitute in local workhouses included old and young: Eppie was quite certain that, but for Silas Marner, she would have been taken to a loveless workhouse. After the passing of the Speenhamland Act of 1795, it became common practice to ensure that all labourers received a minimum income in accordance with the price of bread; unfortunately it was based on supplementation of wages from parish rates, and consequently the farmers, who had to pay most of the rates (cf. SM.xvii), reduced wages. The labourer therefore suffered the indignity of being a pauper when he was fully employed. Many scorned parish relief; Hetty Sorrel thought 'the "parish" was next to the prison in obloquy'. Idleness and crime

increased; poaching became common. Anyone caught attempting
to catch a hare or rabbit could be transported, and the penalty for
sheep-stealing was death. There were riots and outbreaks of
rick-burning in 1816, and even more in 1830, when threshing-
machines and other new labour-saving machinery were smashed,
following the Luddite example in industrial areas. References to
such occurrences are found in *The Mill on the Floss* (II.i, III.ix),
the introduction to *Felix Holt*, and *Middlemarch* (iii, xxxvi, xlvi).
The number of large farms increased, and the area of efficient
farming, with crop-rotation, grew, although the old style of culti-
vation was still much in evidence, with its strips and fallows. There
were tenant-farmers like Dagley who suffered from the neglect of
landowners like Brooke (M.xxxix), and others who were im-
poverished as a result of inefficient or corrupt administration of
estates, like that inherited by Harold Transome. Many small
farmers were driven out of business, and both ne'er-do-wells and
honest men took the opportunity to emigrate rather than face the
law or continuing hardships at home. Injustices and oppression
were fearlessly exposed by William Cobbett in his *Weekly Political
Register*. The New Poor Law of 1834 made things worse: outdoor
relief was abolished; workhouse inmates had to prove their
integrity by accepting 'less eligible' labour than was available
outside; and husband and wife were separated to prevent child-
bearing. The new workhouses were built by groups of parishes,
and therefore known as 'unions'. Each union had a paid visiting
chaplain (cf. SCL1.ii) and a board of guardians elected by the
ratepayers, but centralized administration resulted in ruthlessness
and bumbledom.

Although, like the inhabitants of Frick (M.lvi), the mass of the
people were not directly affected by parliamentary reform, the
urge towards it was undoubtedly fomented by popular grievances.
The demand was for an increase in the electorate, and a more
equitable distribution of the seats. Large new towns such as
Birmingham, Leeds, and Manchester had no representation,
while ancient towns which had dwindled in size often had two
members of Parliament. These constituted 'pocket boroughs' and
'rotten boroughs', the former so small that their representation
was completely controlled by local magnates, the franchise of the
latter being in the hands of corporations or privileged minorities.
County representation was the preserve of landowners who were
responsible for the enclosure acts and corn laws; the franchise was

vested in forty-shilling freeholders, including many yeomen farmers, although their number had been reduced in recent years. The iniquity of the system was recognised in government circles; Huskisson proposed the disfranchisement of small ancient boroughs and a transfer of seats to the larger non-represented or under-represented towns. With a new parliament as a result of George IV's death in 1830, parliamentary reform became a major issue. The first reform bill was defeated in April 1831. The election associated with Mr Brooke's inglorious campaign in *Middlemarch* produced a larger reforming majority, but the bill which followed in June was defeated in October 1831. Rioting resulted in Nottingham and Derby, and more alarmingly in Bristol, with mob-demonstrations in London. A third reform bill was launched in December; although it failed when it came up for its third reading in the House of Lords the following May (cf. M.lxxxiv), opposition was overcome, and the bill became law on 4 June 1832. To the forty-shilling freeholders in the counties it added copyhold tenants of land valued at £10; leaseholders of land valued at £10, where the lease was for sixty years or more, or at £50, where the lease held for at least twenty years; and land-tenants who paid annual rents of £50 or more. In boroughs quali-fying for parliamentary representation, the franchise was secured for householders (owners or tenants) of property with a minimum rateable value of £10.

In her introduction to *Felix Holt*, George Eliot states that the view of reform among country people in the period of agitation before the passing of the First Reform Bill was 'a confused combination of rick-burners, trades-union, Nottingham riots, and in general whatever required the calling-out of the yeomanry'. The rioting of this novel is based on her recollections of what took place in Nuneaton during the election of December 1832, after the passing of the bill. The subject was suggested by the demand for the extension of the franchise which preceded the Second Reform Bill of 1867.

There were no police at the opening of the nineteenth century. Had there been, much mob violence would never have flared up, and 'the massacre of Peterloo' (1819), when magistrates used yeomanry against a huge demonstration of Lancashire cotton workers, would have been avoided. Parish constables were appointed by local justices of the peace (cf. SM.vii), and watchmen hired in towns, particularly against thieves. Criminals took refuge in suburban slums, or moved from one rural district to another. The police force which Robert Peel set up for the London area in 1829 saved the capital from the kind of violence which got out of hand in Bristol during the Reform Bill agitation. By degrees, his example was followed in various parts of the country, but it remained easy for criminals to escape from policed to unpoliced counties until a co-ordinated police system was established. Developing from 1856 onwards, it led to public order, and a marked diminution in crime.

The Municipal Corporations Act of 1835, after an investigation by commissioners under the secretaryship of Joseph Parkes, Radical father of one of George Eliot's closest friends, led to the removal of a mass of corruption, and transferred control from oligarchies of Churchmen, Tory lawyers, and agents of nobility to middle-class, rate-paying citizens, including Dissenters. Early advances were slow, but they paved the way for the municipal amenities and safeguards which the western world now takes for granted.

Fashions in dress for the New Year's Eve dance at Squire Cass's (SM.xi) and Captain Wybrow's departure for Bath (SCL2.iv) are a reminder of Jane Austen's world. Further reference to the era of spas occurs in *Felix Holt* (iii): Treby Magna in the early years of the nineteenth century was a 'respectable market-town', where farmers 'praised Mr Pitt and the war as keeping up prices and religion'; then came the canal, followed by coal mines two miles off at Sproxton, with the discovery of a saline spring 'which suggested to a too constructive brain the possibility of turning Treby Magna into a fashionable watering-place'. Despite opposition, handsome buildings were erected, and a guide-book printed; but the spa never flourished, and the town 'took on the more complex life brought by mines and manufactures, which belong more directly to the great circulating system of the nation than to the local system to which they have been superadded'. The emphasis is incidental, but it indicates the importance George Eliot attached (and expressed through Caleb Garth) to the role of industry and transport in national life.

During this period canals still provided the best form of transport for heavy goods. Local roads were precarious, especially in winter, when they were miry and often deeply rutted, as *Silas Marner* reminds us. The main turnpike roads were well surfaced as a result of Macadam's scientific engineering, and there were regular coach

services to all towns in the country. By the time of the First Reform
Bill the era of 'gigmanity' was very evident. Prosperous middle-
class farmers such as Robert Evans usually owned gigs, and George
Eliot in her introduction to *Felix Holt* pictures one of them,
'weighing down one side of an olive-green gig' on his way to
market, and probably regarding coach-passengers with com-
placent contempt.

Most country people habitually turned to the Church of England
for moral and spiritual strength, but dissenting chapels were on the
increase among the poorer and more industrialized areas. The
church in Lantern Yard at the end of the eighteenth century (SM.i)
is not to be identified with any of the well-established dissenting
sects, but it exemplifies the kind of extreme sectarianism to which
nonconformity was inevitably prone in small communities, and is a
forerunner of the hole-and-corner religion which placed stiff-
necked judgment before knowledge, disinterestedness, and that
reasonableness which Matthew Arnold pleaded for in *Culture and
Anarchy*. There were old-fashioned Methodists (and in the eyes of
outsiders, all Dissenters were 'Methodists') who 'believed in present
miracles, in instantaneous conversions, in revelation by dreams
and visions; they drew lots, and sought for Divine guidance by
opening the Bible at hazard; having a literal way of interpreting
the Scriptures' (AB.iii).

Slow to change, the Church of England pursued its more sober
course. Metrical psalms were still commonly sung in the early part
of the nineteenth century, though hymn-books were becoming
familiar to many parish congregations, especially in Evangelical
areas. Music was provided by instrumentalists of varying quality.
From her references elsewhere (AB.xviii, SM.vi), it seems that the
bassoon and the two key-bugles of Shepperton Church were drawn
from George Eliot's memories of Chilvers Coton; likewise the
wheelwright leader of the choir (SM), 'a carpenter understood to
have an amazing power of singing "counter"' (SCL1.i). His
presence could lighten the burden of the parish-clerk, whose
duties included leading the responses and singing. Some of the
Shepperton congregation remembered the Sternhold and Hopkins
version of the psalms, and regretted their replacement by the 'new'
metrical version of Tate and Brady (which dated back to 1696).
Although many were unable to read, they joined in the singing, for
words and tunes soon became familiar to regular worshippers. A
passage deleted from 'Amos Barton' describes the awe with which

Mary Evans regarded the choir in her early childhood, when they visited Griff House at Christmas 'for their yearly money and beer', and she clung to her mother's apron with 'a sort of polytheistic awe', as if 'these psalmodizing tosspots' were 'Olympian deities in disguise'.

But for the Evangelical fervour of the eighteenth century, and its continuance into the nineteenth, the Church of England would not have been a great spiritual force. The counteracting Oxford or Tractarian movement, which began in 1833, attempted to restore the authority of the Church in national life by reaffirming its essential catholicity and the apostolic succession of its ministry; it ended in High Church ritualism. Unfortunately John Wesley's Methodist movement had led to secession from the Church of England after his death in 1791. These Methodists, like Mary Evans' aunt, were Arminian, believing in the forgiveness of the penitent. Followers of Whitefield, the most representative leader of that other great strand in the religious revival of the eighteenth century, accepted the Calvinist doctrine of predestination, which divided the 'elect' from those doomed to suffer eternal perdition. Such Evangelicals were to be found in the Church of England, one of them being John Newton, whose preaching at Olney inevitably revived the poet Cowper's 'castaway' conviction that 'hatred and vengeance' would be his 'eternal portion'. By and large the rigours of Calvinistic teaching declined steadily in the early part of the nineteenth century, and for all practical purposes many Church Evangelicals rejected Calvinism completely. In more industrial areas they were generally a great success; in the more traditional towns they encountered opposition from inveterate supporters of Church and State. Ministers with the zeal and pertinacity of Mr Tryan (SCL3) could be a great spiritual power, and a source of solace and succour among the poor and needy in towns where neglect more often created openings for dissenting churches. His organization, with the aid of women assistants, of a lending library for the converted suggests that he must have shared Sir Anthony Absolute's view that a circulating library in a town was 'an ever-green tree of diabolical knowledge'. Amos Barton had less appeal and intelligence, though he believed he was shrewd in combating dissent with Low Church doctrine and 'a High-Church assertion of ecclesiastical powers and functions'. Like Patrick Brontë, he had been strongly influenced by Charles Simeon at Cambridge; at Shepperton he promoted the reading among his parishioners of evangelical pamphlets published by the Religious Tract Society. Though he liked to appear strong-minded, he was no more sure of his tenets than of his English; he inclined to the Calvinism of Newton and Scott, and needed only 'a very little unwonted reading and unwonted discussion' to feel convinced that 'an Episcopalian Establishment was much more than unobjectionable'.

Amos Barton was a poor curate, employed by an incumbent at a time when 'a man could hold three small livings, starve a curate a-piece on two of them, and live badly himself on the third'. Many absentee parsons were rich; the State Church was an exceedingly wealthy part of the established order, and some bishops enjoyed enormous incomes. Their resistance to the Reform Bill inflamed political opinion, and added to the growing opposition created by nonconformist denominations. But for internal reforms and a more equitable distribution of its wealth, the Church could have been disestablished, as was expected about 1850. Mr Irwine, though a pluralist and a friend of the Donnithornes, represents some of the better features of rural clergy at the end of the eighteenth century; Mr Gilfil belongs to a slightly earlier period, and has farming interests. Both are refined, friendly, and respected by their parishioners; their accent is on upright living and good works; their sermons are moral and practical, and they set an example by helping the poor and needy. More than thirty years later the farming parson (SCL1.vi) and the sporting parson, represented by John Lingon, a great huntsman who supports cock-fighting (FH.ii), were still to be found in the country. Mr Cadwallader's main interest is in fishing. Fred Vincy is expected to enter the church for the sake of gentility. Mr Farebrother finds it irreconcilable with his scientific views, but preaches excellent sermons; his chief consolation is card-playing, especially for gain, in days 'when Evangelicalism had cast a certain suspicion as of plague-infection over the few amusements which survived in the provinces'.

Evangelicalism helped to preserve the Church, and to ensure a peaceful process of reformation in times of hardship and injustice; its humanitarianism formed a link between Dissenters on the one hand and the Church and the established order on the other. Nonconformist chapels continued to spring up throughout the country, especially in industrial areas, partly in reaction to Church of England torpor, partly as a result of class and political divisions. Raveloe is 'aloof from the currents of industrial energy and Puritan earnestness'; 'no looms here, no Dissent', Dorothea Brooke finds in Lowick. Among the dissenting sects, the Independents (or Congregationalists, as they were becoming increasingly known) are most to the fore in George Eliot's fiction. Although the gentility who listen to Mr Crewe's inaudible sermons assume that their chief attributes are 'prayer without book, red brick, and hypocrisy', the intellectual and social tradition of the Independents was considerable; their political memory was distinctly Cromwellian. Rufus Lyon's Independent chapel in Malthouse Yard could not have been unenlightened; despite the Calvinistic leanings which make him doubtful about Wesley's Arminian doctrine (FH.v), he is gentle, learned, and wise. Had there not been a good influence at work in the Independent chapel known as Salem at Milby (SCL3), Mr Jerome could not have remained its chief member; its respectability is indicated by its gigmanity. The Baptists were not a flourishing group in this town, for 'the doctrine of adult baptism, struggling under a heavy load of debt, had let off half its chapel area as a ribbon-shop'; its Methodism was to be found only in 'dirty corners'. In many 'fashionable quarters' of the country it denoted 'nothing more than low-pitched gables up dingy streets, sleek grocers, sponging preachers, and hypocritical jargon'. There were Church families at Milby who attended Salem and thought that, though 'Dissent might be a weakness', there was after all 'no great harm in it'. George Eliot's views were more liberal, placing 'the generous stirring of neighbourly goodness' above all schism (AB.iii).

Mr Lyon's reservations about Wesley may have been tinctured with anti-Catholicism, for Calvinists found the Arminian heresy Romish in tendency; he had regarded Esther's mother as 'an unregenerate Catholic' before falling in love with her. In 1829, as a result of Irish agitation for Catholic representation at Westminster (supported as a principle of social justice by many Independents, but opposed by many Wesleyans), the Catholic Emancipation Act was passed, much to the discomfiture of the Tories, after Wellington and Peel had given way for fear of civil war in Ireland. This act removed all major civil and political disabilities from the Catholics, and increased their unpopularity among the people, as well as with the less liberal upper-class Protestants. Both Mr Brooke and Mr Casaubon are suspect in Mrs Cadwallader's eyes after taking Peel's side; Mr Tulliver and Mr Deane, seeing Wellington in a new light, speak slightingly of his conduct at

Waterloo; and the Independent minister Mr Spray subtly distinguishes between 'his fervent belief in the right of the Catholics to the franchise and his fervent belief in their eternal perdition' (MF.I.xii).

Two references in *Daniel Deronda* to a later period call for comment. The first (xlii) is on the equality of the Jews: like Catholics and Dissenters, they had been enabled to accept most public offices by the repeal of the Test and Corporation Acts in 1828, but they had to wait until 1858 before they were allowed to become members of Parliament. The second concerns rates for the maintenance of Church of England buildings: for many years Dissenters had complained against a compulsory levy regardless of creed, but it was not until 1866 that the Church Rate Abolition Bill was passed (lxiv).

Perhaps nothing illustrates more the blind self-interest of the ruling classes in nineteenth-century England, the richest nation in the world, with its vast imperial resources and its growing trade, than their failure to provide compulsory elementary education before 1870. One reason for conceding it was the proof afforded by the 1867 International Exhibition in Paris that British industrial enterprise was being outstripped by that of countries which were better educated; another, which had hitherto been considered a reason for opposing it, was the recognition that the working classes, after being enfranchised in 1867, threatened to become the main controlling factor in the economy. It had become necessary, Robert Lowe declared, to educate 'our future masters'. More than a century later, it is clear that they have not yet been well educated for their responsible role, and that the truths of George Eliot's 'Address to Working Men' (ostensibly by Felix Holt) are continually ignored, with consequent retardation of progress and prosperity.

Silas Marner takes us back to a period when ignorance and superstition (in medicine, ghosts, and the Devil, for example) prevailed; 'demon-worship' might be found among grey-haired rustics, and Dolly Winthrop's hazy idea of 'Them above' is more pagan than Christian. If night-schools like Bartle Massey's (AB.xxi) were near, they could be attended by adults; similarly, young children could be sent to 'dame schools', which provided supervision and some instruction, if parents were willing to spend a few pence per week. There were charity schools in some towns; many children in Coventry attended a year or two before starting work at the age of nine or ten. Clergy like Mr Stelling would take a few pupils as boarders; and small boarding-schools were becoming fashionable, especially for girls. Higher education for boys consisted largely of Latin grammar-grind, with some mathematics, chiefly Euclid; the emphasis for girls was on 'accomplishments' (elocution, singing, music, painting) and languages. Tom Tulliver's education had little practical value, and Maggie's was no preparation for life. The drudgery of a governess's life in home or school was dreaded by most educated young women, who had scant scope for their talents. Private academies scarcely better than Dotheboys Hall existed; Mr Tulliver decides that, whatever school he sends Tom to, it will be 'a place where the lads spend their time i' summat else besides blacking the family's shoes, and getting up the potatoes'. There were ancient grammar schools (for boys), many of which had boarding accommodation; but they were small and ineffectual. About the year 1830, before Churches (principally the Church of England) increased the number of elementary schools, and 'public' school expansion provided more places for the sons of the wealthy, education was 'almost entirely a matter of luck – usually of ill-luck'. The only chance of escaping a Mr Stelling or (worse still perhaps) a draper's son who, intended for the Church, had ended his college dissipations with an imprudent marriage, fell to those fathers who were on the foundation of a grammar school, 'where two or three boys could have, all to themselves, the advantages of a large and lofty building, together with a head-master, toothless, dim-eyed, and deaf, whose erudite indistinctness and inattention were engrossed by them at the rate of three hundred pounds a-head – a ripe scholar, doubtless, when first appointed; but all the ripeness beneath the sun has a further stage less esteemed in the market' (MF.II.iv). Here George Eliot probably remembered 'Milby' (Nuneaton), where the curate Mr Crewe (whose sermons were 'inaudible') 'imparted the education of a gentle man – that is to say, an arduous inacquaintance with Latin through the medium of the Eton Grammar – to three pupils in the upper grammar-school'; he had 'once had a large private school in connection with the grammar-school, had numbered a nobleman or two among his pupils, and made 'a large fortune out of his school and curacy' (SCL3.ii). Oxford and Cambridge provided university education principally for the wealthy; poorer students who found their way there, usually to enter the Church, and survived 'the Eleusinian mysteries', were often as unscholarly as Mr Barton (SCL1.ii), and sometimes worse. Although George Eliot was far from militant in the cause of women's liberation, she was decidedly in favour of their higher education, a movement which gathered some momentum, even at university level, in the second half of the century. How much she valued the role of women in a progressive society is emphasized in her essay 'Woman in France', hinted at in *Daniel Deronda* (end xi), and implicit to an incalculable degree in the unenlightened role of Rosamond Lydgate (who had all the 'accomplishments') and in Dorothea's frustrated idealism and restricted opportunities. In the penultimate paragraph of the first edition of *Middlemarch* George Eliot states that the 'knowledge' derived by the latter from her education was synonymous with 'motley ignorance'.

The ancient universities of Oxford and Cambridge continued in their conservative courses with snobbish disregard for scientific and technological progress. They were finishing schools of a kind for the sons of the aristocratic and wealthy classes; and they prepared students for the Church, law, and medicine. The University of London originated in 1826, largely to provide opportunities for scientists and Dissenters; Owens College, Manchester, followed; and from 1871 to 1881, when science was at last making an impact on Oxford and Cambridge, several civic universities were initiated, all offering courses for scientists.

The tardiness and moderation (as it proved in the twentieth century) of this development, like the delayed approval of basic elementary education for all in 1870, reflects the short-sighted philistinism of upper classes who had become prosperous too easily. This was due partly to colonial exploitation, even more to resources which had made England the leading industrial country in the world. Trade at home and overseas had been speeded up by the steam-engine. Starting in 1825, the railway system had developed to such an extent that it had taken much business from the canal companies; as it grew, stage-coaches disappeared. Huskisson had been run over and killed at the opening of the Manchester–Liverpool railway in September 1830 (M.xli). The Rugby and Coventry lines to Nuneaton were opened respectively in 1847 and 1850. Railways had been regarded as a menace (FH.xx), especially by women (M.lvi). Landowners and others whose property was likely to be affected were naturally up in arms, and often took advantage of rustic ignorance to raise opposition to the 'invasion' of their land; one objection was the effect on hunting.

A scene in *Middlemarch* (lvi) shows 'six or seven men in smock-frocks with hay-forks in their hands making an offensive approach towards the four railway agents'. Their view was that railways were 'good for the big folks to make money out on', but of no more use to the poor than the canals. George Eliot's sympathies are with Caleb Garth, who tries to reason with them. His support for improvements in transport reflects his belief in 'the indispensable might of that myriad-headed, myriad-handed labour by which the social body is fed, clothed, and housed'.

Ignorance, prejudice, and even superstition, impeded medical progress. When Silas Marner's preparation of foxglove 'worked wonders' with Sally Oates at the beginning of the century, villagers thought he could dispense charms as the Wise Woman of Tarley had done; there were women in Raveloe who had worn the Wise Woman's little bags round their necks to avoid bearing idiot children. Mrs Glegg carried in her pocket a mutton-bone inherited from her grandmother as a precaution against cramp. Leeches were commonly used by doctors. As Dame Fripp was believed to have the power to make them bite, she was called in to apply leeches supplied from Mr Pilgrim's surgery when patients were attacked with inflammation (SCL2.i). The age of the barber-surgeon was over, but phlebotomy was practised by one school of doctors. Pratt of Milby ascribed all diseases to debility, and prescribed port-wine and quinine; Mr Pilgrim believed that 'the evil principle in the human system was plethora', and 'made war against it with cupping, blistering, and cathartics'. Similarly in Middlemarch about 1830 Wrench stood for 'the strengthening treatment' and Toller for 'the lowering system'; 'the heroic times of copious bleeding and blistering had not yet departed'. Unlicensed practitioners like Felix Holt's father acquired reputation and no mean income from the sale of soothing medicines, the only good effect of which was generally psychological.

There were three types of medical doctor: the physician (principally a consultant), the surgeon, and the apothecary (one of whose functions was to supply drugs). Dr Kimble was one of the country apothecaries who 'enjoyed that title without authority of diploma' (SM.xi); he had served a long apprenticeship. After 1815 it was necessary to study further and take an examination to qualify as a medical practitioner or surgeon apothecary. In resisting 'the irrational severance between medical and surgical knowledge', Lydgate represents the new type of doctor, but he is more than a general practitioner, for his main ambition is in research. The proficiency of schools of medicine is indicated by his progress from London to Edinburgh, and thence to higher studies in Paris; Oxford and Cambridge did not go far, and were not very reliable. Many hospitals had been raised in England by charities and subscription, but it was not until 1848 that the Public Health Act set up a General Board of Health with the power to establish local health authorities. These local powers were vested in town councils; elsewhere local boards of health could be created *de novo*. George Eliot knew from her husband's consultations with German specialists how essential research was for medical progress in England, and they were both impressed by the work of Dr Allbutt at the 'fine hospital' in Leeds which they visited in 1868, not long before she decided to write *Middlemarch*. In Lydgate's career she is really voicing her regret that genius which might benefit humanity at large should be doomed to remain lodged with him useless. His best self defeated, he acquires a lucrative practice, alternating seasonally between London and one of the fashionable Continental spas.

Marian Evans' final rejection of the ancient theological assumptions of the Christian churches began with her study of Hennell; it was confirmed by the discoveries of geologists and astronomers, by discussions with scientists and philosophers (Henry Spencer in particular), and by familiarity with their writings, when she was virtually editor of *The Westminster Review*. Darwin's theories caught the limelight through controversy with the Church, but there was little in them that was significantly new to the scientific world. Marian Evans found *The Origin of Species* interesting, but criticized its 'want of luminous and orderly presentation' (Journal, 23.xi.59); the Development Theory produced 'a feeble impression' on her 'compared with the mystery that lies under the processes' (5.xii.59). For her God remained, as with Feuerbach, the hypostatization of the goodness and love which spring in human hearts.

She was not strictly a Positivist, but her religion must have been strengthened by the basic humanitarianism of Comte's Positive doctrines. Her familiarity with them was strengthened by Harriet Martineau's abridgment *The Positive Philosophy of Auguste Comte*, and a work by Lewes on the more scientific aspects of Comtism. During the same period, when she worked for *The Westminster Review*, she became acquainted with J. S. Mill, who is said to have confirmed her religious and philosophical outlook; he was one of the most progressive intellectual leaders, and an advocate of Comte's religion of humanity. In 1859 she became friendly with the Congreves. Before her marriage, when she lived at Coventry, Mrs Congreve, daughter of the surgeon who attended Robert Evans during his last illness, met Marian and was much impressed by her; she was to become one of George Eliot's most devoted friends. Dr Congreve, after meeting Comte in Paris, had resigned his Fellowship at Wadham College, Oxford, where Frederic Harrison, E. S. Beesly, and J. H. Bridges had been his students; his ambition was to make Positivism a social-religious force in England. Bridges, Beesly, Harrison, and Congreve were the principal translators of Comte's massive works. 'My gratitude increases continually for the illumination Comte has contributed to my life', George Eliot wrote to Mrs Congreve in January 1867, a few months before attending Dr Congreve's lectures on Positivism. She had been 'greatly moved' by the *Discours Préliminaire* in October 1863, and not long before her death her husband J. W. Cross read Dr Bridges' translation of it to her. 'This volume was one of her especial favourites', he wrote, adding, 'For all Comte's writing she had a feeling of high admiration, intense interest, and very deep sympathy. I do not think I ever heard her speak of any writer with a more grateful sense of obligation for enlightenment.'

In 1861 George Eliot had expressed the view that, though Comte was a great thinker who deserved reverence, Positivism was 'one-sided'. She was unsympathetic to his policy of institutionalizing spiritual power, just as she was opposed to Congreve's ritualistic role when he set up a church for the new religion. Basically, however, she must have agreed with the imperatives which motivated Comte's elaborate systematizing and pontification: the subordination of self-interest to altruism and general welfare; the insistence that education and science are fundamental to progress, and that religion needs to be founded on scientific truth; above all, the necessity to stimulate moral energy or will, for the achievement of social justice through the development of humanitarian feelings. The 'effective bond of human action is feeling', George Eliot wrote late in her life. Perhaps she thought the movement too intellectual and academic; it produced a sect, and she distrusted sectarianism. Undoubtedly it influenced contemporary reform, but it could have no direct effect on the public at large. 'If Comte had introduced Christ among the worthies in his calendar it would have made Positivism tolerable to thousands who, from position, family connection, or early education, now decry what in their heart of hearts they hold to contain the germs of a true system', Hardy wrote when George Eliot's death 'set him thinking about Positivism'. She knew that aesthetic teaching which appeals to the heart and the imagination is more effective than anything doctrinaire, and her religion of humanity still lives in her novels; in, for instance, the repentant Janet Dempster or Dolly Winthrop, or the vanquished Lydgate. Frederic Harrison hoped that George Eliot would write a Positive work in poetry. A discussion with Dr Allbutt in August 1868 (before her visit to Leeds) prompted her suggestion that 'the highest possible religion' might not have been 'evolved and accepted' by a society whose moral standards were not very high during a time of 'religious decay'. She told him that 'the inspiring principle' which alone had given her courage to write was that of presenting life to give her readers 'a clearer conception and a more active admiration of those vital elements which bind men together and give a higher worthiness to their existence'. In *Middlemarch* (although she was writing about an earlier period) she presents the kind of England in which Positivism hoped to make headway. As a researcher, Lydgate had wished to follow Bichat, one of those men whose service to mankind Comte had honoured when he named the months of his calendar for the Positivist Era which began with the French Revolution. Comte believed in orderly, enlightened, and continued progress, and in this respect at least had something in common with the author of *Felix Holt*.

Essays and Reviews

George Eliot's first essays, like her last, were published in fictional disguise. The five short pieces which Mary Evans contributed to Charles Bray's local newspaper in the winter of 1846–7 show a lapidary attention to style, sustained care in presentation, interest in Scott's novels, and the influence of Wordsworth. She expresses her pantheism in terms which echo 'Intimations of Immortality', her Platonic idealism (the love of 'the good, the true, the beautiful') being based on the assumption that the spirit has its home in the eternal mind. Man's highest destiny transcends the worldly, but it is rooted in childhood and the common feelings of humanity; like Wordsworth's, as expressed in 'To a Skylark', it is 'True to the kindred points of Heaven and Home'. George Eliot's religion was destined to change radically, but the experience underlying 'The Wisdom of the Child' is essentially that which prompted her to write nearly thirty years later (on the rootlessness of Gwendolen Harleth's childhood), 'The best introduction to astronomy is to think of the nightly heavens as a little lot of stars belonging to one's own homestead' (DD.iii). The most significant of the newspaper articles, however, is a little fable with a great moral which takes a number of forms in George Eliot's fiction from first to last (see pp. 97–8). Taking advantage of her fictional screen in the last of her five essays, Mary Evans satirizes provincial snobbery, and has her own heterodox position in mind when she states that respectable ladies with strong orthodox views may snub 'any woman not an heiress', though she is 'as full of talents or of good works as a Sir Philip Sidney or a John Howard'.

Her first review, on Mackay's *The Progress of the Intellect* (WR January 1851), is mainly an exposition of the mythical in religion, the Hebrew especially. It indicates her acceptance of Comte's belief that the furtherance of human knowledge and happiness depends on science and the study of the actual. Much can be learned from the errors of the past, but the key to future revelation is the recognition of undeviating law in the universe and of the 'inexorable law of consequences' in the moral world. This view imparts new life to the study of the past; the belief that religion is 'the crown and consummation' of philosophy (science) holds promise for the future.

'Woman in France' (WR October 1854) is devoted principally to Victor Cousin's *Madame de Sablé*. It was femine 'tact, wit, and personal radiance' which created the atmosphere of the *salon*. French women enjoyed a culture superior to that of English women in the seventeenth and eighteenth centuries because they shared ideas and common interests with men. With the typical attitude of contemporary Englishmen in mind (it was still like that of Mr Brooke in *Middlemarch*), Marian Evans asserts that such equality is a requisite for 'true womanly culture' and for 'true social well-being'; the *salon* did not create '*bas bleus* or dreamy moralizers, ignorant of the world and of human nature, but intelligent observers of character and events'. Her scientific interests create new analogies; declaring that women had a vital influence on literature in France alone, she compares it to an electric current which gives crispness and definition to language. She cannot resist a reference to George Sand, that peerless artist who combines Rousseau's eloquence and love of nature with clear depiction of character and deep tragic passion. In 'the wondrous chemistry of the affections and sentiments' women are naturally different from men. They should remain true to their experience, and write as women. Their peculiar endowment is 'a necessary complement to the truth and beauty of life'. Once this is accepted, we have a marriage of minds blending thought and feeling into a 'rainbow of promise for the harvest of human happiness'. Lawrence, at the time of writing *The Rainbow* and *Women in Love*, would have found much to commend in this manifesto.

'Woman in France', her first commission at Weimar, expresses Marian's convictions after marrying Lewes. The interest of 'Three Months in Weimar' (*Fraser's Magazine*, June 1855) is mainly historical and biographical. In its early description one can see the developing novelist. Ironically, after paying tribute to the 'hardy simplicity' of Goethe's study, in contrast to the elegant Gothic of Scott's at Abbotsford, she can stress the seasonal migration of the Germans to 'the Baths' with the Johnsonian Latinity of 'As birds nidify in the spring . . .'. Still relying on her Weimar journal, she continued the next month with 'Liszt, Wagner, and Weimar', testifying admiringly in defence of Liszt's character, and predicting that as a composer he would be more than a coruscating meteor. She describes three of Wagner's operas at length, strikes a cautionary note against contemporary prejudice, and stresses the artistic unity of his music, drama, and spectacle.

The review of *Westward Ho!* and *Constance Herbert* (WR July 1855) evokes some of Marian's best writing. She takes Kingsley to task for weakening his artistic effects by preaching; he rides two steeds, Pegasus and his hobby, and becomes a poor copy of Carlyle when he attempts to make the second keep pace with 'the great Scotchman's fiery Tartar horse'. She takes exception to Kingsley's anti-scientific assurance, and questions the doctrine of renunciation as it is proclaimed by Geraldine Jewsbury in *Constance Herbert*. The conventional doctrine of ultimate rewards is not a proper foundation for true moral development, which cannot exist without 'the immediate impulse of love and justice'. A similar lack of realism in attributing a husband's alienation to his wife's 'entire devotion' makes her regret that the author fails to create a better understanding of woman's true position.

How far Marian Evans had changed as a religious thinker since her adolescence may be judged from 'Evangelical Teaching: Dr. Cumming' (WR October 1855): 'Where is that Goshen of mediocrity in which a smattering of science and learning will pass for profound instruction, where platitudes will be accepted as wisdom, bigoted narrowness as holy zeal, unctuous egoism as God-given piety? Let such a man become an evangelical preacher . . .'. After studying Dr Cumming's writings she comes to the following conclusions:

> We fancy he is called, in the more refined evangelical circles, an 'intellectual preacher'; by the plainer sort of Christians, a 'flowery preacher'; and we are inclined to think that the more spiritually-minded class of believers, who look with greater anxiety for the kingdom of God within them than for the visible advent of Christ in 1864, will be likely to find Dr. Cumming's declamatory flights and historico-prophetical exercitations as little better than 'clouts o' cauld parritch'.

She did not find the kingdom of God within the theologian, but a perverted moral judgment which he shared with all evangelical believers, regarding those outside the fold, especially Romanists, without humanity or understanding, and insisting that justice, sympathy, and charity exist, not for human reasons but simply for the glory of God. She insists that 'human nature is stronger and wider than religious systems', and that the idea of God cannot be dissociated from humanity and moral values. Marian Evans is a formidable polemicist, quick to see illogicalities and inconsistencies where 'hardihood of assertion is surpassed by the suicidal character of the argument'. Her style is trenchant, reasoned though forthright, and sustained with unflagging energy. It is no wonder that the article produced a strong impression. According to Charles Lewes, it was the first writing which convinced his father that his wife had genius, rather than great talent, as a writer. In this kind of contest she shows that she is well-armed with knowledge of her subject, intellectual perspicacity, and realistic faith. Her criticism is invigorating by virtue of its positive implications.

In comparing Mary Wollstonecraft and Margaret Fuller (*Leader*, 13.x.55), Marian is not militant on the question of women's rights; she believes that the champions of women are overzealous. She sympathizes with Margaret Fuller's view that there are no positions which some women cannot fill, and argues for a removal of all restrictions on the development and culture of women. A comment on Mary Wollstonecraft's style underlines where she differs from her. It is 'nothing if not rational; she has no erudition, and her grave pages are lit up by no ray of fancy'. Marian Evans is habitually grave and rational in her articles, but her erudition provides admirable illustrations and quotations (here from *The Princess*), and her lively intellect and poetic sense illuminate her reasoning with original rays of fancy from many sources.

Her definition of a writer's effectiveness is significant. It is not in what he announces or demonstrates but in his power to influence others, to rouse them to activities which result in discovery, and to awaken in them a sense of right and wrong, or a desire for the truth, and the energy to live by it whatever the cost. Thomas Carlyle is such a writer (*Leader*, 27.x.55), and her impressions of him lead her to conclusions which indicate deep appreciation and sound critical judgment. No reader who relishes him would wish his style different, any more than he would wish 'Gothic architecture not to be Gothic, or Raffaelle not to be

Raffaelesque'. His pictorial or concrete presentation is perhaps greater than his philosophy.

Four articles written by Marian on Heine in 1865–6 did much to introduce him to English readers. In 'German Wit: Heinrich Heine' (WR January 1856) she gives an account of his life, and then turns to an evaluation of his poetry and prose. Her preliminary analysis of wit and humour shows the complexity of the differentiation between the two, but her conclusion that wit is *reasoning raised to a higher power* falls short of her earlier definitions; and the implied contrast, when she states that humour, by association with the sympathetic emotions, 'continually passes into poetry', suggests that a nineteenth-century view of poetry, which is narrower than that of the seventeenth or the twentieth, has led to some confusion. From French wit without humour to German humour without wit, she passes to Heine. He is an exception, combining with 'Teutonic imagination, sensibility, and humour' an *esprit* 'that would make him brilliant among the most brilliant of Frenchmen'. Her appraisal of his writing is intensive, evoking many qualities with cameo-like precision, and affording an excellent illustration of her power to recall imaginative experience distinctly both in detail and generality.

Two masterly little essays (*Leader*, 12.i.56, 29.iii.56) relate to historical criticism and Genesis and to the *Antigone* of Sophocles. The first bears testimony to immense scholarship and intellectual vision; the second, to largeness of mind and balanced judgment. Wherever views of loyalty or moral sense create opposition in society or State (and Marian could not have written this without considering her own position), the conflict between Antigone and Creon is renewed, and neither is wholly right or wrong.

On the basic necessity for truth to life in art Marian agrees with Ruskin. A sentence in her review of the third volume of his *Modern Painters* (WR April 1856) points forward to her laudation of Dutch paintings in *Adam Bede*:

> The truth of infinite value that he teaches is *realism* – the doctrine that all truth and beauty are to be attained by a humble and faithful study of nature, and not by substituting vague forms, bred by imagination on the mists of feeling, in place of definite, substantial reality.

'The thorough acceptance of this doctrine would remould our life', she adds, in the conviction that

The fundamental principles of all just thought and beautiful action or creation are the same, and in making clear to ourselves what is best and noblest in art, we are making clear to ourselves what is best and noblest in morals; in learning how to estimate the artistic products of a particular age according to the mental attitude and external life of that age, we are widening our sympathy and deepening the basis of our tolerance and charity.

'The Natural History of German Life' (WR July 1856) is devoted principally to the study of two books by Riehl, an author whom Marian admired because he studied the conditions of rural life at first hand, and not in the light of theory or preconceptions. One of his conclusions seemed important to her, and is relevant to the modern world. German society is different from French or English or Italian, and therefore '*a universal social policy has no validity except on paper*, and can never be carried into successful practice'; 'to apply the same social theory to these nations indiscriminately', she adds, with reference to Scott (*The Pirate*, iv), 'is about as wise a procedure as Triptolemus Yellowley's application of the agricultural directions in Virgil's "Georgics" to his farm in the Shetland Isles'. In conformity with her natural history parallelism, she observes that in Europe more than in England the nature of man 'has its roots intertwined with the past, and can only be developed by allowing these roots to remain undisturbed while the process of development is going on, until that perfect ripeness of the seed which carries with it a life independent of the root'. George Eliot's approval of Riehl's 'clear-eyed' conservatism is inherent in *Felix Holt*.

The most interesting part of her review gives an earnest of the rural England which was to appear in her first stories and novels. German peasantry reminded her of English tenant-farmers and their labourers fifty years earlier, and she sketches a farmhouse interior which evokes that of Mrs Poyser (see pp. 48−9). More important is her condemnation of 'cockney sentimentality' in the depiction of rustic life. What we need has been accomplished for the Germans by Riehl. The failure of the English to present the people as they really are is 'a grave evil', for 'the greatest benefit we owe to the artist, whether painter, poet, or novelist, is the extension of our sympathies'; 'it *is* serious that our sympathy with the perennial joys and struggles, the toil, the tragedy, and the humour in the life of our more heavily-laden fellow-men, should be perverted, and turned towards a false object instead of the true one'. (In this it seems clear that Marian's convictions are the stronger for having read Ruskin.) Reacting strongly against idyllicism, she paints a picture more true to Crabbe than consistent with her own works, but only to insist on the need for truth and understanding:

> Idyllic ploughmen are jocund when they drive their team afield; idyllic shepherds make bashful love under hawthorn bushes; idyllic villagers dance in the chequered shade and refresh themselves, not immoderately, with spicy nut-brown ale. But no one who has seen much of actual ploughmen thinks them jocund; no one who is well acquainted with the English peasantry can pronounce them merry. The slow gaze, in which no sense of beauty beams, no humour twinkles, – the slow utterance, and the heavy slouching walk, remind one rather of that melancholy animal the camel, than of the sturdy countryman, with striped stockings, red waistcoat, and hat aside, who represents the traditional English peasant.

Observe a company of haymakers, and the scene is 'smiling':

> Approach nearer, and you will certainly find that haymaking time is a time for joking, especially if there are women among the labourers; but the coarse laugh that bursts out every now and then, and expresses the triumphant taunt, is as far as possible from your conception of idyllic merriment. That delicious effervescence of the mind which we call fun, has no equivalent for the northern peasant, except tipsy revelry; the only realm of fancy and imagination for the English clown exists at the bottom of the third quart pot.

Nor are the rustics above cheating and stealing: 'The selfish instincts are not subdued by the sight of buttercups, nor is integrity in the least established by that classic rural occupation, sheep-washing. To make men moral, something more is requisite than to turn them out to grass.'

Perhaps the kind of burlesque in which the youthful Jane Austen indulged is a more suitable medium than a substantial review for the criticism of those contemporary follies in fiction which are the subject of 'Silly Novels by Lady Novelists' (WR October 1856). They are discussed in general terms and with reference to several

novels. Heroines are wonderfully gifted, and happy endings are inevitable for them, whatever their trials. For authors 'inexperienced
in every form of poverty except poverty of brains', high society
backgrounds are *de rigueur*. Absurdites of high-flown style,
fictional clichés, and fashionable relics of romantic antiquity are
amply illustrated. The *oracular* novel elicits the remark that the
ability of a lady writer to present actual life is inversely propor-
tional to her 'confident eloquence about God and the other world'.
The Evangelical or *white neck-cloth* species presents the fashionable world in another type of costume. The *modern-antique*, 'the
least readable of silly women's novels', gives rise to comments which
could apply to *Romola* (see p. 144). Unfortunately pretentious lady
novelists are encouraged by reviewers' puffery, while women
writers of genius are subject to moderate praise or severe criticism.
Harriet Martineau, Currer Bell (Charlotte Brontë), and Mrs
Gaskell have been 'treated as cavalierly as if they had been men'.
The weakness of feminine fiction is due hardly more to 'want of
intellectual power' than to the 'want of those moral qualities that
contribute to literary excellence − patient diligence, a sense of the
responsibility involved in publication, and an appreciation of the
sacredness of the writer's art'. As the novel is more 'free from rigid
requirements' than any other form of art, it holds a fatal fascina-
tion for incompetent women. 'Like crystalline masses, it may take
any form, and yet be beautiful; we have only to pour in the right
elements − genuine observation, humour, and passion.' This is
'clear-eyed' criticism, and one wishes that Marian Evans had found
time to enlarge on the creative art she was contemplating, especially with reference to works of authors she most admired.

Further implications are to be found in her review of three
novels (WR October 1856). She criticizes the sentimentality and
dogmatism of a Swedish novel, and the exaggerated effects or
theatricality of Charles Reade's *It is Never Too Late to Mend*. One
difference between talent and genius in fiction is that the great
writer is 'thoroughly possessed by his creation − he lives *in* his
characters'. She finds the same glow in Mrs Stowe's *Dred* as in
Scott's *Old Mortality*. Humour 'preserves her from extravagance
and monotony', but her negroes are so good that 'the most terribly
tragic element' in the race question, 'the Nemesis lurking in the
vices of the oppressed', is overlooked.

'Worldliness and Other-Worldliness: The Poet Young' (WR
January 1857) was begun in April 1856, laid aside first for the

article on Riehl, then for the writing of 'Amos Barton', and not completed until December. Following the biographical and critical method of *The Lives of the Poets*, Marian achieves a more arresting style than Johnson's, with frequent injections of mordant satirical wit. It is the longest and in some ways the most important of her essays, but its trenchancy in the cause of humanism could have been more effective had the critical analysis of Young's poetry been less extensive.

The satirical note is struck at the outset with the hauling up of 'a remarkable individual of the species *divine*' from the natural history of men in the eighteenth century. He is 'a paradoxical specimen . . . a sort of cross between a sycophant and a psalmist: a poet whose imagination is alternately fired by the "Last Day" and by a creation of peers', one who will 'feel something more than private disgust if his meritorious efforts in directing men's attention to another world are not rewarded by substantial preferment in this'. 'His spiritual man recognises no motives more familiar than Golgotha and "the skies"; it walks in graveyards, or it soars among the stars.' This curious creature is Edward Young, author of *Night Thoughts*, a poem which George Eliot had admired almost unreservedly in her youth. The reason for her volte-face is religious; although 'the sweet garden-breath of early enjoyment still lingers about many a page', *Night Thoughts* is condemned because it is 'the reflex of a mind in which the higher human sympathies were inactive'.

Sycophancy is found in Young's poetry from first to last. He began with two poems, 'The Last Day' and 'An Epistle' (to Lord Lansdowne); (the suppressed dedication of the former to Queen Anne is swollen with the kind of fulsome absurdity in her triumphal progress and reception on high which characterizes Southey's laudation of George III in *A Vision of Judgement*). 'On the accession of George the Second, Young found the same transcendent merits in him as in his predecessor, and celebrated them in a style of poetry previously unattempted by him — the Pindaric ode, a poetic form which helped him to surpass himself in furious bombast.' In *Night Thoughts* he declares that God is his patron, but 'not at all to the prejudice of some half-dozen lords, duchesses, and right honourables, who have the privilege of sharing finely-turned compliments with their co-patron'.

In prose and poetry, rhymed and blank verse, satire, odes, and meditations, the same Young is found, 'the same narrow circle of thoughts, the same love of abstractions, the same telescopic view of human things, the same appetency towards antithetic apothegm and rhapsodic climax'. The most arresting lines in his tragedies anticipate some of the finer passages in *Night Thoughts*; his characters are 'only transparent shadows through which we see the bewigged *embonpoint* of the didactic poet, excogitating epigrams or ecstatic soliloquies by the light of a candle fixed in a skull'. The outburst of genius in the earlier books of *Night Thoughts* is attributable to 'the freedom of blank verse and the presence of a genuine emotion', though it often 'slides into rhetoric'. He shows a 'startling vigour' of imagery, and 'occasional grandeur' of thought. His merits being known, Marian merely glances at them, preferring to dwell on his radical insincerity and the indefensibility of his religious views.

'When a poet floats in the empyrean, and only takes a bird's-eye view of the earth, some people accept the mere fact of his soaring for sublimity, and mistake his dim vision of earth for proximity to heaven.' Marian rejects the view that 'a mortal joy' is 'Far beneath/A soul immortal': 'Happily for human nature, we are sure no man really believes that. Which of us has the impiety not to feel that our souls are only too narrow for the joy of looking into the trusting eyes of our children, of reposing on the love of a husband or wife, — nay, of listening to the divine voice of music, or watching the calm brightness of autumn afternoons?' Earth for Young meant 'lords and levees, duchesses and Dalilahs, South-Sea dreams and illegal percentage; and the only things distinctly preferable to these are, eternity and the stars. Deprive Young of this antithesis, and more than half his eloquence would be shrivelled up.'

His *want of genuine emotion* is seen in his 'adherence to abstractions'; 'we never find him dwelling on virtue or religion as it really exists . . . in courageous effort for unselfish ends, in the internal triumph of justice and pity over personal resentment, in all the sublime self-renunciation and sweet charities which are found in the details of ordinary life'. The 'angel' in man is 'to be developed by vituperating this world and exalting the next'. Most reprehensible is Young's translation of Paul's text into the view that but for immortality it would be to our advantage to banish moral restraints and live for ambition or self-indulgence, 'Nor care though mankind perish'. It is no wonder, in the light of this, that Marian Evans came to feel that man had yet to find an adequate religion. Her answer is:

> I am just and honest, not because I expect to live in another world, but because, having felt the pain of injustice and dishonesty towards myself, I have a fellow-feeling with other men, who would suffer the same pain if I were unjust or dishonest towards them. . . . Through my union and fellowship with the men and women I *have* seen, I feel a like, though a fainter, sympathy with those I have *not* seen; and I am able so to live in imagination with the generations to come, that their good is not alien to me, and is a stimulus to me to labour for ends which may not benefit myself, but will benefit them.

She holds that there is no necessary link between a future state and 'the widening and strengthening of our sympathetic nature'. 'Nay, to us it is conceivable that in some minds the deep pathos lying in the thought of human mortality — that we are here for a little while and then vanish away, that this earthly life is all that is given to our loved ones and to our many suffering fellow-men — lies nearer the fountains of moral emotion than the conception of extended existence.'

Young's religion is self-centred; it is 'egoism turned heavenward', or '"ambition, pleasure, and the love of gain", directed towards the joys of the future life instead of the present'. His 'argumentative insistence' in end-stopped lines is contrasted with 'that melodious flow of utterance which belongs to thought when it is carried along in a stream of feeling' in Cowper, who, instead of regarding all earthly things as 'dross', finds enjoyment and beauty in common objects, in both the animate and inanimate world. 'His large and tender heart embraces the most every-day forms of human life'; his deep humanity makes him look forward, not with Young to 'Heaven's own pure day' and the world's end, but to the millennium on earth. Marian Evans finds in Young 'that deficient human sympathy, that impiety towards the present and the visible, which flies for its motives, its sanctities, and its religion, to the remote, the vague, and the unknown'. In Cowper she finds 'that genuine love which cherishes things in proportion to their nearness, and feels its reverence grow in proportion to the intimacy of its knowledge'. These affirmations disclose the foundation of both her faith and her fiction.

First Phase of Fiction

SCENES OF CLERICAL LIFE

Although George Eliot's first three stories reveal varying strengths and weaknesses, they undoubtedly mark successive stages of sustained progress in the evolution of a novelist. They also indicate that the transition to fiction was not always easy or felicitous for an essayist with pronounced convictions on life and literature.

In 'Silly Novels by Lady Novelists' she had insisted that the 'real drama of Evangelicalism' was to be found, not in the fashionable world of society (as might be deduced from contemporary novels) but 'among the middle and lower classes', especially in industrial areas. She had witnessed it in Nuneaton during the ministry of the 'Mr Tryan' of 'Janet's Repentance', and acquired a large fund of impressions and hearsay pertaining to local clergy from her parents, from family worship, and further observations of ministers and services while she was at school. Such interests were fostered by her subsequent friendship with Maria Lewis. Her nostalgic return in imagination to her youth and childhood at home was naturally activated by the years of separation which rigid convention had imposed, and it is not surprising that her first fictional venture relates to a clergyman closely associated with her family, though his Evangelicalism was mixed, like much else in his character.

She had another reason for choosing 'clerical' subjects. Though her outlook changed, she remained deeply religious at heart. Her study of Feuerbach confirmed her conviction that the basis of true religion is the love which proceeds from the human heart alone; as she wrote late in life (10.xii.74), she 'could not have cared to write any representation of human life' if she had felt that social and moral development were dependent on 'conceptions of what is not man'. For her 'the idea of God' as 'a high spiritual influence' came from 'the ideal of a goodness' which is 'entirely human'. Discussing

77

her religion earlier with Harriet Beecher Stowe, she stated that 'a religion more perfect than any yet prevalent' was needed, with the emphasis not so much on 'personal consolation' as on 'a more deeply-awing sense of responsibility to man, springing from sympathy with that which of all things is most certainly known to us, the difficulty of the human lot' (8.v.69). It was not by his preaching or his acts that Amos Barton eventually touched 'the spring of goodness' in his parishioners; 'his recent troubles had called out their better sympathies, and that is always a source of love'. Similarly George Eliot strengthens her humanitarian cause, not by preaching but by stirring her readers' hearts.

Lewes could not have been unmindful of such views when he recommended 'Amos Barton' to John Blackwood as the first of a series of tales presenting the 'actual life' of country clergy solely from a human angle. He emphasized that the tone would be sympathetic throughout; numerous religious stories had introduced doctrine, but none had represented the clergy 'with the humours, sorrows, and troubles of other men' since *The Vicar of Wakefield* and Jane Austen, he added.

Although he accepted the story and found it 'very pleasant reading', Blackwood's approval was qualified. He liked the humour of the descriptions, and thought the death of Amos's wife Milly 'powerfully done', but the conclusion seemed lame, and he ventured to believe that the author fell into 'the error of trying too much to explain the characters of his actors instead of allowing them to evolve in the action of the story'. Here he was exercising his tact, for 'Amos Barton' contains technical weaknesses which reflect inexpert authorship. It is workmanlike rather than artistic, close in texture, and instinct with gifts capable of development in a variety of ways. Its unevenness may be illustrated in contrasting scenes, from those which are undramatically descriptive and from others which reveal unmistakable character in sustained dialogue. 'Amos Barton' demonstrates in both the dialogue of comment and the dialogue of action that George Eliot could achieve what to Lewes was 'the highest quality of fiction − dramatic representation'.

In two 'choric' scenes characters meet at Cross Farm, home of the aged Mrs Patten, who at one time adored her husband and now adores her money. Although more implacably disposed towards Janet Gibbs, the niece who, she is convinced, expects a large legacy from her, she derives as much pleasure from the thought of balking expectations as Featherstone does *vis-à-vis* his nephew Fred Vincy in *Middlemarch*. She has always done her duty, having 'known women, as their cheeses swelled a shame to be seen, when their husbands had counted on the cheese-money to make up their rent'. Yet they had three gowns to her one; 'if I'm not to be saved, I know a many as are in a bad way'. Her guests are the Hackits and her doctor Mr Pilgrim, who decreases the tempo of his speech for the sake of emphasis 'as a hen, when advertising her accouchement, passes at irregular intervals from pianissimo semiquavers to fortissimo crotchets'. In deference to Mrs Hackit, one of his best clients, he limits disapproval of her views to 'a succession of little snorts, something like the treble grunts of a guinea-pig'. The four are old friends and, although the ladies cannot agree over Amos Barton, their discussion is nicely tempered by geniality and discretion. At the approach of winter, Janet's undue anxiety about her aunt's health brings Mrs Hackit and Pilgrim hurriedly to Mrs Patten's bedside, where the conversation soon turns to Barton's disgraceful conduct in allowing the Countess to live at his house month after month, to the detriment of his children and his ailing wife. Like Mr Farquhar and Mr Ely in a previous scene, when Amos's susceptibility to the Countess's flattery is discussed, they are the voice of public opinion.

Such gossip and comment promote the story, giving it breadth and preliminary humour. On the other hand, the delineations of the clergy who meet at Milby vicarage, interesting though they are as background figures, are static. George Eliot's powers of invention were reduced by her preoccupation with recollections. One of the seven clergy could have been introduced more effectively in a 'choric' scene; for, as 'the true parish priest, the pastor beloved', helpful in need, 'encouraging rather than severe', able to preach intelligibly 'because he can call a spade a spade, and knows how to disencumber ideas of their wordy frippery', Mr Cleves is Mr Barton's foil. These clergymen assume an interesting role when they discuss his domestic situation and the scandal he is creating, before they settle to the business of the Clerical Meeting, which is excluded as 'esoteric' and 'perhaps dangerous to our repose of mind'.

Nanny, the Bartons' maid, loves her mistress. When she hears the voice of calumny, she is so indignant that little is needed to inflame her anger. The spark falls on the November morning of Mrs Hackit and Mr Pilgrim's visit to Cross Farm, and the sting of Nanny's outburst, 'a-livin' on other folks, an' bringin' a bad name on 'em into the bargain', ends with welcome abruptness the long parasitic stay of the Countess at the Bartons'. Nanny's flare-up is brief, but it exemplifies more significantly than the emphatic tones of Mr Pilgrim or the lisping pomposities of Mr Farquhar that faculty of 'dramatic ventriloquism' which Lewes thought 'the rarest of all'.

'The Countess had left, but alas, the bills she had contributed to swell still remained; so did the exiguity of the children's clothing, which also was partly an indirect consequence of her presence; and so, too, did the coolness and alienation in the parishioners . . .'. Barton's blindness at the expense of his family, and of his beautiful, self-sacrificing wife Milly in particular, arises from a self-assurance which made him disregard other people's views. He has no vices, but he is not very intelligent. His preaching is 'as evangelical as anything to be heard in the Independent Chapel', yet it needs 'very little unwonted reading and unwonted discussion' to convince him that 'an Episcopalian Establishment' is 'much more than unobjectionable'; on many points he begins to feel that his opinions are 'a little too far-sighted and profound to be crudely and suddenly communicated to ordinary minds'. The Countess flatters his pretensions, and raises his hope of preferment. His inadequacies as a parish priest are highlighted by his visit to the workhouse, where his want of imagination renders his religious exposition unintelligible, just as his insensitive tactlessness closes the heart of the pathetic snuff-loving Mrs Brick, and induces him to use the threat of hell-fire, Brocklehurst-wise, in reasoning with a child of seven on his reported misbehaviour.

Like that of the Clerical Meeting, this 'College' picture is divided into portrait description and dramatic realization. In retrospect it stands out as a whole, almost independently of the story, exemplifying the change of mode which characterizes much of the presentation. Like *The Mill on the Floss*, 'Amos Barton' begins with nostalgic recollections, rather in the style of Charles Lamb (recurring briefly in the address to the reader which is prompted by thoughts of cups of tea enriched with farmhouse cream). Between this lingering reminiscential start and the swift economical movement which brings the story to its close, there are frequent shifts and some abrupt transitions. The link between scenes in the 'College' chapter is Amos Barton, whom we accompany imaginatively; the narrative pauses for visual presentation, character-analysis, and retrospect; through dialogue and narrative description we are made aware of the curate's problems at home and in the parish;

after the workhouse visit he prepares for the Clerical Meeting from which we are rightly excluded. The structuring is often ingenuous and unprofessional. Minor changes to the present historic tense are less jarring; sometimes they help to create vivid impressions, but the device is overworked and, at one point where the author's memory of home environment revives, it introduces an awkward inconsistency:

> The College was a huge square stone building, standing on the best apology for an elevation of ground that could be seen for about ten miles around Shepperton. A flat ugly district this; depressing enough to look at even on the brightest days. The roads are black with coal-dust, the brick houses dingy with smoke; and at that time − the time of handloom weavers − every other cottage had a loom at its window . . .

George Eliot cannot resist the intrusion of personal reminiscence and views. The memory of 'Shepperton' takes her back beyond the period of the story to her childhood and the old church and choir; one autobiographical passage was discarded, but the whole recollection, with its delightful evocations, belongs more properly to the love story of Mr Gilfil. Her comments on life and the narrative (ii) indicate the difficulty she experienced in confining herself to fiction from the outset. A long address to the representative reader ('my dear madam') arises from the commonplaceness of her hero (v); it comes from the author of 'Silly Novels by Lady Novelists'. Unfortunately the tone changes from the positive and persuasive to the superior and dismissive:

> Depend on it, you would gain unspeakably if you would learn with me to see some of the poetry and the pathos, the tragedy and the comedy, lying in the experience of a human soul that looks out through dull grey eyes, and that speaks in a voice of quite ordinary tones. . . . As it is, you can, if you please, decline to pursue my story farther; and you will easily find reading more to your taste, since I learn from the newspapers that many remarkable novels, full of striking situations, thrilling incidents, and eloquent writing, have appeared only within the last season.

All that is relevant is said more winningly in a brief paragraph (vii) which ends: 'I wish to stir your sympathy with commonplace troubles — to win your tears for real sorrow: sorrow such as may live next door to you — such as walks neither in rags nor in velvet, but in very ordinary decent apparel.'

Amos lives not so much from his imperfections as from his final affliction. The death of the wife whom he loved, but whose patient endurance he never appreciated until he lost her, is deeply moving, as John Blackwood found; and tragic regret is enhanced by the author's appeal:

> O the anguish of that thought that we can never atone to our dead for the stinted affection we gave them, for the light answers we returned to their plaints or their pleadings, for the little reverence we showed to that sacred human soul that lived so close to us, and was the divinest thing God had given us to know!

Traces of Victorian sentimentality are faint; the reactions of the children are differentiated convincingly and movingly at the bedside of their dying mother and at her burial; relief comes with the kindness of neighbours in the spring. To most modern readers Amos's grief when he visits the grave by moonlight is more convincing than its expression, but few would disagree with Lewes that the pathos of the story is better than its fun. The comedy and wit of 'Amos Barton' are incidental, and the wit is not very memorable. It varies from the intellectual and esoteric to word-play, facetious Latinity and circumlocution, and obvious Dickensian syllepsis when John, servant in the household of Mr Bridmain and the Countess, approaches Mrs Barton nervously with a gravy tureen and an odour of the stable.

In the seasonal parallelism which supplies a subdued colouring to the story, we can see a characteristic feature of the author. Troubles thicken and Mrs Barton's health declines as winter approaches; snow lies thick on the graves when she is buried. The 'fatal frost' thaws as sympathy reopens the hearts of parishioners towards Amos, and cold faces look kind again. The children's happiness with loving neighbours in the spring coincides with the opening of the restored church 'in all its splendour'; and, years later, Amos revisits Milly's grave 'in the calm and softened light of an autumnal afternoon' with his eldest daughter Patty, who 'makes the evening sunshine of his life'.

*   *   *

Like 'Amos Barton', 'Mr Gilfil's Love-Story' begins with leisurely recollections, and accelerates artistically as tension increases. With longer unbroken sequences, less obtrusive personal notes, and more even and assured prose, it achieves a smoother, rather distinctive continuity, though none of its characters creates as strong an impression as Amos. Mr Gilfil lingers sympathetically, but with less definition, in the memory, for he is not quite at the centre of the narrative, and the story is less real, much as it gains from the introduction of glimpses of community life in short dramatic scenes.

It begins with his death, thirty years before the time of writing. The author's memories of Astley ('Knebley') and Arbury Hall ('Cheverel Manor'), the housekeeper's room (iv) in particular, are evident, but the main story belongs to a period about thirty years before her birth. The opening chapter is woven around observations and anecdotes which she heard from her parents; through the Hackits and Mrs Patten it creates a link with 'Amos Barton', whetting the reader's curiosity to know more about the late vicar and his marriage. For this, the main scene and dramatis personae are presented in the second chapter, on a June evening in 1788, at a critical point when Captain Wybrow excites Caterina's jealousy. With interest focused on the heroine, the next chapter takes us further back in time to Italy, describing how Caterina became Sir Christopher Cheverel's ward. There follows an account of her up-bringing at Cheverel Manor during the period of its 'architectural metamorphosis' in fashionable Gothic style. The drama to which we are introduced in the second chapter then continues without let. Perhaps the presentation of Caterina's origin and girlhood could have been limited with advantage to a paragraph or two, but the narrative is nicely dovetailed, the description is never too weighty, and preliminary flashbacks succeed in creating wider and deeper human interest than would a chronological sequence of the same events.

In 'Mr Gilfil's Love-Story' the author is most herself when she writes about the life she knew in the Midlands. The story of the Countess (which is almost wholly imaginary; see pp. 258–9) is the least convincing part of 'Amos Barton', but it is less improbable than that of Caterina, entirely an invention suggested by the marriage of a local vicar to a collier's daughter, whose singing had been cultivated by an Italian music master at Arbury Hall. Reflecting a conventional view of the Italian temperament, it develops Caterina's jealousy to a histrionic climax which seems quite foreign to the author of 'Silly Novels by Lady Novelists'. Captain Wybrow's frivolous behaviour when his marriage to Miss Assher is approaching is taken as a cruel insult, and this, preying on feverish susceptibility, leads to violent reactions, and finally to a fierce resolve to stab him to the heart. John Blackwood felt uncomfortable when he read the first part of the story, wondering whether 'the excellent Gilfil' was not 'too abjectly devoted a lover for a man of character', and whether it would not be better to make Caterina 'a little less openly devoted' to 'the insufferable Wybrow'. George Eliot refused 'to alter anything in relation to the delineation or development of character' which she felt to be psychologically true. 'My artistic bent is directed not at all to the presentation of eminently irreproachable characters, but to the presentation of mixed human beings in such a way as to call forth tolerant judgment, pity, and sympathy', she added (18.ii.57). The critical question hinges less, however, on 'mixed' characters than on improbabilities of behaviour and chance rather than extreme possibilities. Lewes was struck by the 'subtle truth' in the 'complex motives' which made the story exciting, and one cannot fail to be impressed by the steps repeatedly taken to give conviction to the development of both Caterina's mental derangement and the stages of her slow recovery.

Allied to the theatrical crisis of her story is the minor improbability of a long soliloquy in which Captain Wybrow twice reminds us of his precarious health. 'These palpitations may carry me off', he tells Caterina when her anger upsets him in the first act of the drama (ii). Both the frequency and the manner of such warnings impose a strain on the reader's credulity; and the two weaker features of the narrative merge in sensational climax when Caterina, 'the incarnation of a fierce purpose, rather than a woman', hurries to the Rookery, and finds him dead in her path. The irony of circumstance by which jealousy, first of Mr Gilfil, then of Miss Assher, inflames the vengeful mind against Wybrow, is well contrived; Gilfil's suppressed feelings (conveyed alliteratively in 'If it were not for Sir Christopher, I should like to pound him into paste to poison puppies like himself') lead to a remark in a letter designed to help Caterina, and the irony of its effect is equalled in the sequel, hatred giving way to her old love when she finds Wybrow dead.

Among the finer imaginative effects comes the recurrent bird image in association with Caterina, Sir Christopher's 'singing-bird'. When news reaches Cheverel Manor that she is alive with Dorcas, Gilfil gallops to see her, hoping he will be in time to cherish his little bird with 'the sweet throat that trembled with love and music'. A victim of chance (overpowering emotions as well as events), she is presented early as a poor bird destined to flutter and dash its soft breast against 'the hard iron bars of the inevitable'. This Carlylean symbol must have appealed to Hardy, as would the philosophical conclusion of the chapter describing the evening of Miss Assher's arrival. At length Caterina falls asleep from sheer exhaustion, her 'poor little heart' bruised with 'a weight too heavy for it'. Nature maintains her inexorable course — the stars, the tides, the sun, the stream of human thought and deed:

> What were our little Tina and her trouble in this mighty torrent, rushing from one awful unknown to another? Lighter than the smallest centre of quivering life in the water-drop, hidden and uncared for as the pulse of anguish in the breast of the tiniest bird that has fluttered down to its nest with the long-sought food, and has found the nest torn and empty.

Here we have the perspective of detachment, but there are hints of sentimentality in the 'poor little' bird imagery, which are renewed when Caterina returns from Mosslands, the home of Mr Bates, and a 'nest' to her from childhood: his remarks on Miss Assher's beauty have reduced her to the state of 'a poor wounded leveret painfully dragging its little body through the sweet clover-tufts', though the sunlight beams through the trees 'like a Shechinah, or visible divine presence'. The irony of the contrast may counter-balance momentary sentimental indulgences, but it cannot remove them.

Elsewhere there is a harmony between the outer scene and Caterina's feelings. When she can no longer bear to see Wybrow admiring Miss Assher, she retires to her bedroom. The moonlight is dreary, 'robbed of all its tenderness and repose by the hard driving wind'; the trees are harassed, the shivering grass makes her quake with sympathetic cold, and the willows by the pond seem agitated and helpless like herself. The description combines sub-jectivity of impression with the pathetic fallacy, and there is a suggestion of the latter in the author's comment on 'the cessation of threatening symptoms' which allays Wybrow's anxiety (and Gilfil's) about his health: 'All earthly things have their lull: even on nights when the most unappeasable wind is raging, there will be a moment of stillness before it crashes among the boughs again, and storms against the windows, and howls like a thousand lost demons through the key-holes.' The imagery reminds us of Caterina's unrelieved grief, but the brief parallel soon turns to the irony of sunny days which smile on the family gladness but do nothing to allay the 'tempest' within her; only when she reaches her room does it break out every night in 'loud whispers and sobs'.

There is less recourse to the present historic than in 'Amos Barton'. It is used most effectively in the moonlight passage already referred to, but more noticeably when it conveys Gilfil's perturbation lest Caterina, her mind unhinged by Wybrow's death, has committed suicide. Following a stream hidden among trees, he suddenly notices something white behind a bough. Mistaking it for her dress, he seems to see her 'dear dead face upturned' but, as he approaches agonizingly, the white object moves, and a waterfowl spreads its wings and flies off screaming.

On a smaller scale, 'Mr Gilfil's Love-Story' creates a sense of rural community like that of *Adam Bede*. From the scene on the lawn outside the Manor, where Lady Cheverel appears like one of Sir Joshua Reynolds' stately ladies, to Dorcas and her family, there is a wide social gradation, introducing characters and scenes of varied interest. Among those who play a secondary role, Lady Assher, who dribbles on 'like a leaky shower-bath' and is full of good advice and recollections of the late Sir John, is one of the less forgettable. Lady Cheverel is a submissive nonentity, but Sir Christopher, who likes his way, shows his wise humanity in an interview with Mrs Hartopp, a widow who is anxious to retain her husband's farm. Wybrow's death unmans him, and he realizes how proud and obstinate he has been to his sister, who had lost one of her sons a short time previously. 'We can hardly learn humility and tenderness enough except by suffering', Maynard Gilfil comments, speaking for George Eliot.

Mr Bates, a bachelor memorable for his Yorkshire accent and friendliness, has a red complexion and a way of walking with his head hanging forward and rolling from side to side which give him 'the air of a Bacchus in a blue apron', as if, 'in the present reduced circumstances of Olympus', he had taken to the management of his own vines. This and the table, 'high enough surely for Homer's gods', in the housekeeper's room at Cheverel Manor, where Bates habitually enjoys 'the feast of gossip and the flow of grog', may not have been lost on the imagination of Thomas Hardy (see p. 247).

One February day, 'when the sun is shining with a promise of approaching spring', music plays its part in Caterina's recovery. As her fingers wander with 'their old sweet method' among the keys of the harpsichord, her soul floats 'in its true familiar element of delicious sound, as the water-plant that lies withered and shrunken on the ground expands into freedom and beauty when once more bathed in its native flood'. Appropriately she sings Sir Christopher's favourite tune *'Che farò senza Eurydice?'* in Gilfil's hearing, for he faithfully awaits her restoration. Their marriage is happy but short-lived. Caterina dies in child-labour, and takes his love 'with her into deep silence for evermore'.

No doubt his sorrows made him respected among his parishioners, and enlarged his sense of fellowship in his later years, for, as George Eliot writes with reference to his unbroken love for Caterina, 'It is so with the human relations that rest on the deep emotional sympathy of affection: every new day and night of joy and sorrow is a new ground, a new consecration, for the love that is nourished by memories as well as hopes . . .'. As a preacher he inclined not to spiritual doctrine but to the practical virtues. His humour and kindness endeared him to children; and dirty Dame Fripp, 'a very rare church-goer', borrowed old crape from Mrs Hackit to attend his funeral, not from 'theological' motives (she remained 'as indifferent to the means of grace as ever') but because she remembered his generosity. His most biting criticism was reserved for 'the evil doing of the rich man'. Many oddities grew from his hard sorrow, just as odd excrescences develop over the wounds of trees where their finest branches have been lopped off. Gilfil was like a lopped oak, but 'the heart of him was sound, the grain was of the finest'; he had never lost the 'brave, faithful, tender nature' he had evinced in his 'first and only love'.

*   *   *

The crucial subject of 'Janet's Repentance' is the irreligion or inhumanity proceeding from sectarian religion (of which the modern world is continually reminded in outrage and controversy) and its transcendence in a humanity which is above creed and casuistry. Janet is an orthodox believer, convinced ultimately that God will not forsake her, and that she and Mr Tryan will meet after death. In a story which illustrates her faith in the healing power of sympathy and compassion, George Eliot's muted dissent is an irrelevance; she emphasizes 'the margin of ignorance which surrounds all our knowledge', and concedes that 'perhaps the profoundest philosophy could hardly fill it up better' than Tryan's 'Divine Will' (xxii). She believes that 'we reap what we sow', but also, with Wordsworth, that 'nature has love over and above that justice, and gives us shadow and blossom and fruit that spring from no planting of ours' (v). (For the psychological, non-pantheistic basis of this attribution, see p. 231.) Each of the movements towards sectarian hatred and sectarian reconciliation, the one instigated by Dempster, the other inspired by Tryan, finds it finale in a ritualistic procession past Dempster's house in Orchard Street. Janet, one of the anti-Tryanite party who are drawn from the most respectable citizens of Milby, looks down on the first with scorn and merriment; eighteen months later, 'in quiet submissive sorrow', she follows Mr Tryan's coffin. The sympathy that comes from suffering had drawn her to him. Had George Eliot managed her story more artistically, she would probably have included fewer assertions on the subject. It might have been conveyed more poignantly and intensely, but she was unable to bring Tryan and Janet together in a great imaginative action, and the ending of the story suffers in consequence.

The presentation is an amalgam, ranging from social documentation to highly dramatic scenes and the quieter narrative ending. Mr Tryan's idealization may reflect a revival in George Eliot of the religious ardour she experienced when she was a friend of Maria Lewis, herself a fervid supporter of the Evangelical preacher whose 'persecution' is inseparable from Janet's story. The background is indispensable, but George Eliot remembered too much to keep it in proportion, and she lacked the fictional expertise to present it at appropriate points, without holding up the action unduly. The result is that an excellent introduction, wholly dramatic in contrast to her earlier ones, is followed by a Milby chapter which is of considerable interest to the social historian but of almost insuperable dimensions for the general reader. Even after this the story remains at a standstill, while persons of hardly secondary importance are described at length. Satirical irrelevance at this point probably originated from reminiscential indulgence; later, memories of schooldays in Nuneaton assume the autobiographical disguise of boyhood recollections. Not surprisingly Blackwood wished that the author had plunged sooner into her story; he would also have preferred a pleasanter picture of life. This was impossible; either Dempster and Janet had to remain as George Eliot saw them, or the story had to be abandoned as too painful. The persecution was 'a real bit in the religious history of England' about twenty-eight years previously, and everything was 'softened from the fact' as far as art allowed without falsifying. 'The real town was more vicious than my Milby; the real Dempster was far more disgusting than mine; the real Janet alas! had a far sadder end then mine, who will melt away from the reader's sight in purity, happiness, and beauty' (11.vi.57).

The first scene opens in 'loud, rasping' tones, stressing the dominance of Dempster, a great drinker and talker, a bullying sciolist in denominational matters, who is prepared to level the most unscrupulous accusations against his opponents. Evangelicalism, he holds, is demoralizing, and an insult to the 'venerable pastor' Mr Crewe. Descriptive analysis of Milby reveals that the latter delivered inaudible sermons on Sunday, and imparted 'the education of a gentleman' ('an arduous inacquaintance' with Latin grammar such as Tom Tulliver was to suffer) to three pupils in the upper grammar school. He read nothing, but was regarded as learned, for he had once had a large private school attended by a young nobleman or two. Having made a fortune from his curacy and teaching, he enjoyed his avarice in comfort. The Church was torpid in Milby until Mr Tryan gave it new life. Yet, though the place was dull and dingy, spring came to it and (an image which may have suggested the end of Lawrence's *The Rainbow*) rainbows spanned it,

clothing the very roofs and chimneys in a strange transfiguring beauty. And so it was with the human life there, which at first seemed a dismal mixture of griping worldliness, vanity, ostrich feathers, and the fumes of brandy: looking closer, you found some purity, gentleness, and unselfishness, as you may have observed a scented geranium giving forth its wholesome odours amidst blasphemy and gin in a noisy pot-house.

The picture of the select band of Mr Tryan's admiring lady supporters in Mrs Linnet's parlour is acidulated with humour, but the author's interest in fashions of female dress and fancy-work, before Evangelicalism wrought a change for the better in Miss Rebecca's person, creates hampering disproportion. A lighter note is struck with Mrs Linnet's rapid reading of religious books, her interest being confined to the secular portions, especially (since her legs swelled occasionally) in the lives of dropsical divines. Her conversation with Miss Pratt, who finds few in Milby to esteem 'profound learning', and speaks in a superior style sometimes reminiscent of Mary Bennet, revives interest in a story that has hardly begun, throws out proleptic hints, and leads to rising excitement with the appearance of Mr Tryan and news of a mob demonstration in progress against him. Swift changes follow, from the parlour to the assembling crowd, with Dempster's arrival, and his triumphant speech at the end of the first round in his contest with Tryan. Late at night he returns home the worse for drink, and has to let himself in, the knocker which has thundered ominously having produced no response. When Janet appears with candlestick aslant, his language is threatening; he detects that she has been drinking again, and strikes her heavily and repeatedly. The heroine's entry has been long delayed; it is as startling as it is haunting. Her 'grandly-cut features' are imbued with the sorrow that makes beauty more beautiful. Helpless but proud, she does not tremble, but makes one vain appeal, 'O Robert! pity! pity!' When she next appears she has made him 'as neat as a new pin' for the Confirmation service. The irreligion behind religious appearances could scarcely go further.

The Bishop supports Mr Tryan; the decision which had delighted the anti-Tryanites is reversed, and the sectarian battle is renewed. Tryanites are threatened with dismissal by their employers; Dempster concocts a scurrilous 'playbill' for public display, and Janet shows submissive loyalty in penning the original at his dictation. She would give her crooked guinea and all the luck it might bring her to have Tryan beaten, since she 'can't endure the sight of the man coming to harass dear old Mr and Mrs Crewe in their last days'. Tryan suffers acutely from the ensuing scorn and hatred, and finds brief respite in the summer paradise of Mr Jerome's garden, orchard, and pasture. Though a dissenter, Jerome is George Eliot's ideal. He is above polemics, and welcomes Tryan as if to say, 'Ah, friends, this pleasant world is a sad one, too, isn't it? Let us help one another, let us help one another.' 'That any living being should want, was his chief sorrow; that any rational being should waste, was the next.' Like her china, his wife is handsome and old-fashioned, a foretaste of Mrs Poyser, with an acute sense of time (though it is recorded with wide variation in the White House) and a sharp tongue: 'you're al'ys a-findin' faut wi' my chany, because

I bought it myself afore I was married. But let me tell you, I knowed how to choose chany if I didn't know how to choose a husband.' Like most of George Eliot's young children, their granddaughter sounds adenoidal.

The Evangelicalism which steadily gained ground in Milby is critically evaluated: 'folly often mistook itself for wisdom, ignorance gave itself airs of knowledge, and selfishness, turning its eyes upward, called itself religion'. Yet it encouraged purity of heart, 'that idea of duty, that recognition of something to be lived for beyond the mere satisfaction of self'. Janet resists Mr Tryan's teaching; not until she discovers that his life is threatened with consumption does 'fellowship in suffering' allow her to sympathize with him. Meanwhile luck has turned against Dempster professionally; with the death of his mother, his good angel leaves him, and he drinks more heavily. Janet, who suffers in consequence, finds relief in self-pity. In drunken rage, he behaves abominably, provokes her defiance, and, after midnight and the departure of his guests, thrusts her out in her nightdress. The stony street, the north-east wind, and the darkness express her plight. Later the upper-storey windows, crimsoned with sunset, herald Dempster's corpse-like return, as he is carried in from the accident which he had precipitated by flogging his horse in a drunken frenzy. In the meantime some relief has been afforded the reader by the servants' comments on him and Janet. His delirious ravings may seem the stuff of melodrama, but they are based on sound medical evidence, as could be expected of George Eliot. The renewal of temptation which Janet resists after Dempster's death is too patently contrived.

Janet, who had taken refuge with Mrs Pettifer, one of Tryan's supporters, turns to him in her despair. To qualify him as a spiritual comforter, George Eliot, assured that 'the tale of the Divine Pity was never yet believed from lips that were not felt to be moved by human pity', gratuitously invents an artificial literary story. She confirms his efficacy with passages on that 'blessed influence of one true loving human soul on another' which is not calculable by algebra or Benthamite reasoning (xxi, xxii). 'The only true knowledge of our fellow-man is that which enables us to feel with him', a truth missed by the 'subtlest analysis of schools and sects' unless 'it be lit up by the love that sees in all forms of human thought and work, the life and death struggles of separate human beings' (x). The life and death struggles of Janet and Mr

Tryan were written to present a truth of which we are reminded as Janet watches day after day by Dempster's death-bed, 'a duty about which all creeds and all philosophies are one'; it is found in the pity, patience, and love which can 'sweep down the miserable choking drift of our quarrels, our debates, our would-be wisdom, and our clamorous selfish desires'. The remainder of the story is rather superfluous, though it confirms Janet's redemption through sympathy, fellowship, and good works. Her altruism is a memorial to Mr Tryan, and the finest reflex of his deep compassion.

ADAM BEDE

John Blackwood's lack of sympathy with the opening chapters of 'Janet's Repentance' made George Eliot decide to conclude *Scenes of Clerical Life* sooner than was intended. She had wished to include 'The Clerical Tutor', a story that may have been transmuted years later to that of Casaubon and Dorothea: when she began to work on 'Miss Brooke' she noted that the subject had been recorded among her 'possible themes' ever since she began to write fiction, and that it would 'probably take new shapes in the development'. Another story she had in mind for the same series was that told her by her aunt in 1839. Little detail was remembered beyond Elizabeth's prison visit to a common girl convicted of murdering her own child, staying the night with her, hearing her confession, and accompanying her to the place of execution. After a discussion with Lewes in December 1856, George Eliot 'began to think of blending' it in a single story with more of her aunt's reminiscences, and with 'points' in her father's early life and character. She had probably envisaged the latter when she wrote her introductory chapter to a novel set in Staffordshire (p. 27).

More confident with experience, George Eliot found she needed 'a large canvas' for the novel she contemplated. It would be 'full of the breath of cows and the scent of hay', she told her publisher. She relied on distant recollections of the country around Ellastone, more on memories of the Park and woods at Arbury and of her father's farm at Griff, and much on her imagination. With typical thoroughness (as professor Haight has indicated) she did considerable research on the period of the novel: from *The Life of John Wesley* she made notes on Methodist beliefs and practices; from *The Gentleman's Magazine* of 1799, on the weather, the times when flowers bloomed and fruit ripened, wages and bread prices, coming of age celebrations at Belvoir Castle, and the Church of England. Only the main outline of the action was planned in advance:

> When I began to write [*Adam Bede*], the only elements I had determined on besides the character of Dinah were the character of Adam, his relation to Arthur Donnithorne and their mutual relations to Hetty . . . the scene in the prison being of course the climax towards which I worked. Everything else grew out of the characters and their mutual relations. Dinah's ultimate relation to Adam was suggested by George, when I had read to him the first part of the first volume: he was so delighted with the presentation of Dinah and so convinced that the readers' interest would centre in her, that he wanted her to be the principal figure at the last. I accepted the idea at once, and from the end of the third chapter worked with it constantly in view.

Adam Bede was published in February 1859, and enjoyed a tremendous success; before the end of the year a third edition in Russian was called for. It did not escape criticism altogether; *The Saturday Review* found the climax melodramatic and the authorial intrusions trying. *The Times* thought it first-rate: 'We need not fear to yield ourselves entirely to all the enchantments of the wizard whose first article of belief is the truism . . . that we are all alike — that the human heart is one.' Charles Reade proclaimed it 'the finest thing since Shakspeare', and Alexandre Dumas *père* thought it the greatest novel of its time.

The novel is divided into six books, of which the first and the fifth are much the longest. The first introduces a variety of characters and settings, and initiates the main story with the mutual infatuation of Hetty Sorrel and Arthur Donnithorne. Interrelations are handled dexterously, with the result that the action is almost continuous; by the end, on the fourth day, it has taken up one-third of the novel. In terms of character, actualizations of place, landscape, and community, its achievement is unusually impressive. With the burial of Adam Bede's father, Adam's dreams of Hetty as he goes to work, his evening visit to see her at the Hall Farm, and night-school at Bartle Massey's, impressions are richly reinforced in the second book. The third is devoted to the celebrations at the Chase in honour of Arthur's coming of age; they also serve to heighten our sense of place and community. At the centre of the novel, they mark the peak of both Arthur and Hetty's illusions; he intends to be a respected, liberal landlord, and she flatters herself that he will marry her. Adam becomes the new manager of the woodlands on the estate. The fourth book opens with threatened harvests ('If only the corn were not ripe enough to be blown out of the husk and scattered as untimely seed!'), followed significantly by Adam's shock when he sees Arthur and Hetty kissing in the Grove; he expresses his anger in blows (*a necessity*, the author felt after Lewes had suggested that Adam's part heretofore had been too passive). Arthur breaks with Hetty and joins his regiment; Hetty consents to an engagement with Adam. The fifth book narrates her departure in despair, and the sequence of events leading to her arrest, trial, and last-minute reprieve. It ends in reconciliation between Adam and Arthur by the tree in the Grove which the former recognises as 'the boundary mark of his youth' and the sign of 'the time when some of his earliest, strongest feelings had left him'. Arthur engages not to return for years, so that the Poysers can stay on at the Hall Farm without sense of disgrace, and Adam continue his managership honourably. With the harvest supper and the marriage of Adam and Dinah, the sixth section provides a happy ending.

The identity of the mysterious horseman, whose questioning excites interest in the gathering on Hayslope Green, creates a suspense which helps to focus attention on Dinah Morris's preaching on the first evening of the story. The little he does to knit it together is seen only in retrospect, for, long before he reappears, he is forgotten. His initial role may have been an afterthought; his one function is crucial to the climax of the action. He is a magistrate, and it is because he is impressed by Adam's bearing at Hetty's trial, and remembers him and the preaching at Hayslope, that he enables Dinah to stay with Hetty during her last hours in prison.

Perhaps George Eliot was left to guess the date of the execution witnessed by her aunt, for her main story runs from June 1799 to March 1800, the imaginary prison scene taking place two years before the actual. The harvest supper occurs more than eighteen months later, and is linked for artistic reasons with the marriage of Adam and Dinah. Mr Irwine 'had seen Adam in the worst moments of his sorrow; and what better harvest from that painful seed-time could there be than this?' The brief epilogue (June 1807) refers to

Arthur's return, the death of Hetty, and a Methodist veto on preaching by women; unlike Elizabeth Evans, Dinah submits to this (significantly with Adam's approval) and finds compensation in other forms of teaching. The chronology of the novel continually reinforces a sense of reality; it is registered by clock and calendar, by seasonal changes and events at home and abroad. Hours pass 'to the loud ticking of the old day-clock and the sound of Adam's tools' as he labours to finish the coffin his father had forgotten; before it strikes ten Seth returns from escorting Dinah to the Hall Farm after her preaching, and it is midnight when Adam breaks off to look out at the stars, before Gyp sets up his premonitory howl. Though it is 'close upon three by the sun' when we first visit the Hall Farm, Mrs Poyser's handsome eight-day clock points to half-past three. On the following day (two days after the story opens), always anxious not to be outwitted by time, she asks Hetty, returning late from her meeting with Arthur in the Chase, whether she expects her to set her clock by gentlefolks' time. In this brief period the subject has ranged from death and the consolations of religion to the illusions of young love (Adam's as well as Hetty's) and the self-delusions of Arthur, intent on amusing himself with Hetty and on finishing Dr Moore's *Zeluco*.

The familiar moral at the opening of this novel, on the misery created by vice, could have been no more than a shallow, evanescent sentiment to him in pursuing the villainous courses of a hero (an army officer like himself) who thought nothing of seduction. Wellmeaning, overconfident, and inexperienced, Arthur looks forward to his coming of age on 30 July. By this time, hay-making is over; 'yet the time of harvest and ingathering is not come, and we tremble at the possible storms that may ruin the precious fruit in the moment of its ripeness' (xxii). The overtones are clear; George Eliot anticipates much, particularly (as her next paragraph shows) the moment when Hetty at Windsor sees the ear-rings bought by Arthur, recalls trying them on in the bright sunshine of 30 July, and wishes she could drown herself. It is while Arthur is looking forward to the events of that day with his admiring godmother Mrs Irwine that the conversation turns to character and appearance (a motif in *Zeluco*, where the topic is discussed at some length with reference to the hero). Mr Irwine declares that nature is too clever even for his mother, who maintains that she can 'tell what men are by their outsides'.

Talking of eyes reminds Arthur of the wizardry of 'The Ancient Mariner'; later he reads Irwine's friend Arthur Young's books.

A more critical contemporary subject for country people, including the Bede family, is the rising cost of bread. From abroad come rumours of the Napoleonic war, with 'the news from Egypt' at the beginning, and possibilities of peace at the harvest supper. Mr Poyser's comments reflect a farmer's self-interest and the ignorance of popular prejudice: 'Th' war's a fine thing for the country, an' how'll you keep up prices wi'out it? An' them French are a wicked sort o' folks, by what I can make out; what can you do better nor fight 'em?'

In conjunction with change and suffering, time expresses the inexorable. After his fruitless search for Hetty, and before learning the worst from Mr Irwine, Adam sits in the rectory hall and watches the hurrying minute-hand of the clock with its 'loud hard indifferent tick'. 'In our times of bitter suffering,' George Eliot adds, 'there are almost always these pauses, when our consciousness is benumbed to everything but some trivial perception or sensation.' A passage in 'Mr Gilfil's Love-Story' (v) is even more relevant to *Adam Bede*:

> The inexorable ticking of the clock is like the throb of pain to sensations made keen by a sickening fear. And so it is with the great clockwork of nature. Daisies and buttercups give way to the brown waving grasses, tinged with the warm red sorrel; the waving grasses are swept away, and the meadows lie like emeralds set in the bushy hedgerows; the tawny-tipped corn begins to bow with the weight of the full ear; the reapers are bending amongst it, and it soon stands in sheaves; then, presently, the patches of yellow stubble lie side by side with streaks of dark-red earth, which the plough is turning up in preparation for the new-thrashed seed. And this passage from beauty to beauty, which to the happy is like the flow of a melody, measures for many a human heart the approach of foreseen anguish − seems hurrying on the moment when the shadow of dread will be followed up by the reality of despair.

This conclusion, with its Wordsworthian link between nature and humanity, applies particularly to Hetty Sorrel, whose name may have sprung from George Eliot's earlier imaginative association of red sorrel with seasonal changes and grief. Hetty's cheek is like a rose-petal; her love for Arthur reaches its climax in the summer; her consequent misery, in winter when she seeks shelter in leafless hedgerows, recalling in her red cloak Martha Ray of Wordsworth's poem 'The Thorn', a mad woman who haunts the mossy grave of the child it was thought she had murdered.

The moral significance of changing fortunes which is registered by the seasons is extended to landscape impressions in the Loamshire–Stonyshire antithesis. Whereas the richer natural surroundings of Thrushcross Grange come to express a more civilized and desirable form of life than the wild bleakness of the moors in *Wuthering Heights*, the green wooded Loamshire pastures breed a spiritual torpor and an overriding concern for earthly things in comparison with the bleak and barren hill country around Snowfield. At least this is Dinah's view, but its reiteration undoubtedly forms one of the interwoven motifs of the novel. Up there, she tells Mr Irwine, there are no trees, 'but you see the heavens stretched out like a tent, and you feel the everlasting arms around you'. When Adam rides to Snowfield on the last visit before his marriage, the October sunshine connotes the wisdom and widening of horizons which suffering and sympathy have brought. The scene which reminds him of the familiar pain of the past now appears less harsh, and he is conscious of the overarching sky. A relationship therefore exists between this change and the diptych-like contrast of the two adjacent bedroom scenes (xv), where Hetty, self-centred and vain, performs her narcissistic rites before her mirror, while Dinah looks out of her window at the peaceful fields and the rising moon, and is reminded of 'all the dear people whom she had learned to care for' and of 'the struggles and weariness that might lie before them'. Intuitively she is aware of Hetty's need for guidance, but Hetty repulses her and is soon lost 'in the wood again', dreaming of Arthur with whom she had walked blissfully that evening, as if borne along on a cloud by warm zephyrs. Dinah's missionary zeal is generated by convictions which are identical with George Eliot's. 'The Egoist's Progress' might be the title of more than one of her novels, wrote Viola Meynell; it is to be seen on a larger scale in *Daniel Deronda* than in *Adam Bede*, and is found in one of her first published essays, 'A Little Fable with a Great Moral', the story of two hamadryads, one loving to gaze on her reflection and adorn herself, the other caring only to watch the reflected heavens. The former angrily tears the water-lilies which spoil her mirror, and dies miserably because her image has grown uglier with age. The other finds the lake more beautiful with the years, as a result of men's labours around it; she loves the lilies more and more, never discovers that she is growing old, and dies peacefully. The beauty of the lake may be seen in the autumnal sunshine at the end of *Adam Bede*, and the lilies in the people who were dear to Dinah but of little concern to Hetty. There is too much truth in Mrs Poyser's description of her as 'no better than a peacock', with a heart 'as hard as a pebble'.

George Eliot does not punish Hetty; it would be more true to say that she imposes limitations in pursuit of a theme. There is no improbability in Hetty's self-centredness and foolish fancies, and the author's imaginative sympathy is unquestionable. The psychological realism of Arthur Donnithorne's repeated failure (despite the promptings of his better judgment) to withstand temptation, and of the moral evasiveness with which he subsequently drugs his conscience, shows remarkable understanding. Yet the expression of Hetty's growing helplessness and despair in scene after scene of poignant detail (the final stages of which are artistically withheld until she confesses to Dinah) gives ample evidence of deep, sustained, creative feeling, and constitutes one of George Eliot's great achievements in tragic vision. Nevertheless, whatever the laws of a period when a boy of ten was hanged for stealing a silk handkerchief, Hetty's life had to be saved. Arthur's arrival in the nick of time was a kind of melodrama George Eliot was prepared to risk with Victorian readers. Though she would not have agreed with Trollope, who thought a novel could not be too sensational if it preserved 'truth of description, truth of character, human truth as to men and women', she would, if truth had to be sacrificed, have accepted Hardy's principle that improbability of incident matters less in fiction than improbabilities of character. *Adam Bede* impresses by the number and variety of characters who live and are long remembered.

Of these the most notable is Mrs Poyser. Adam, Hetty, Arthur, and Dinah are the main figures in the plot, and their story takes us beyond Hayslope and the Chase to Snowfield, Windsor, and Stoniton. Yet the Hall Farm occupies a central place in the novel, and it is Mrs Poyser's domain. Joshua Rann's complaints about the Methodists (v) afford a fine sample of George Eliot's gift for sustained humour in dialect; with Mrs Poyser it wells up without fail. She is keen and practical, quick-witted and shrewish in disapproval. Bartle Massey has a sharp anti-feminist tongue, but she can hold her own with him, telling him finally that some folk's tongues are like clocks 'as run on strikin' . . . because there's summat wrong i' their own inside'. Yet, as Adam tells Bartle, her heart is tender. Her sayings are original, fresh from the author's mint (25.ii.59) and worthy of Shakespeare. Just as Adam's figurative expressions are apt to be drawn from his craft, and his mother's from household items, Mrs Poyser's have their idiosyncratic fitness. She has nothing to say against Craig, the gardener at the Chase, except that it is a pity he can't be hatched again, and hatched differently; he seems to her 'like a cock as thinks the sun's rose o'purpose to hear him crow'. Methodist preachers are no better than bare-ribbed runts on a common, whereas the sight of Mr Irwine 'i' the desk of a Sunday' is like 'looking at a full crop o' wheat, or a pasture with a fine dairy o' cows in it'. In principle she judges people as she finds them: 'Some cheeses are made o' skimmed milk and some o' new milk, and it's no matter what you call 'em, you may tell which is which by the look and the smell.' The scene (xx) in which the tables are turned on her (or, as Mr Poyser remarks, her own whip flies in her face), after she has berated Molly for tripping and smashing crockery, is unusually near the farcical for George Eliot. It is a relief to find that Hetty has a sense of humour, though her aunt takes it amiss and ominously declares that it is to Dinah they must turn in time of trouble. Mrs Poyser comes into her own when the cunning old Squire arrives with a proposal 'to effect a little exchange' for the benefit of Thurle at the Chase Farm. Once she takes over, she keeps up the assault, voicing complaints about conditions at the Hall Farm with the liveliest exaggeration. Only Poyser would put up with it: 'a maggot must be born i' the rotten cheese to like it', she reckons. By this time the Squire is hurrying off, but she pursues him with accusations, and tells him he may go on spinning underhand ways of doing them a mischief with Old Harry his friend. Whatever the consequences, she must have her say. In the end, knowing nothing of future circumstances which will make them wish to leave, she and Mr Poyser conclude that their tenure is not in danger.

Mr Irwine may not be the ideal rector, but he is probably the most admirable character in *Adam Bede*. Had he not had his mother and 'two hopelessly-maiden sisters' to support, he might have married. No zealot, he has epicurean tastes, and indulges in hunting and shooting. He is courteous, kind, tactful, philosophical, and tolerant (as is shown when his parish-clerk Joshua Rann makes his protest against the Methodists). More interested in Church history than in theology, and in people's characters rather than their opinions, he accepts human failings, but possesses a subtlety of moral fibre which endows him with 'unwearying tenderness for obscure and monotonous suffering'. He responds to the call of duty. When the news comes of Hetty's arrest, he is Adam's counsellor and friend; and he does not spare himself during her trial. In his old age, Adam realizes how superior Irwine had been to one of his successors. Mr Ryde was strict, and an expert in doctrinal matters, but gradually he had lost the hearts of his parishioners. Mr Irwine had preached short moral sermons, and won people's affection and respect by tolerance and good will, not by doctrine. When Adam asserts that 'religion's something else besides notions', and that it is feelings that 'sets people doing the right thing', he speaks for his author; Mr Irwine, more splendidly and dramatically than Mr Gilfil, embodies her belief. Had Arthur Donnithorne taken him into his confidence, his honour might have been saved; like the moral of *Zeluco*, the implications of the rector's views on blaming circumstances for wrongdoing, and on the pitilessness of consequences, are lost on him.

Had we known more of Hetty's past, she might have been more intelligible.

> A human life, I think, should be well rooted in some spot of a native land, where it may get the love of tender kinship for the face of earth, for the labours men go forth to, for the sounds and accents that haunt it, for whatever will give that early home a familiar unmistakable difference amidst the future widening of knowledge: a spot where the definiteness of early memories may be inwrought with affection, and kindly acquaintance with all neighbours, even to the dogs and donkeys, may spread not by sentimental effort and reflection, but as a sweet habit of the blood (DD.iii).

Unlike Dinah, who establishes friendly relations very quickly, Hetty has every opportunity with her aunt but develops no sense of attachment. She is like a plant with 'hardly any roots', and 'could have cast all her past life behind her' (xv). Mrs Poyser is not a heartless woman, and her criticisms of her niece are confirmed by Adam's mother, a shrewd intuitive judge of character and relationships. More importantly they are George Eliot's: 'we must learn to accommodate ourselves to the discovery that some of those cunningly-fashioned instruments called human souls have only a very limited range of music, and will not vibrate in the least under a touch that fills others with tremulous rapture or quivering agony'. Hetty shows little or no affection towards the Poyser children; she is indifferent to the sorrows of the Bede family when Thias is drowned, and to Adam, though it suits her to entice him from time to time into her net of 'coquettish tyranny'. She feels nothing but 'cold triumph' over his attachment, and their ultimate engagement is a desperate remedy which promotes no warm feelings towards him. Hers is 'a luxurious and vain nature, not a passionate one'. Arthur dazzles her, as if he is an Olympian god; in 'young ignorance' she spins 'a light web of folly and vain hopes which may one day close round her and press upon her, a rancorous poisoned garment, changing all at once her fluttering, trivial butterfly sensations into a life of deep human anguish'. Hetty's nature is described in terms of butterflies and birds; she is kitten-like; her beauty has a false air of innocence like that of a young star-browed calf which can play one up. These resemblances, with the statements that she dreads bodily hardship because she has 'the luxurious nature of a round, soft-coated pet animal', and clings to life in her ultimate despair like 'the hunted wounded brute', have no dehumanizing connotations. They convey (as well as partial similitudes can) an objective analysis of Hetty; finally, an intense awareness of her suffering. More open to criticism, in view of the pitiless nemesis to which she is condemned, is the heavy irony of 'How she will dote on her children! She is almost a child herself, and the little pink round things will hang about her like florets round the central flower . . .'. Had this been presented subjectively (for it expresses very closely what Adam thought about Hetty), the irony would have been tragic. As it is, the authorial detachment seems inclement; 'people who love downy peaches', George Eliot adds, 'are apt not to think of the stone, and sometimes jar their teeth terribly against it'.

A more decidedly 'mixed' or imperfect character than Dinah (whose function as a foil to Hetty is dramatized in contiguous early scenes), Adam, in one respect at least, is an example to Arthur, who envies him the power he believes he possesses to master a wrongful wish as easily as he would knock down a drunkard who quarrelled with him. Adam replies, 'I've seen pretty clear, ever since I could cast up a sum, as you can never do what's wrong without breeding sin and trouble. . . . It's like a bit o' bad workmanship — you never see th' end o' the mischief it'll do.' After their fight, Adam can accept no amends, but stands like 'an immovable obstacle', 'an embodiment of what Arthur most shrank from believing in — the irrevocableness of his own wrong-doing'. He is a practical man who thinks 'it's better to see when your perpendicular's true' than to imagine a ghost, and to use good timber for repairs than theorize about setting the world to rights. Of such men George Eliot wrote, thinking about her father, 'Their lives have no discernible echo beyond the neighbourhood where they dwelt, but you are almost sure to find there some good piece of road, some building, some application of mineral produce, some improvement in farming practice, some reform of parish abuses, with which their names are associated by one or two generations after them' (xix). A supporter of the Carlylean gospel of work, Adam holds that 'there's the sperrit o' God in all things and all times — week-day as well as Sunday — and i' the great works and inventions . . . and if a man does bits o' jobs out o' working hours — builds a oven for's wife to save her from going to the bakehouse, or scrats at his bit o' garden and makes two potatoes grow instead o' one, he's doing more good, and he's just as near to God, as if he was running after some preacher and a-praying and a-groaning.' He feels it is 'a man's plain duty' to do his work thoroughly; solid work lasts, and 'if it's only laying a floor down, somebody's the better for it being done well, besides the man as does it'. We should aim at leaving the world a better place than we find it. Yet Adam has to learn that there is more in life than good workmanship. 'Perhaps nothing 'ud be a lesson to us if it didn't come too late', he reflects when he looks back on his hard, unforgiving judgment of his father. He is captivated by Hetty's beauty (which is *impersonal* rather than an index of her soul), but he lives to think more deeply as a result of the sorrow her tragedy brings him; he becomes more sympathetic, more affectionate to his mother, more indulgent to Seth, and sets a greater store on friendship, with the Poysers and Dinah especially.

Even so, he is not very percipient. He had spun a web of illusion around Hetty, and it needs his mother's perception to make him realize that Dinah is in love with him. Seth knows that she will let no 'fondness for the creature' divert her from the path marked out for her by God. When Adam declares his love, she tells him that she had begun to hunger after 'an equal love' from him, and wrestled with the temptation because she thought his heart was not hers. She does not consent to marry him until she knows it is 'the

Divine Will'. This Methodist thinking is not unacceptable to the God-fearing Adam, the fruit of whose unhappy experience is a vision beyond uprightness of action, an awareness not only of the sanctity of human feelings but also of 'deep speritial things in religion' (xvii). The Feuerbachian implications of the change in Dinah are clear, but one wishes that George Eliot had dramatized more of 'the slight words, the timid looks, the tremulous touches, by which two human souls approach each other gradually, like two little quivering rain-streams' until 'they mingle into one'. If the union of Adam and Dinah is not altogether convincing, it is because a religious interpretation prevails, and too much is left to the reader's imagination.

Most of George Eliot's secondary and incidental characters are memorably presented, and nowhere more than in *Adam Bede*. Adam's devoted, but rather lugubrious and over-querulous, mother Elizabeth is an obvious contrast to that inveterate misogynist, the lively, sharp-tongued Bartle Massey. Seth Bede and Mr Poyser are often almost inevitably reduced to passive roles, and for that reason, though they appear more often, create a less distinct impression than that grand old lady Mrs Irwine. Several background figures besides Joshua Rann are vividly sketched. Among them are Mr Craig, the opinionated Scotch gardener; Wiry Ben; Mr Casson, landlord of the Donnithorne Arms, swollen with a sense of his importance and dignity; and blowsy Bess Cranage, the blacksmith's daughter, as incurably addicted to trinkets and self-admiration as the beautiful Hetty. Some of these minor characters live by virtue of pictorial detail so distinct that it suggests childhood memories; none more so than shrunken old Martin Poyser in the large wicker-bottomed armchair by the chimney-nook, his blue handkerchief over his head, as he gazes at the flickering fire or sunbeams, spies pins or counts the quarries on the floor, or watches the hand of the clock and detects a rhythm in its tick. Another unforgettable ancient is seen but once, at the harvest supper: bent-kneed Kester Bale, who excelled in everything he turned his hand to on the farm, particularly in the art and craft of thatching. Other workers at the feast are a reminder that the pastoral world of *Adam Bede* is not idyllic: 'when Tityrus and Meliboeus happen to be on the same farm, they are not sentimentally polite to each other'; nor is stealing unknown. A realistic comment on 'jocose talk' among haymakers (xix) is another reminder of Marian Evans' essay on Riehl (pp. 71–2).

When a story hinges largely on the illusions of three young people, recurrent irony is almost inevitable. George Eliot's is less subtle than Jane Austen's, and less contrived than Hardy's; it is sometimes obvious, and generally less effective as a reflection of character than in its tragic overtones. Hetty's blush when she is startled by Adam's approach in the Hall Farm garden kindles his hopes, but she has been thinking of Arthur; she is not the first woman to behave more gently to a devoted lover because she has fallen in love with another. At the dinner in Arthur's honour, Mary Burge sees Adam looking at Hetty when she is cross with Totty, and takes comfort in the thought that he will know how to judge beauty in a woman with a bad temper; in fact, he thinks Hetty 'the prettiest thing in the world'; if he could have his way, nothing should vex her again. Subsequent events underscore Arthur's immature overconfidence a little earlier, as he imagines the children present telling their children when he is 'the old squire' how superior he had been compared with his own son. From this to the felicity of the Poysers' dialogue late in the evening is more than one remove. Whatever his wife's views on 'pleasurin' days', Mr Poyser has enjoyed himself. As they drive home, he expresses his delight that they have both been given pride of place. 'An' Hetty too − *she* never had such a partner before − a fine young gentleman in reg'mentals. It'll serve you to talk on, Hetty, when you're an old woman − how you danced wi' th' young Squire the day he come o' age.' There is irony too in the death of the old Squire, immediately before Hetty's imprisonment and Arthur's disgrace come to light. Mrs Irwine rejoices that she will live to see her favourite 'making good times on the estate, like a generous-hearted fellow as he is'; she is confident that he will be as 'happy as a king', and this is precisely how he feels when he lands at Liverpool, on his return from Ireland. Irony is reflected more than once in Nature's smile: when Adam, returning from work with buoyant hopes, sees Hetty compromised in the Grove; when she leaves the Hall Farm in despair after her betrothal to Adam; and when he sets out happily, expecting to find her at Snowfield. This 'harsh contrast' of nature's indifference to the human lot is the subject of authorial comment (xxvii). Nature's mood cannot harmonize with all, for while some grieve others are happy. 'We are children of a large family, and must learn, as such children do, not to expect that our hurts will be made much of − to be content with little nurture and caressing, and help each other the more.'

In its context this very simple and unexceptionable plea undoubtedly expresses George Eliot's sympathy with the basic humanitarian principles of Positivism. Inevitably her presentation of life is coloured by her outlook. Much in *Adam Bede* stems from the conviction that true religion depends on love that is active on behalf of our fellow-men. The old Methodists had strange superstitious beliefs and practices, but they had 'very sublime feelings'; what matters is 'the generous stirring of neighbourly kindness' (iii), and this is what Dinah preaches and practices. In Hetty it remains dormant. Mr Irwine's success with his parishioners is due to the fostering and hallowing of 'family affections and neighbourly duties'; the subject of his address at Thias Bede's funeral — 'how the present moment is all we can call our own for works of mercy, of righteous dealing, and of family tenderness' — is Positivist at heart. Adam believes in a weekday religion of working to the best of one's ability, but the spiritual maturity he derives from suffering is seen in the enhanced value he attaches to sympathy, friendship, and love.

George Eliot's vision of life was deepened and enriched by her humanistic philosophy; her problem was to reconcile the urge of the moral essayist with the demands of imaginative fiction. Though she could not expect the freedom enjoyed by Fielding (M.xv), she had to take the reader into her confidence. She never digresses, but her intrusions can be irritating. In *Adam Bede* she speaks on love, Nature, Nemesis, and the spiritual and moral growth wrought by suffering. The one occasion when she holds up the story unduly (bringing her armchair to the proscenium, in the manner she aptly ascribes to Fielding) is at the opening of the second book, where the chapter title 'In which the Story Pauses a Little' has a familiar Fielding ring. Her subject is the need for fidelity to life in fiction, and she extols the truthfulness of Dutch paintings; more importantly, she stresses the need for 'deep human sympathy', especially for ordinary people, and this leads to an appraisal of Mr Irwine's pastoral work. George Eliot's reflections on situations which command our attention are not unwelcome. Arthur Donnithorne's self-extenuation leads to the conclusion that 'Nemesis can seldom forge a sword for herself out of our consciences', since our moral sense conforms to the manners of our society. How human it is to see our mistakes through 'the lens of apologetic ingenuity', the author comments with reference to her aphoristic 'Our deeds determine us, as much as we determine our deeds' (xxix). The conflict of emotions in families (Nature, 'that great tragic dramatist', knitting and dividing us) is the subject of an imaginative paragraph which is calculated to induce a more sympathetic understanding of Adam's persistently over-anxious mother. The death and funeral of Thias Bede bring remorse to Adam for the severity of his criticism, with two brief but moving authorial generalizations on death and the irremediable. In these (end iv, xviii), conjointly with Adam's reflections, there may be autobiographical implications.

How far memory contributed to the wealth of descriptive and imaginative detail in *Adam Bede* must remain conjectural, but there are significant hints. Youthful memories can be enchanting: the thought of Mrs Poyser's whey fills the author's imagination with 'a still, happy dreaminess. And the light music of the dropping whey is in my ears, mingling with the twittering of a bird outside the wire network window – the window overlooking the garden, and shaded by tall Gueldres roses' (xx). Memory can also be deceptive: thinking of an earlier period when the barge was 'the newest locomotive wonder', George Eliot recalls walks through the fields (by the Coventry Canal) from afternoon church (at Chilvers Coton); but her nostalgia for the leisure of this era, now departed with its spinning-wheels, pack-horses, slow waggons, and pedlars calling with bargains on sunny afternoons, induces a euphoric obliviousness of harsher realities. This reminiscential address to the reader (lii) betrays a romantic partiality which is not characteristic of the novel as a whole; nevertheless, it throws light on the origin of an imaginative warmth and glow which is found more abundantly in *Adam Bede* than in any other of George Eliot's novels.

'The greatest benefit we owe to the artist, whether painter, poet, or novelist, is the extension of our sympathies', George Eliot observed in her essay on Riehl. *Adam Bede* is a moving story, combining sorrow and humour, and extending our sympathies at various levels to a wide range of characters. There is no villain; Arthur is betrayed by what is false within. Characters and story are not soon forgotten, but perhaps the most lasting impressions are of places, scenes, and community. Nowhere is this better illustrated than in the chapter devoted to the Sunday funeral of Thias Bede (to be buried under the white thorn, because his wife had set her heart on it, 'on account of a dream as she had'). It begins and ends with the Poysers, and with considerable humour in different veins; it indicates character in dialogue and acts of self-revelation, in events and thoughts (especially in Hetty, whose unhappiness in church is caused by Arthur's absence). Most of all we remember the farmyard scene when the Poysers set off (old Martin holding open the gate), the walk through the fields, the 'perpetual drama' of the hedgerows which fascinates the children Hetty has forgotten, the gossip of spectators during the burial, and the church service which follows, with Joshua Rann in his rusty spectacles admirably supporting Mr Irwine, reading the lesson with naturally rich interpretative voice, and suffering no eclipse in the singing of the psalm. It does not need Adam's regrets to feel the sadness of the occasion. In this visit (as it were) we meet nearly all the people we are familiar with in the neighbourhood. From farm life to bird life, from parishioners to its principal dramatis personae, this chapter is full of lively detail, as continually varied in form of presentation as in subject. No wonder that Anne Mozley, reviewing the novel in *Bentley's Quarterly Review*, wrote, 'We do not know whether our literature anywhere possesses such a closely true picture of purely rural life as *Adam Bede* presents.'

THE MILL ON THE FLOSS

The rift between the inner world and the outer which is the cause of Maggie Tulliver's suffering is the ultimate theme of *The Mill on the Floss*. It springs from George Eliot's condemnation by a Grundyan society, and more intensely from the yearning for reconciliation with her brother Isaac, after her marriage with Lewes. The novel begins with childhood recollections; its real subject gets under way in the last two books. The identification of Isaac with Tom Tulliver is partial, but there can be no mistaking the thought behind 'that fear which springs in us when we love one who is inexorable, unbending, unmodifiable'. To tear away 'the artificial vesture' of civilization, and realize 'primitive mortal needs', such people require, it seems, the threat of common calamity or death. As Maggie rows to rescue Tom, 'strong resurgent love' annihilates all thought of past misunderstanding and wrong, leaving only 'the deep, underlying, unshakable memories of early union', of a time when the outer world seemed only an extension of personality (II.i). The flood which unites them in death had been in the author's mind long before she completed the planning of her novel.

In deciding to ally herself with Lewes to support his children, she showed a higher morality than that of the society which judged her. The story of Maggie Tulliver and Stephen Guest has little in common with hers; Maggie, though sinned against more than sinning, succumbs to temptation, but the course she subsequently follows also shows principles far superior to those which regulate worldly judgment. Her pharisaical brother finds it his duty to exclude her from his home; for reasons outside himself, so too does the charitable and rather saintly Dr Kenn. He admires her integrity, and braves public opinion to support her, only to find, in the teeth of opposition and scandal-mongering, that he has to keep up appearances in order to maintain his rectorial mission. Life, it seems, can bring no final rescue to Maggie; St Ogg's legend belongs to a bygone era (I.xii) and a world of dreams (VI.xiv). On the question affecting the heroine and herself, George Eliot emphasizes the truth that 'moral judgments must remain false and hollow, unless they are checked and enlightened by a perpetual reference to the special circumstances that mark the individual lot'. She censures people like her brother whose moral guidance depends solely on general rules, 'a ready-made patent method' without the discrimination or 'insight that comes from a hardly-earned estimate of temptation, or from a life vivid and intense enough to have created a wide fellow-feeling with all that is human' (VII.ii); Tom Tulliver never develops as Adam Bede did.

Even so, despite the warning of J. W. Cross, the autobiographical element in the novel is usually exaggerated. *The Mill on the Floss* contains childhood reminiscences, but it is impossible to distinguish them with certainty from the fiction which has absorbed them. The deep Round Pool, for instance, is not the pond near Griff House; it has been created by the flooding of a great river. The 'Brother and Sister' poems indicate how some childhood memories have been assimilated to the story, but we should remember that the Tulliver parents bear little resemblance to Mr and Mrs Evans, that the Dodson aunts show only a few, exaggerated, characteristics of the aunts George Eliot remembered, and that the main story of Maggie and Tom in all its ramifications differs very widely from the youthful lives of Mary Evans and her brother. Whatever autobiography enters the account of Maggie's childhood, there can be no doubt that traditional biography has drawn too much of George Eliot's childhood from *The Mill on the Floss*. To some extent this may be due to the opening chapter, which contains vivid kinetic imagery and the most memorable pictorial scene in the novel. The author remembers Arbury Mill, but the little girl who watches the mill-wheel send out 'its diamond jets of water' is Maggie Tulliver. Recollected scenes such as this and that of the Red Deeps, with its rocks, ravines, and firs, are not quite in harmony with a Lincoln-shire landscape; and the author's relative unfamiliarity with the latter suggests one reason why so much of the novel, unlike *Adam Bede*, is devoid of rural background.

Childhood and memory are nonetheless highly relevant to *The Mill on the Floss*. However much life changed for Tom and Maggie, 'the thoughts and loves' of their first years 'would always make part of their lives'. Like his father, and Wordsworth's Michael, Tom develops feelings for his old home which are an essential part of his life; unlike Michael's son, he never betrays them. Nor does Maggie when she recovers from temptation; she remembers loyalties and attachments she cannot surrender. 'But heaven knows where [our] striving might lead us', George Eliot comments, 'if our affections had not a trick of twining round those old . . . things – if the loves and sanctities of our life had no deep immovable roots in memory' (II.i). The absence of such roots is a great misfortune for Hetty Sorrel.

On the strength which comes from childhood attachments, George Eliot writes with Wordsworthian conviction. 'We could never have loved the earth so well if we had had no childhood in it', she affirms. The wood in which she walks (end I.v) recalls 'the sun-shine and the grass in the far-off years which still live in us, and transform our perception into love'; the May day, the flowers 'at my feet', the bird notes, 'the sunshine and the grass', all echo 'Intimations of Immortality'. Yet her presentation of childhood in *The Mill on the Floss* is not romanticized; heaven does not lie about her infant scenes. Most of all we remember incidents depicted with vivid realism in which Tom and Maggie give natural, sometimes fierce, expression to feelings of frustration, resentment, and self-assertion. 'So much of our early gladness vanishes utterly from our memory: we can never recall the joy with which we laid our heads on our mother's bosom or rode on our father's back in childhood; doubtless that joy is wrought up into our nature, as the sunlight of long-past mornings is wrought up in the soft mellowness of the apricot; but it is gone for ever from our imagination, and we can only *believe* in the joy of childhood' (AB.xx).

The child is father of the man. Tom loves to have the upper hand, and can be cruel, even to his sister; he is Rhadamanthine, determined to punish everyone who offends him. Maggie is excitable, impulsive, and imaginative; her greatest need (and this was characteristic of the author in her childhood) is to be loved, especially by her brother; when actuality displeases, she escapes into a world of make-believe, and the link between her inner world and the outer is broken. So it is when she takes refuge with the gipsies, thinking they will admire her superior knowledge, until fear excites her imagination and she is glad to be home. Later, in moods of rebellion against her parents because they are not as she would have them, or against Tom because he thwarts her wishes, she indulges in 'wild romances of a flight from home in search of something less sordid and dreary: she would go to some great man − Walter Scott, perhaps − and tell him how wretched and how clever she was, and he would surely do something for her'. She is cleverer than Tom, but leaves school 'with a soul untrained for inevitable struggles', 'quite without that knowledge of the irreversible laws within and without her, which, governing the habits, becomes morality, and, developing the feelings of submission and dependence, becomes religion'. The uselessness of Tom's expensive education (almost certainly reflecting *some* of Isaac Evans' experiences at Foleshill) is the subject of some heavy satire; it makes him long for home (memories of which 'come before him in a sort of calenture'), and does nothing to qualify him for a profession, though it gives him 'a slight deposit of polish'; worse still, it fails to humanize him and make him more tolerant (VI.iii).

Character is destiny, but not the whole of it (VI.vi), and among the circumstances affecting the destiny of Tom and Maggie nothing is more crucial than their father's character. With a reference to Dandy Dinmont in Scott's *Guy Mannering*, George Eliot had drawn attention, in her essay on Riehl, to the countryman's 'inveterate habit of litigation', citing it as perhaps the worst result of his 'unreasoning persistency'. Proud, blundering, and litigious, Mr Tulliver is blindly set on a disastrous course. Had he been less impulsive and stubborn, he would not have entangled the skein of his life financially; and the chances are not only that he would have kept the mill and been spared degradation and ignominy, but that Maggie would have enjoyed more freedom and happiness, and thereby have developed greater poise and judgment in her personal relationships. Egoism, however, asserts that 'a male Tulliver' is 'far more than equal to four female Dodsons', including Mrs Glegg. It is the chance of things that the money he needs to be independent of her has to be borrowed from one of Wakem's clients. 'Mr Tulliver had a destiny as well as Oedipus, and in this case he might plead, like Oedipus, that his deed was inflicted on him rather than committed by him.' The world is puzzling to his limited intelligence, but he will have his way. He chooses a wife who will not tell him 'the rights o' things', accepts Riley's opinion that a clerical gentleman is qualified to prepare Tom for any career, wrecks his own life and that of his family, and after giving way to savage, revengeful impulses, when family honour is redeemed by the full payment of his debts, dies, leaving Tom to inherit his undying hatred of Wakem as a sacred duty. There are people in whom 'predominance is a law of life', and their tragedy 'goes on from generation to generation', in the conflicts perhaps of 'young souls, hungry for joy, under a lot made suddenly hard to them' (III.i). If there is conflict for Tom, it is external − with Maggie. Hers is deep, and suppressed for long periods; circumstances (which include character) determine that it can never be fully resolved, not even in the final reconciliation with Tom.

After stating that her imagination habitually strove after 'as full a vision of the medium in which a character moves as of the character itself', George Eliot claimed that her reasons for giving details of Florentine life and history in *Romola* were identical with those which made her give details of village life in *Silas Marner* or of 'the "Dodson" life, out of which were developed the destinies of poor Tom and Maggie' (8.viii.63). Tom shows Dodson qualities unrelentingly and Maggie suffers in consequence. Her father is primarily responsible for the train of events which leads to her tragedy, but the Dodsons represent the conventional society which condemns her. Fortunately, despite the satire to which they are subjected, they provide a counterpoise of comedy. When *The Times* reviewer described them as 'odious', stressed their 'Pharisaical rigidity', and judged their respectability in clearing family debts 'mean and uninteresting' compared with Bohemian life, George Eliot was 'rather aghast', and defended their virtues (27.v.60). She had found poetry in ruined castles by the Rhine but none in dismal remains of villages by the Rhone; the lives of their inhabitants, she felt, were part of 'a gross sum of obscure vitality' destined to be 'swept into the same oblivion with the generations of ants and beavers'. She can sympathize with readers who think similarly of the emmit-like Dodsons and Tullivers and conclude that their life was sordid, 'irradiated by no sublime principles, no romantic visions, no active, self-renouncing faith'. But their pride, she insists, was 'wholesome' in many respects, 'since it identified honour with perfect integrity, thoroughness of work, and faithfulness to admitted rules'. Tullivers differ from Dodsons in being warmly affectionate, and sometimes generously imprudent or rashly hot-tempered. Nothing is nobler in Tulliver than the remission of the Moss family debts; sister Gritty's woes weigh more heavily with him than his own dire needs; 'we're our mother's children', he remembers, and he thinks that, if he is hard on Gritty, his 'little wench' Maggie might one day be made to suffer by Tom. Naturally the Dodsons regard faults in Bessy's children as Tulliver traits, but the religion of the two families is similar, and it consists in revering what is customary and respectable, in being honest and rich, richer than expected at death, and in winning public esteem by their wills towards kindred, even those who had not been a credit to them. These they would not forsake or ignore; 'would not let them want bread, but only require them to eat it with bitter herbs'.

Though Mrs Tulliver, condemned to years of privation and suffering as a result of her husband's improvidence, is a sorrowful figure, she excites amusement by her early disclosure that the best sheets are kept ready 'to lay us out in'; should Tulliver die on the morrow, they are 'mangled beautiful' and lavendered for him. The most comical of the four Dodson sisters is Mrs Pullet, the lugubrious hypochondriac of Garum Firs, a rather Dickensian figure in a somewhat Dickensian home with white railings and gates, glittering weathercocks, and garden walks paved with pebbles in beautiful patterns. Cleanliness takes precedence over use: substitutes are provided to keep the front door scraper and mat in impeccable order; the stair-carpet is rolled up and laid by in a spare room; and furniture in a bedroom of funereal solemnity is shrouded in white. Two storeroom shelves are filled with her medicine bottles, and Mr Pullet will not allow any of them to be sold, as he thinks they should be seen when his wife is 'gone'. Her two obsessions are death and fine clothes, and she makes her first appearance in tears which are respectably renewed over the death of a neighbour, and in large buckram sleeves (too wide to enter Mrs Tulliver's without brushing both shoulders), with several bracelets on each arm, an architectural bonnet, and delicate ribbon-strings. At Garum Firs she takes sister Bessy (Mrs Tulliver) to the shuttered funereal bedroom to display the new bonnet she keeps locked in her wardrobe. Pullet, who is paying for it, had told her it must be the best at Garum Church. As she adjusts its trimmings, she observes that she may not live to wear it again; when it is locked away, she begins to cry, telling Bessy that, if she should never see the bonnet again until she is 'dead and gone', she will remember seeing it that day. The Dodson religion suggests neither life nor happiness. Mrs Glegg's obsession is economizing and anticipating how well off she will be when she is widowed. It is a source of pleasure that nimble-witted Bob Jakin with his rule of thumb is more than a match for her miserliness, but she wins our esteem when she takes Tom severely to task for refusing to admit his sister, insists that Maggie should be given the benefit of the doubt until the truth is known, and invites her to share her home. She keeps her best curled front for special occasions; the silk gown which she wears when she visits the Tullivers betrays 'certain constellations of small yellow spots' and a clothes-chest mustiness which indicate that it belongs to 'a stratum of garments just old enough to have come recently into wear'. She things that Bessy is 'far too well drest, considering', and too proud to dress Maggie in 'the good clothing' she has given her ('from the primeval strata of her wardrobe'). Mrs Deane, sister Glegg, and sister Pullet form a trio of Job's comforters when Bessy's 'teraphim' have to be sold; 'there was a general family sense that a judgment had fallen on Mr Tulliver, which it would be an impiety to counteract by too much kindness'. When Wakem bought the mill, and offered him the managership, they were unanimous in thinking that the opportunity had come for Tulliver 'to provide for his wife and daughter without any assistance from his wife's relations'.

Although the centrality of Maggie in the novel is slow to emerge, it was planned early, for the title which George Eliot had in mind when she finished her first volume was 'Sister Maggie'. Provisionally it had been 'The Tullivers' or, possibly, 'St Ogg's on the Floss'. Later alternatives were 'The House of Tulliver' and 'The Tulliver Family', with 'Life on the Floss' as the subtitle. Then, on Blackwood's recommendation, 'The Mill on the Floss' was accepted, though the author thought it sounded 'laborious' and had to point out that the mill stood on a tributary of the Floss. After working on the novel during the greater part of 1859, she finished the second volume in January 1860, and the third nine weeks later. Maggie's critical role becomes increasingly evident in the final phase of her father's life; then suddenly, with the opening of the sixth book, it comes to the fore and continues unabated to the end. George Eliot accepted Sir Edward Lytton's criticism that 'the tragedy is not adequately prepared', and admitted that the 'epic breadth' into which she had been beguiled in the first two volumes had caused 'a want of proportionate fulness in the treatment of the third' which she would always regret. Later she said that her delight in 'the pictures of childhood' in the first volume had created a disproportion which made it impossible to develop as much as she wished the concluding tragedy, to which she had looked forward 'with much attention and premeditation from the beginning'. These pictures include our introduction to the Dodson families, and visits to two of their homes; if they suffer from superabundance, it is more welcome than some of the superfluities which will be found elsewhere in the first two volumes.

The 'golden gates' of Tom and Maggie's childhood are passed when their schooldays are brought abruptly to an end. So far their lives have been sheltered, not without discord and pain. Tom has suffered at school, and his days there seem to be without relief, except when he is visited by Maggie or looks forward to returning home, or when Mr Poulter boasts of his Peninsular War experiences and performs his sword-exercise (with a grievous sequel for Tom during Maggie's second visit). So desperately did he need friendship at the Stellings' that he would gladly play with their child Laura when she could hardly walk. Philip Wakem told exciting war stories, but friendship with him was out of the question for Tom as soon as his father began his lawsuit against Wakem's clients. With Mr Tulliver's failure, Tom had to leave school totally unprepared for life or suitable work, and in the grip of a relentless will to avenge his father. He has a blind heroic nature. With Mr Deane, one can admire the tenacity with which (helped very considerably by Bob Jakin's business acumen) he labours to redeem his father's debts. In this, as he shows at the outset, over the indebtedness of his uncle Moss and the family obligation to Luke, he is the soul of honour. Unfortunately circumstances dictate that the atavistic revenge lust in Tom works on his inveterate will to dominate and hurt his sister; his cruelty to Maggie *vis-à-vis* Philip Wakem almost expunges whatever sympathy he earns. The nature of Philip is superior to that of his father, and they in turn are decidedly more civilized than Tom and his father. When Philip divulges his love of Maggie, his father's reconciliation with him, bearing in mind the unprovoked and merciless assault he had suffered from Mr Tulliver, is noble compared with Tom's tyrannical sense of family duty.

What Tom suffers is left to the imagination. When the mill is sold, we are told that his heart endured 'the most unmixed pain, for Maggie, with all her keen susceptibility, yet felt as if the sorrow made larger room for her love to flow in, and gave breathing-space to her passionate nature'. A true boy 'would rather go and slay the Nemean lion, or perform any round of heroic labours, than endure perpetual appeals to his pity, for evils over which he can make no conquest' (III.viii). Unlike Maggie, Tom can become absorbed in prolonged but heroic exertion to save the situation. In reply to the reviewer in *Macmillan's Magazine* who found him, 'so far as his light goes', a finer character than his sister, despite the author's 'disdain' for him and her 'evident yearning' over Maggie, George Eliot wrote (4.iv.61): 'as if he could have respected Tom, if I had not painted him with respect; the exhibition of the *right* on both sides being the very soul of my intention'. Her prior claim (27.v.60) that he was 'painted with as much love and pity as Maggie' is not altogether convincing. He has a laudable Dodson doggedness, consistency, and rectitude; but, though his sub-jugation of feelings to will is an asset in business, his self-assertion (at the expense of sympathy and understanding) over his sister is disastrous. When Lucy Deane reveals Wakem's readiness to receive Maggie 'with all the honours of a daughter-in-law', Tom displays 'the positive and negative qualities that create severity', including not only self-control but 'a disposition to exert control over others'. He has not grown up; his dominant boyhood attitude towards his sister shows a shift from 'I shall always take care of you' to 'you must mind what I say'. Her return from her unfortunate escapade with Stephen Guest is met with his final outburst of Tulliver rage.

It is no wonder that Maggie grew up in awe of him. They had often been happy together, and she yearned for his love. On being wrenched from school, they were united 'in the sense that they had one father and one sorrow'. When Tom speaks harshly to her, as he does when his prospects seem bleak, she is despondent: 'if life had no love in it, what else was there for Maggie? . . . There is no hopelessness so sad as that of early youth, when the soul is made up of wants, and has no long memories, no superadded life in the life of others.' Maggie was 'full of eager, passionate longings for all that was beautiful and glad; thirsty for all knowledge; with an ear straining after dreamy music that died away and would not come near to her; with a blind, unconscious yearning for something that would link together the wonderful impressions of this mysterious life, and give her soul a sense of home in it'. Hers was a 'conflict between the inward impulse and outward fact, which is the lot of every imaginative and passionate nature'. She had loved music, but now there is none for her except at church, and the longing for happiness comes to her like musical strains. In *The Imitation of Christ* by Thomas à Kempis, one of the books brought by her devoted Bob Jakin, she reads the lesson of renunciation, and thinks it the key to a happy life, not yet realizing that 'renunciation remains sorrow, though a sorrow borne willingly'. So in loneliness, from her thirteenth to her seventeenth year, she finds consolation in religion, and learns to remain submissive despite 'some volcanic upheavings of imprisoned passions', her own life 'still a drama' in which her part has to be 'played with intensity' (IV.iii).

Philip Wakem remembers the affection she had shown him during her second visit to Mr Stelling's, and hopes to meet her by chance in the Red Deeps. Just before their first meeting by the Scotch firs, her appearance conveys 'a sense of opposing elements, of which a fierce collision is imminent'. When he hears how death-like her loneliness is, he remonstrates with her for making a virtue of self-sacrifice, and insists that they can never give up longing and wishing while they are 'thoroughly alive', a truth which seems to be imaged in the firs, with their red stems soaring higher after storms have broken the ends of their branches. When she argues that her life is determined by her father's will, he urges that a continuation of their friendship could heal their wounds; and the words are music to her. She is sorry for Philip, knowing that her father's vindictiveness is unjustifiable. The thought of meeting in secret hurts her conscience, but the 'music' swells out again 'like chimes borne onward by a recurrent breeze, persuading her that the wrong lay all in the faults and weaknesses of others'. The conflict continues; in retrospect, her interview appears like 'an opening in the rocky wall which shut in the narrow valley of humiliation' and excluded 'memory-haunting earthly delights'. When next they meet, she tells him she has never been satisfied with a *little* of any-thing; she has never felt she had enough music; and it is better for

her 'to do without earthly happiness altogether'. She is tall and
beautiful, a healthy young woman; and Philip is in love with her,
though passion never enters her thought, as he knows. They continue to meet secretly until he declares his love, and she says she
could hardly love anyone better, though they cannot even be
friends. Tom's suspicions are aroused, and he extorts Maggie's
confessions, makes her swear on his father's Bible that she will
never meet or speak to Philip again in private, then accompanies
her to her rendezvous and addresses Philip so abominably that she
is forced to protest: Tom has always been hard and cruel to her,
and is pharisaical, thanking God for shining virtues which are
'mere darkness' compared with her love. As in *Jane Eyre*, the
cloven tree is the symbol of love's interdiction. Tom's virtues are
shown when he clears his father's debts, but he sows tares as well as
wheat. More than ever is Maggie the victim of circumstance.
Another sorrow brings them together briefly when their father dies
after his paroxysm of rage against Wakem. 'Tom, forgive me – let
us always love each other', she pleads, but the hope born of the
moment is illusory.

Time passes, and Maggie, preferring independence to a life
with Aunt Pullet, submits to a dreary situation in a distant school
until she can endure it no longer. Mrs Deane (for whom the novel
has little room) has died, and Mrs Tulliver is staying with Lucy
when Maggie comes to join them for a spring holiday. Mr Deane is
the right-hand man of Guest and Co., and Stephen Guest, 'whose
diamond ring, attar of roses, and air of nonchalant leisure' are 'the
graceful and odoriferous result of the largest oil-mill and the most
extensive wharf in St Ogg's' (and a sign of superior vulgarity) is
Lucy's accepted lover. Maggie's return to the old scenes has the
inevitable effect of making her continued life of renunciation seem
hard and distasteful. Stephen is overpowered by her beauty; and
his blush, as he bows on being introduced to her, is such a new and
agreeable experience for her that she is in danger of forgetting
Philip. She is not impressed by Stephen's foppish airs or by the
artificiality of his compliments, yet, after boating with him and
cousin Lucy, and hearing him sing, she retires with vague feelings
'of love and beauty and delight' similar to those conjured up in the
past by poetry, romance, and reverie. Such is the effect of long
privation on a 'highly-strung, hungry nature'. Stephen thought it
'perfectly natural and safe to admire beauty and enjoy looking at
it'. His attentions, George Eliot emphasizes, 'could have had no

perceptible effect on a thoroughly well-educated young lady, with a perfectly balanced mind, who had had all the advantages of fortune, training, and refined society'. No other words in the novel go so far to explain the tragedy of Maggie Tulliver, or to indicate the gap between her upbringing and the author's.

While Stephen and Maggie meet in her presence, each 'oppressively conscious' of the other, 'even to the finger-ends', Lucy dreams of the charming quartet they will have when Maggie marries Philip, an event she believes she will be able to contrive. Yet Tom remains obdurate, as Maggie finds when she asks to be absolved from her pledge. He is not opposed to her meeting Philip occasionally in company, but he does not trust her; he insists that he is kind in doing what he knows is good for her, and that he will abandon her if she thinks of Philip as a lover again. As it is, Maggie hardly trusts herself; a 'new element' having been brought into her 'starved life' by Stephen, Philip has become 'a sort of outward conscience to her', and she needs to turn to him as a safeguard:

> Her tranquil, tender affection for Philip, with its root deep down in her childhood, and its memories of long quiet talk confirming by distinct successive impressions the first instinctive bias — the fact that in him the appeal was more strongly to her pity and womanly devotedness than to her vanity or other egoistic excitability of her nature, seemed now to make a sort of sacred place, a sanctuary where she could find refuge from an alluring influence which the best part of herself must resist, which must bring horrible tumult within, wretchedness without.

Not only does she like to hear Stephen sing; the music moves her with 'inexorable power', and she is affected by the gentle solicitude towards her which he cannot repress. At such times the thought of luxury, adoration, and culture is a temptation; but soon 'passion, and affection, and long deep memories of early discipline and effort, of early claims on her love and pity' get the better of vanity, and she tells Lucy that, but for separation from her brother, it would be 'the best and highest lot' for her to marry Philip. Such is the conflict which makes Dr Kenn judge that she is troubled at heart when he meets her for the first time.

Like Arthur Donnithorne, Stephen knows that he is behaving irresponsibly, and resolves to be more sensible. He knows as little about Maggie as she of him; their attraction is physical. At Park

House he does not dance with her, but observes her with 'devouring' eyes; in the conservatory he is seized by 'a mad impulse' which makes him suddenly clasp her wrist and shower her arm with kisses. She turns furiously on him, ashamed that momentary happiness spells treachery to Lucy and Philip, and 'to her own better soul'. Stephen is dizzy with the conflict of love, rage, 'despair at his want of self-mastery, and despair that he had offended Maggie'. She believes she has regained self-command, and that her attachment remains unchanged. Stephen seeks her out at aunt Moss's because he cannot resist his passion, and argues, when he hears that she is virtually engaged to Philip, that her engagement and his own are 'unnatural'; if she loves him as he loves her, their feelings are overriding. Contending that such feelings conflict with the ties that their former lives have made 'natural' for each of them, she pleads with him not to urge her further *because* she loves him. The confession may come as a shock, and the question is whether the reader is sufficiently prepared for it. It is not Maggie's higher nature which responds to Stephen; her instinctive response has been like that of 'a lovely wild animal timid and struggling under caresses'. Her resistance to the sensual explains the violence of her reaction in the conservatory scene; and preliminary hints of it may be seen in the expression of pain Dr Kenn sees in her face, and her enigmatic statement that she must leave the neighbourhood (VI.ix). Stephen promises to honour her wishes, but the sequel is more the result of chance and his fond selfish hopes than of Maggie's weakness.

Yet her weakness persists; the erotic spell lulls her into thinking with Stephen that 'they might still snatch moments of mute confession' before parting, and, though 'the old voices' reassert 'all the memories of early striving', 'all the deep pity for another's pain, which had been nurtured in her through years of affection and hardship', and 'all the divine presentiment of something higher than mere personal enjoyment', the lure of a life of ease and luxury makes her succumb to the opium of dreams, as she did in childhood when experience was unkind. It is by chance that she accompanies him when they are 'borne along by the tide'; and she acts as if she has no will of her own. They glide without thought in an 'enchanted haze', the scene admirably symbolizing and psychologizing Maggie's suspension of judgment until it is too late. When Lytton protested against this failure of principle, George Eliot insisted that 'Maggie's position towards Stephen' was 'too

vital a part' of her 'whole conception and purpose' for her to accept
its condemnation:

> If I am wrong there — if I did not really know what my heroine
> would feel and do under the circumstances in which I deliber-
> ately placed her, I ought not to have written this book at all, but
> quite a different book, if any. If the ethics of art do not admit
> the truthful presentation of a character essentially noble but
> liable to great error — error that is anguish to its own nobleness
> — *then*, it seems to me, the ethics of art are too narrow, and
> must be widened to correspond with a widening psychology.

The choice of a noble character liable to error may have been a
logical sequence to the idealization of Dinah Morris, but no doubt
many Victorian readers, like the reviewer in *The Guardian*, felt
that there are temptations in life which should not be observed too
closely. The 'flagrant blemish' in the novel which displayed the
author's 'magnificent and matchless powers' most fully worked
Swinburne into a welter of seething indignation: Maggie's lapse
was surely 'the last word of realism', the 'last abyss of cynicism'; it
was a plague-spot, a degradation to 'the very crown and flower of
George Eliot's wonderful and most noble work'.

All that is noblest in Maggie Tulliver is purged by her error.
When she wakes she knows that she has blotted her life with irrevocable wrong, bringing sorrow into lives 'knit up with hers by trust
and love'. She does not believe, with Stephen, that a natural
impulse justifies treachery and cruelty. But for selfish delusions she
would never have betrayed Lucy and Philip. She could never marry
Stephen with her 'whole heart and soul', for she had never consented to it with her whole mind; marrying him would have rent her
from all that was 'dear and holy' in her past. The Tulliver— Dodson
inheritance has its higher moral values, and its shortcomings can
generate the thirst for a nobler life. To Stephen's outburst that she
is robbing him of *his* happiness, the reply is: 'We can only choose
whether we will indulge ourselves in the present moment, or
whether we will renounce that, for the sake of obeying the divine
voice within us — for the sake of being true to all the motives that
sanctify our lives. I know this belief is hard: it has slipped away from
me again and again; but I have felt that if I let it go for ever, I
should have no light through the darkness of this life.'

Perhaps the Philip–Stephen dichotomy of love had some influence on Lawrence in planning *Sons and Lovers*, the open-
endedness of which might be considered in critical contrast to the
overwhelming resolution of *The Mill on the Floss*. From the outset
George Eliot's novel contains many forewarnings of death by
water, and the idea of life as a river develops in its closing stages.
Maggie's destiny is hidden, 'and we must wait for it to reveal itself
like the course of an unmapped river: we only know that the river
is full and rapid, and that for all rivers there is the same final
home'. As she listens to Stephen's singing, she is 'borne along by a
wave too strong for her'; as she is 'borne along by the tide' with
him, he asks her to recognise that it is carrying them away from
the 'unnatural bonds' of convention. 'Delicious visions' flow over
her 'like a soft stream', making her 'entirely passive' and lulling
her to sleep. When she leaves Stephen and seeks the haven of
home, she recalls 'all the tremulous delights of his presence with
her that made existence an easy floating in a stream of joy,
instead of a quiet resolved endurance and effort'. Unlike the
metaphorical river, the predetermined flood is, it appears, wholly
actual; it can hardly be equated with 'the depths in life' of which
Tom is made suddenly aware, for, though they had 'lain beyond
his vision', they had been familiar to Maggie in renunciation and
distress. One might wonder whether the machinery which
destroys brother and sister has overtones which anticipate
Arnold's 'machinery' (the mistaking of means for ends) in *Culture
and Anarchy*: whether the implication is that, in particular
circumstances (VII.ii), the code of conventional morality may
destroy life in those who are either rigidly activated by it like Tom
(and Isaac Evans) or unjustly condemned by it like Maggie. Lack
of internal evidence for this interpretation of the huge fragments
of wooden machinery in the river of life suggests that the ending is
to be taken at its face value, and that George Eliot had worked
towards it, confident of its power to move and finalize. The
emotional appeal of 'In their death they were not divided' was
strong. Had the fatal flood been imaginatively integrated with the
psychological symbolism of the river, it would have been more
satisfactory. As it is, it may move readers powerfully; some may
associate with it, as perhaps George Eliot did, 'Many waters
cannot quench love, neither can the floods drown it' from *The
Song of Solomon*; others may regard it as arbitrary and somewhat
melodramatic.

TWO STORIES, FROM GRAVE TO GAY

'The Lifted Veil' was begun at Richmond when George Eliot felt 'too stupid for more important work'. At the end of March 1859, when the success of *Adam Bede* made Blackwood eager for another tale, she informed him that she had a slight one which could be ready in a few days; she did not regard it highly, but her 'private critic' Lewes thought it striking and original; she described it as 'of an outré kind – not a *jeu d'esprit*, but a *jeu de mélancolie*'. It was finished at the end of April, and appeared in *Maga* the following July. A proposal (which she declined) from Blackwood in 1873 to include it in a miscellany caused George Eliot to re-appraise her story; she liked the creative idea, thought it justified the 'painfulness' of the story, and wrote an elucidatory epigraph:

> Give me no light, great heaven, but such as turns
> To energy of human fellowship;
> No powers save the growing heritage
> That makes completer manhood.

Five years later 'The Lifted Veil' was included with *Silas Marner* and 'Brother Jacob' in the Cabinet Edition of her complete works. Unfortunately it is no longer readily available, for it is not only striking and original, as Lewes saw; it springs from a visionary foreboding of our modern spiritual moribundity.

The story is fascinatingly told. Latimer, the narrator, was unfortunate in his childhood; he lost his sight for a period, and the mother who lovingly tended him. His elder brother Alfred was sent to Eton and Oxford 'for the sake of making connections'. In accordance with the wishes of his father, a phlegmatic banker whom he held in awe, Latimer was crammed with science; Mr Letherall's phrenological test revealing his deficiencies, he was taught science and classification because he had no aptitude in them but was 'hungry for human deeds and human emotions'. At sixteen he was sent to Geneva to complete his education, and there the beauty of mountains and sky (which George Eliot remembered from her stay in 1849) seemed to surround him with love such as he had never known since his mother's death. He made one friend, a medical student who was to become famous.

This happier life was ended by a severe illness. When his father talked about the journey home they would take via Prague,

Latimer had a vision of a parched city; he knew it was not a dream, and wondered whether it could be poetically inspired. Later, when overwrought with anxiety, he had a vision of a slim young woman with blond hair, whose features and expression were like a cutting wind. He had been reading German lyrics, and her pale-green dress and the leaflike border round her hair made him think of a water-pixie. Hardly had he recovered from his trance when he saw her with his father, and fainted. Her name was Bertha Grant.

Soon afterwards Latimer discovered that he could follow the mental processes of persons he met. The result was disillusionment, for he found that the fine words and kindly deeds 'which used to make the web of their characters' were the product of suppressed egoism, puerilities, meanness, and 'indolent make-shift thoughts'. When Alfred joined the party at Basle, his assurance that Bertha preferred him provoked Latimer's hatred. Among those around him, Bertha was the one exception to his 'unhappy gift of insight'. For this reason, though she was self-centred, sarcastic, cynical, and averse to his poetry and 'enthusiasm for the great and good', she exercised complete tyranny over his mind; physical attraction undoubtedly affected his imagination. She encouraged his illusions, always remaining an 'oasis of mystery in the dreary desert of knowledge' which came to him preternaturally. In Vienna, after gazing at Giorgione's picture of the cruel-eyed woman, said to resemble Lucrezia Borgia, he felt an arm slipped within his and a light hand gently pressing his wrist. The poisoned sensation created by the picture returned; he lost sight of his surroundings, and seemed to be in a darkness from which there emerged a scene at home with Bertha, to whom he was married. He saw her cruel eyes, the green jewels and green leaves on her white ball-dress, the great emerald brooch (a studded serpent with diamond eyes) on her bosom, and her pitiless soul. They hated each other.

Soon after reaching Prague, Latimer's fears were confirmed: his prevision of the city proved right in its most distinctive detail. Yet he was still a slave to Bertha's 'siren melody', and his jealousy remained unchanged until Alfred was killed while hunting. His father's affection and approval of his prospective marriage to Bertha made Latimer happier than he had been since childhood, even though she was more distant after Alfred's death. Yet this screen served only to bring him more under her power: 'no matter how empty the adytum, so that the veil be thick enough', for 'doubt and hope and effort' are always the breath of life. Bertha affected him like hashish, and sweet illusions overcame the warnings of prevision. Through the crowded excitements of their early marriage, Bertha's self remained shrouded from him; gradually they grew estranged; when his father died, the veil was withdrawn, and 'the terrible moment of complete illumination' came:

> I saw that the darkness had hidden no landscape from me, but only a blank prosaic wall: from that evening forth, through the sickening years which followed, I saw all round the narrow room of this woman's soul — saw petty artifice and mere negation where I had delighted to believe in coy sensibilities and in wit at war with latent feeling — saw the light floating vanities of the girl defining themselves into the systematic coquetry, the scheming selfishness, of the woman — saw repulsion and antipathy harden into cruel hatred, giving pain only for the sake of wreaking itself.

Now that he was no longer deceived by his imagination, Bertha was powerless. Some of Latimer's involuntary betrayals made her suspect his abnormal power of penetration; and she hoped he would commit suicide. Years passed; then, one January evening, she appeared in her white ball-dress, with the glittering serpent, like a familiar demon, on her breast, the exact fulfilment of the Vienna vision. He had a vague dread that the new maid she had appointed would appear in a sickening vision as the evil genius in the 'dreary drama' of his life. As all that was personal in him seemed to die, his relations with his fellow-men became deadened, and visions like that of Prague came more frequently and vividly; in all there was something unknown and pitiless, and beyond all, and recurring, there was the vision of his death. His faith was annihilated, for there can be no religion for the unloving and the unloved, 'no worship but a worship of devils'.

When his medical friend, now famous, visited him, their old sympathy could not be revived. Latimer had lost his abnormal awareness, and lived continually in his own solitary future. The maid fell ill suddenly and, when nothing could be done to save her life, Latimer's friend sought permission to experiment as soon as she lost consciousness. A blood-transfusion revived her for a brief period, long enough for her to accuse Bertha of intending to kill her husband with the poison she (the maid) had acquired for her. The scene seemed of one texture with the rest of Latimer's existence; horror was his 'familiar'. From that time he and Bertha lived apart. He wandered abroad until he came to die in Devon. Sometimes when he rested in a favourite spot, his heart went out to the men, women, and children who were becoming known to him; then the old disillusioning insight drove him away 'to live continually with the Unknown Presence revealed and yet hidden by the moving curtain of the earth and sky'. Now he knows exactly when he will die, and with the approach of death his double consciousness never leaves him. He longs for life; having thirsted for the unknown, he wishes to stay with the known. He reflects cynically that people will sympathize when he is dead; 'it is the living only who cannot be forgiven — the living only from whom men's indulgence and reverence are held off, like the rain by the hard east wind'. The bitter irony which follows, 'While the heart beats, bruise it . . .; while the creative brain can still throb with the sense of injustice, with the yearning for brotherly recognition . . .', suggests that the melancholy which oppressed George Eliot at the inception of 'The Lifted Veil' may have included, even originated from, thoughts of the relatives and friends who shunned her (cf. pp. 31–2). The story, it should be remembered, was written while *The Mill on the Floss* was much in mind (cf. pp. 107–8).

Its wider 'creative idea' came from Shelley's sonnet:

Lift not the painted veil which those who live
Call Life: though unreal shapes be pictured there,
And it but mimic all we would believe
With colours idly spread, — behind, lurk Fear
And Hope, twin Destinies; who ever weave
Their shadows, o'er the chasm, sightless and drear.
I knew one who had lifted it — he sought,
For his lost heart was tender, things to love,
But found them not, alas! nor was there aught
The world contains, the which he could approve.
Through the unheeding many he did move,
A splendour among shadows, a bright blot
Upon this gloomy scene, a Spirit that strove
For truth, and like the Preacher found it not.

Latimer's double consciousness is identical with Shelley's 'twin

Destinies' of hope and fear, and it flows like 'two parallel streams which never mingle'. Overcome by hope, or temptation, he ignores the warning visions and becomes Bertha's willing victim. Mindful perhaps of Arthur Donnithorne, George Eliot mentions 'the presentiments that spring from an insight at war with passion', and states that Latimer's visions were like 'presentiments intensified to horror'. 'There is no short cut, no patent tram-road, to wisdom', she adds.

The ultimate theme of 'The Lifted Veil' is more general and significant; it is comparable to that of *Silas Marner* in reverse. Complete the story by returning to the beginning, and the complementary appropriateness of the epigraph becomes clearer, as if in recoil from a climactic horror of hatred and hopelessness to a humanitarian faith without which life is empty and purposeless. The more Latimer is cut off from his fellow-men and spiritually deadened, the more subject he is to visions like that of Prague. From one angle the horror is like that of Kurtz in Conrad's *Heart of Darkness*, but the city of the vision in 'The Lifted Veil' has no commercial connotations; it has some resemblance to the city of the dead in *The Waste Land*, but it is not merely a vision of life as seen by the narrator; it reflects his negativism when all that is loving and personal dies within him. Perhaps the vision emerged in George Eliot's prophetic soul after contemplating a future godless civilization without a new religion of brotherhood and love. The arrested sunshine is like T. S. Eliot's desert. It makes the city look thirsty, and the river (which might have been 'the river of life') a sheet of metal. The bridge along which the visionary walks (in the brief transit of life) seems unending, and its blackened statues, with their blank gaze, ancient garments, and saintly crowns, appear to be the real inhabitants and proprietors of the place, 'while the busy, trivial men and women, hurrying to and fro' are a 'a swarm of ephemeral visitants infesting it for a day'. It might be thought that the occupants of the time-fretted buildings were descended from those statues; 'urged by no fear or hope', they worship wearily in stifling churches, and remain doomed 'to live on in the rigidity of habit', without 'the repose of night or the new birth of morning'. The scene epitomizes a state of spiritual deadness or 'death-in-life' amid the memorials of a past religious age.

*   *   *

'The Lifted Veil' and 'Brother Jacob' are poles apart, the one deep and dark, the other light and bordering on the farcical. If the one is a *jeu de mélancolie*, the other is a *jeu d'esprit* which may appear 'outré' by George Eliot standards. 'Brother Jacob' was written for the fun of it; its pace is satisfying, and it is never dull. Her only story without high seriousness, it suggests that she might have benefited had she been encouraged to write a few more diversions in fiction. Originally 'Mr David Faux, Confectioner', then 'The Idiot Brother', it was written in the summer of 1860, probably as a relief from preparations for *Romola*, before she was inspired to write *Silas Marner*. She described it as a slight tale, but it was offered to Sampson Low for 250 guineas. George Smith, anxious to secure her work, offered the same sum for it; and, after the disappointing sales of *Romola*, she made it a compensatory gift for publication in *The Cornhill Magazine*, where it appeared anonymously in July 1864. At the end of 1866 John Blackwood decided that 'The Lifted Veil' and 'Brother Jacob' were better omitted from 'the recognised series' of George Eliot's works; both were 'as clever as can be' but there was 'a painful want of light' about them. He was as mystified by the implications of the first as he was by the author's motivation in the second.

'Brother Jacob' is steeped in mock-serious humour; it has fine ironical moments; and its suspense is judiciously managed throughout. Few authors have chosen a confectioner as a disreputable hero. After being wed to his apprenticeship by a sweet tooth, David Faux, with his unprepossessing visage and patronym, dreams of making a fortune in the West Indies, where a princess might fall in love with him and give him jewels; he would marry her if it suited him. By pertinacity and cunning he manages to escape his idiot brother Jacob and emigrate with his stolen guineas from Liverpool. Nearly six years later a Mr Edward Freely rents a vacant shop in the marketplace at Grimworth; his window display, when the shutters are removed to indicate that business has commenced, is a sight to bring tears to a Dutch painter, and even more to the children who gather open-eyed outside.

The rector's wife regards bandy-legged Mr Freely, with his sallow complexion and buff cravat, as very civil and obliging, unusually intelligent for a confectioner, and a man of strict principles, to judge from his remarks on the dishonesty of other tradesmen. He is a regular church-goer, and his business prospers. It would be a melancholy task to describe 'the gradual corruption of Grimworth manners from their primitive simplicity', George

Eliot writes, were it not 'cheered by the prospect of the fine peripateia or downfall by which the progress of the corruption was ultimately checked'. Mr Steene, the veterinary surgeon, no longer sharing his wife's interest in romantic poetry about the Orient, as he had done before marriage, must have mince-pies for a Christmas-Eve party; and Mrs Steene, eager to regain the esteem of a husband more interested in his food than in the bulbul of literary romance, succumbs to temptation and buys them at Freely's. With her recommendation the 'infection' spreads, and gradually the confectioner follows his commodities into Grimworth homes, charming Desdemonas with accounts of his astonishing adventures abroad. Things begin to look serious when Penny Palfrey falls in love with him, and he cunningly cultivates the friendship of her parents; more serious still, when he persuades her father that he has relatives of rank including an admiral (whose portrait in a good light is indistinguishable from that of Nelson), and gains his consent to marry her. By chance, after talking of a West Indian estate he might inherit, Mr Freely learns that Jonathan Faux, his father, has died, and that if he gets in touch with a certain attorney he will hear something to his advantage.

All David Faux's plans to make a fortune in the West Indies had come to nought, though he gained a sum or two for 'charitably abstaining from mentioning some other people's misdemeanours'. A real chance to make money is irresistible, but Faux's greed is his undoing: to receive his share of the family legacy (due subtraction being made for the stolen guineas) he has to disclose his actual position in the presence of both his eldest brother and the attorney. The news soon reaches Jacob, and when Mr Freely is at home discussing his imminent marriage with the Palfreys, and saying (after Mrs Palfrey has seen a family likeness between him and the admiral) that his family are 'too high' to take much notice of him, his smock-frocked idiot brother arrives, clutching his pitchfork. Jacob is not only affectionate but fascinated by pies and lozenges: how to get rid of him, and save his face, is beyond Faux's ingenuity. With the arrival of the eldest brother, the game is up.

Perhaps readers, including Blackwood, found themselves embarrassed by a story in which an idiot plays an important role. Certainly Jacob creates amusing scenes, but always at the expense of a brother whose covert designs he hinders and ultimately foils. Wordsworth 'never wrote anything with so much glee' as 'The Idiot Boy', and George Eliot, with this example before her, probably never wrote anything with more glee than 'The Idiot Brother'; in neither is fun directed against an unfortunate creature. Such is Jacob's unpredictability that he might have 'puzzled the astute heroes of M. de Balzac, whose foresight is so remarkably at home in the future'. With his pitchfork he poses a threat to nefarious schemes, and the trick with the lozenges which David plays in a vain attempt to distract attention from the stolen guineas ultimately plays a part in his undoing. Jacob's role as the unconscious guardian of the law allies itself with his brotherly love to win the reader's sympathy. Successive changes in the title of the story seem to confirm the prior importance of this moral role, even though our interest is with a calculating scoundrel from first to last. The epigraph and conclusion supply a moral, which, however appropriate, does not make 'Brother Jacob' a serious tale. George Eliot's nemesis is hidden (as she says) in an unexpected form. Soon after its completion, she turned to another tale of stolen guineas, radically different in tone.

A Transitional Period

SILAS MARNER

While in Florence, George Eliot had been 'fired with the idea' of writing *Romola*, but lack of confidence, especially in undertaking a kind of novel which did not conform to her readers' expectations, made her resolve 'first to write another English story' (28.viii.60). The only fiction she completed in the summer of 1860, after her return from Italy and before removing to 10 Harewood Square, was 'Brother Jacob'. Whether she made progress in planning her other English story, or spent more time on *Romola*, is conjectural, for the idea of her new novel came to her in her new home, thrusting itself 'between me and the other book I was meditating'. 'Silas Marner, the Weaver of Raveloe' unfolded as 'a story of old-fashioned village life' from 'the merest millet-seed of thought', and 'came *across* my other plans by a sudden inspiration'. 'It came to me first of all, quite suddenly, as a sort of legendary tale, suggested by my recollection of having once, in early childhood, seen a linen-weaver with a bag on his back; but, as my mind dwelt on the subject, I became inclined to a more realistic treatment.' By the end of November little more than sixty manuscript pages had been written, but good progress was made after settling at 16 Blandford Square in December, and the novel was finished on 10 March 1861.

John Blackwood found the first hundred pages very sad, and wished for a more 'cheery' picture with 'higher specimens of humanity', but (he went on to say, before engaging in further superlatives) 'you paint so naturally that in your hands the veriest earthworms become most interesting perfect studies in fact'. In reply, George Eliot confessed that, since Wordsworth was dead, she would not have believed that her tale could interest anyone had not Mr Lewes been 'strongly arrested' by it. She hoped Blackwood would not find it altogether sad, 'since it sets − or is intended to set − in a strong light the remedial influences of pure, natural human relations'. 'The Nemesis is a very mild one', she added. She had thought the story 'lent itself best to metrical rather than prose fiction, especially in all that relates to the psychology of Silas', although this would have meant less scope for humour (24.ii.61). We must be grateful that the author preferred to express psychological realism and country life, with humour and genuine feelings, in the less circumscribed medium of prose. At heart the novel is like a parable irradiated with poetic light; it is endowed with a miraculous quality, the probability of which is not questioned because it is inherent in the art of the narrative. It is what we would rather have happen than what we expect to happen, but it is saved from sentimentality by being set in a small imaginary world which is unflinchingly true to life. With its 'fairy-tale' element, *Silas Marner* is a particularly fine example of realistic romance.

George Eliot's reference to poetry in connection with the 'psychology' of Silas recalls some of the poems in *Lyrical Ballads* and Wordsworth's aim in writing them: 'to illustrate the manner in which our feelings and ideas are associated in a state of excitement . . . to follow the fluxes and refluxes of the mind when agitated by the great and simple affections of our nature'. Indebtedness to 'Michael' is acknowledged in the title-page epigraph:

> A child, more than all other gifts
> That earth can offer to declining man,
> Brings hope with it, and forward-looking thoughts.

The lines which follow almost immediately in Wordsworth's poem suggest a further influence on the story:

> Exceeding was the love he bare to him,
> His heart and his heart's joy! For often-times
> Old Michael, while he was a babe in arms,
> Had done him female service, not alone
> For pastime and delight, as is the use
> Of fathers, but with patient mind enforced
> To acts of tenderness . . .

The thought that human love is more precious than gold has been realized so widely throughout the ages that the existence of a parallel (noted by Mathilde Blind) to the central story of *Silas Marner* in *Jermola the Potter* by the Polish author Kraszewski need occasion no surprise. Though it was published in 1857, it seems unlikely that George Eliot knew this novel, nor can it be assumed that she was consciously aware of any literary indebtedness. Yet the pivotal idea on which her imagination worked may have come (as suggested by David R. Carroll) from *The Winter's Tale* (III.iii). In *Silas Marner* the child, drawn by a bright glancing light on the white ground, leaves its dying mother, toddles through the snow and freezing wind to the open door of the weaver's cottage and squats before the blazing hearth, where, after recovering from his trance, he sees her lying asleep, and mistakes her curly yellow hair for his lost gold. The love she awakens in him and his adoption of her bring life, community participation, and happiness to a man who had become almost as mechanical and dead as the machine he operates. In Shakespeare the association of winter with gold and the child who is found derives from the title of the play; the parallel with *Silas Marner* is furthered by the supposition of fairy or Providential agency, and possibly by 'a squire's child':

> *Shepherd*. Heavy matters, heavy matters! But look thee here, boy. Now bless thyself; thou met'st with things dying, I with things new-born. Here's a sight for thee; look thee, a bearing-cloth for a squire's child! Look thee here; take up, take up, boy; open't. So, let's see — it was told me I should be rich by the fairies. This is some changeling. Open't. What's within, boy?
> *Clown*. You're a made old man; if the sins of your youth are forgiven you, you're well to live. Gold! all gold!
> *Shepherd*. This is fairy gold, boy, and 'twill prove so. Up with't, keep it close. Home, home, the next way.

Personal reasons may be suspected for the overriding appeal of the theme. When the idea of *Silas Marner* 'came *across*' George Eliot's other plans, she was forty years old; she had chosen to have no children, possibly for the sake of her career, perhaps because she feared that children of parents ostracized by society might suffer innocently, probably for financial reasons, Lewes having to support his legal wife and give his sons the best education he could afford. The success of *Adam Bede* and *The Mill on the Floss* had brought prospects of relative affluence, yet she had often 'to struggle against a selfish longing for repose', and must have known

Above Mary Anne Evans' birthplace, South Farm, Arbury

Below Griff House, Mary Evans' home, 1820–41. (The two-storeyed extension on the right was built later.)

Above Robert Evans' birthplace, Roston Common

Below Norbury Church, where he sang in the choir

Above Bartle Massey's cottage

Below the Bromley Davenport Arms, Ellastone, original of 'the Donnithorne Arms'

3

Above the dame school near Griff House

Below the pond to the right of the garden behind Griff House

Above the church, Astley ('Knebley')

Below Arbury Mill

Above the church, Chilvers Coton ('Shepperton')

Below the vicarage, Chilvers Coton

Above Arbury Hall ('Cheverel Manor')

Below the church and vicarage, Nuneaton ('Milby')

Above Bird Grove, Foleshill
Below left Robert Evans
Below right Mary Anne Evans (by Sara Hennell)

Above Bird Grove

Below Rosehill, home of the Brays

Marian Evans: *Left* from a painting by M.D'Albert Durade, 1850   *Right* from a photograph thought to be taken in 1854 or 1855

Above the workhouse or 'College of the Poor', Chilvers Coton
Below the tomb of Mrs Emma Gwyther ('Milly Barton'), Chilvers Coton

Above original of Mrs Pettifer's

Left entrance to the Bull Hotel, Nuneaton ('the Red Lion', 'Milby')

Below entrance in Church Street, Nuneaton (original of Janet Dempster's)

Above Herbert Spencer, 1858   *Below left* Griff Hollows ('the Red Deeps')   *Below right* the Old Hall, Gainsborough ('St Ogg's')

Left John Blackwood (portrait by Sir John Watson Gordon, 1857)

Below George Eliot (by Samuel Laurence, in chalks, 1860)

Title-page 'vignettes' (Blackwood edition):
Above Shepperton Church
Below the Hall Farm

'the vignettes . . . are charming' (George Eliot to John Blackwood, 30 January 1877): *Above* Dorlcote Mill   *Below* Raveloe

'Mrs Poyser, following the old Squire beyond the door' — *Adam Bede*

'Tom, looking before him, saw death rushing on them' — *The Mill on the Floss*

19

'powerless, under the double presence of an inexplicable surprise and a hurrying influx of memories' – *Silas Marner*

'She turned her back on Florence, not meaning to look at it till the monks were quite out of sight' – *Romola* (engraved by W. J. Linton for *The Cornhill Magazine* from the illustration by Frederic Leighton). For pictorial reasons the artist has ignored some of the narrative detail.

21

George Eliot (by Frederick Burton, in chalks, 1865). *The National Portrait Gallery*

Above the Priory drawing-room

Below the Heights, Witley

Right 4 Cheyne Walk, Chelsea

Left John Walter Cross in 1870 or earlier

yearnings for motherhood, as well as that reverence for life which makes us 'feel a certain awe in the presence of a little child, such as we feel before some quiet majesty or beauty in the earth or sky — before a steady glowing planet, or a full-flowered eglantine, or the bending trees over a silent pathway' (xiii). When she and Lewes brought their eldest boy Charles from Switzerland to live with them in London, she experienced intense happiness, was delighted that he accepted her as mother, and loved to play Beethoven with him. He was 'the most entirely lovable human animal of seventeen and a half' she had ever met or heard of, and he grew 'dearer every day'. The companionship excited feelings of fulfilment more precious than prospective wealth in one who knew what it meant to be shunned by society. They not only prompted the 'millet-seed of thought'; they provided the fertile conditions for its rapid imaginative growth.

George Eliot's boldest and most inspired stroke in designing her story was the choice for her hero of a poor linen-weaver who, after being despised and rejected, settled in a remote country village where, as an alien, suspect and shunned, he lived a myopic solitary life of soul-destroying mechanical activity, motivated solely by the miserly appetite for gold. His realization that there are treasures on earth beyond the reach of thieves is not only a striking illustration of George Eliot's humanistic gospel ('the ideal of a goodness entirely human') but the basis for those imaginative contrasts and dramatic emphases which make the narrative unusually memorable. One such effect depends on the great scene at the Rainbow, which has a centrality of function in creating a lively sense of village community; fundamentally they depend on the interweaving of two antithetical stories, of Silas and of the squandering, festive, squirarchical Cass family. These stories develop contemporaneously, their linkage depending principally on the two major events in Silas's Raveloe life, the theft of his gold by Dunstan Cass and the advent of the child it suits Godfrey Cass to disown. The greatest change in Silas's life follows: from desolate monotony to affection, companionship, neighbourliness, and the restoration of faith. Such is the implication of the biblical name which is given the child (from Isaiah, lxii.4): 'Thou shalt no more be termed Forsaken; neither shall thy land any more be termed Desolate: but thou shalt be called Hephzibah, and thy land Beulah: for the Lord delighteth in thee, and thy land shall be married.'

The most pervasive Wordsworthian influence on *Silas Marner* probably came from George Eliot's critical reading of *The Excursion*. There are obvious differences: whereas Silas is simple, and his regeneration springs from human love, Wordsworth's solitary is an intellectual, and the hope finally raised of his renewed faith is based on God's redeeming love, though earlier (V.1012–16) the stress is on love, divine or human. In both works the influx of life and love is associated with nature and sunshine, though in *Silas Marner* they have no transcendental connotations.

Silas is a cataleptic who, in his earlier years, belonged to a narrow religious sect in a dingy town. Members of his Church believed in healing by prayer, so much so that Silas, who had inherited knowledge of medicinal herbs from his mother, began to imagine the search for them in the fields a sinful pleasure. His trance during a prayer-meeting was believed to be a divine visitation; a second fit enabled William Dane, whom he regarded as a devoted friend, to fasten the imputation of theft upon him (Dane's motivation becoming clear when he marries Silas's sweetheart). The church did not approve of legal prosecution; instead, lots were drawn after prayer, with the result that Silas was found guilty, and concluded that there was 'no just God that governs the earth righteously'. When he migrates he has lost both his love and his faith. The coincidence of his seizure with the event initiating this double loss is balanced later by the coincidence of another seizure with Eppie's entry into his home and life. Out of context, these crucial coincidences suggest the merest possibility and risky authorial contrivance; yet, unlike George Eliot's patent manoeuvring to ensure the temptations of Janet Dempster and Maggie Tulliver, these chance occurrences are so artistically assimilated that they seem natural and create no suspension of imaginative belief.

The migration of this pallid young man to Raveloe in 'that far-off time' when rustics regarded unusual people and events with suspicion concludes the first act of a drama which is set with deliberate imprecision in a period extending from the latter part of the eighteenth century to the years of Mant's Bible and an increasing poor-rate (xvii) almost immediately after the Napoleonic war. Fifteen years pass before we see Silas at Raveloe in the 'early years' of the nineteenth century, and the villagers know no more about him than when he came, except that he has made a lot of money; just before Christmas all his hoarded gold is stolen. There is talk of peace, and Squire Cass (like Mr Poyser) is afraid prices

will fall. New Year's Eve brings Eppie. Part II opens about sixteen
years later, with another interval of fifteen years in the narrative.
The autumn sunshine reflects Silas's age and happiness, and the
story ends aptly with Eppie's marriage the following spring.

There is no radical change in Silas Marner before Eppie's
arrival. He was cut off from the past, and the Power in which he
had trusted seemed remote in a country district where men lived in
'careless abundance' (as Dinah Morris observed in Loamshire),
and women (like the Dodson sisters) seemed to be 'laying up a stock
of linen for the life to come'; hence Silas's financial gain, though
he had almost lost his soul, for he had no purpose but to make
money, and wove mechanically, like the spider, 'from pure impulse, without reflection'. When the illness of the cobbler's wife
reminded him of his mother's fatal disease, and pity stirred him to
provide herbal relief, a link with the past was established which
'might have been the beginning of his rescue from the insect-like
existence into which his nature had shrunk'. But the numerous
callers who assumed he was 'a wise man' capable of charms and
miraculous cures were discouraged by his honest disclaimers, and
he worked unceasingly until by 'constant mechanical relation to
the objects of his life' he 'produced the same sort of impression as a
handle or a crooked tube, which has no meaning standing apart'.
Changes in his inner life are expressed in terms of nature. His grief
when he breaks the pot which had been his companion for years
shows that even in 'this stage of withering' the 'sap of affection' was
not dead. Only at night when he counted his gold was he happy;
when it was stolen, his 'withering desolation' reduced him to 'a
blank like that which meets a plodding ant when the earth has
broken away on its homeward path'. Christmas kindnesses and the
visits of Mr Macey and Dolly Winthrop (even her lard-cakes inscribed with sacred letters) did not move him; he was glad to be left
alone 'that he might weave again and moan at his ease'. 'The
fountains of human love and divine faith had not yet been
unlocked, and his soul was still the shrunken rivulet, with only this
difference, that its little groove of sand was blocked up, and it
wandered confusedly against dark obstruction.'

Silas had been told that hearing the old year rung out and the
new rung in would bring him luck, perhaps the return of his gold;
and his excitement helps to bring on the seizure which arrests him
when he is about to close the door, after failing to notice something
approach. Recovering consciousness, he sees his gold miraculously

restored; so it seems to his blurred vision until he clutches it and finds not 'hard coin' but soft warm curls. The child reminds him of his little sister, his old home, and the streets leading to Lantern Yard; old quiverings of tenderness revive and 'old impressions of awe at the presentiment of some Power presiding over his life'. Moral revival, as in *The Mill on the Floss*, is attributed to memory of old feelings and loyalties, but the explicable coincidence has the numinous suggestiveness of a visitation: 'the door was open. The money's gone I don't know where, and this is come from I don't know where'. The open door in Revelation, the receiving of a little child in the Gospels, and the association of these two images with the coming of God's kingdom, may have been in George Eliot's mind when she imagined the turning-point in Marner's life. Her gospel is Feuerbachian; the love which renovates Silas, and is externalized in sunshine and flowers, is human, from the tenderness that Eppie awakens to that which responds to neighbourly help and sympathy. He does not know what christening and church-going mean, but he acts for Eppie's good; his 'gold had kept his thoughts in an ever-repeated circle', but she gives him hope for the future, warming him into joy because *she* had joy, as the sunshine did 'the old winter-flies that came crawling forth in the early spring'; such too is her effect on others, 'stirring the human kindness in all eyes that looked on her'. The 'sunshine' which makes him unfold and tremble gradually into full consciousness needs no reference to a supramundane agency such as Dolly Winthrop's 'Them above', a survival of pagan superstition in a church-centred peasantry. George Eliot's humanitarian religion is clear without preaching; she shows the human factors at work, and quietly observes that, though men are no longer saved from destruction by angels, 'a hand is put into theirs, which leads them forth gently towards a calm and bright land, so that they look no more backward; and the hand may be a little child's'.

The central figure on the other side of the Raveloe picture is Godfrey Cass, whose 'mild' Nemesis is to be the want of something that would make him (unlike Silas) 'look forward more'. George Eliot operates the law of consequences, but her delineation of this victim of weakness and chance shows great understanding and sympathy. Blackmailed by his brother Dunstan and afraid of being disinherited on the score of his secret marriage to an ex-barmaid who has become an opium-addict, he is 'almost as helpless as an uprooted tree'. Good resolutions defer to hope; he would 'rather trust to casualties than to his own resolve', rather go on sitting at the feast like Damocles, 'with the sword hanging over him and terror in his heart, than rush away into the cold darkness'. With the loss of Wildfire and Dunstan's failure to return, he has to confess that he received Fowler's rent and gave it to his brother; his father is furious, but the situation becomes more alarming when he tells Godfrey that if the shilly-shallying does not stop, and he does not make up his mind to marry Nancy Lammeter, he himself will propose for him. Godfrey still trusts to 'some throw of fortune's dice'; like Tito Melema and Gwendolen Harleth, he gambles with Chance, the 'evil principle' of which 'religion' is 'the orderly sequence by which the seed brings forth a crop after its kind'. In the portrayal of his character, psychological realism is nowhere more piquant than when, after recognising his child in Silas's arms and hearing that the mother is probably dead, he experiences a terror that the woman might *not* be dead. This fear may be 'an ugly inmate' in a kindly disposition, but 'no disposition is a security from evil wishes to a man whose happiness hangs on duplicity', the author adds, as if she has Tito already in mind. The sequel shows that, had Godfrey claimed the child, his marriage with Nancy might have been happier.

In Raveloe, 'aloof from the currents of industrial energy and Puritan earnestness', life continues much as in Fielding's eighteenth century. Society is hierarchical, and the poor think the rich 'entirely in the right of it to lead a jolly life'. George Eliot presents a composite picture of their dissoluteness and humour, class superiority and kindness, roughness and nobility. Had the Squire's wife not died long before, the Red House would have been the better for 'that presence of the wife and mother which is the fountain of wholesome love and fear in parlour and kitchen'; Godfrey and Dunstan had grown up in neglect and idleness. Small squires and yeomen regarded the war as providential, and high prices for produce created extravagant habits; the deer-hound of slovenly, idle Squire Cass consumes enough beef at breakfast 'to make a poor man's holiday dinner'. Both Godfrey and his wife Nancy are rather to be pitied; he is all he should be to her, but their childlessness makes her worry for his sake, and he thinks it a retribution. Living in accordance with traditional principles, she judges that the adoption of Eppie which he recommends is contrary to the will of Providence. When the discovery of Dunstan's crime shocks Godfrey into confession, he is astonished that, instead of being indignant, she regrets that the child had not been theirs from the first. Blind, class-bound prejudice makes it difficult to see how deep affection can 'go along with callous palms and scant means'. It seems natural to him that Eppie would prefer to be a lady; in the end he asserts that it is his duty to take care of her lest she marry 'some low working-man'. Even though Nancy understands Eppie's natural feelings, she insists on her duty to her legal father. Eppie's word is final: she can think of no other home than Silas's; she was not brought up to be a lady; she likes working-class folk and their houses; and (she ends passionately) 'I'm promised to marry a working-man, as'll live with father, and help me to take care of him.' The defeat is complete; Godfrey accepts it as his nemesis.

When he knows that his first wife is dead, he is afraid that confession will destroy his chance of happiness with Nancy; by a process of self-deception he ironically concludes that he would be much happier without possession of the child. The passage bears brief testimony to the general truth of the author's psychological imagination. It is exemplified at some length when Silas finds that his gold has disappeared, as well as in such detail as the fateful recollection of the forgotten twine which is prompted by the string he habitually uses for roasting meat, and which leaves the way clear for Dunstan to enter during his absence.

More discreet in manner and proportion than in her earlier works, George Eliot's comments raise no egotistical barriers in the way of the reader. The style generally is pleasing, with some happy incidental humour: when Silas makes his dramatic appearance at the Rainbow, the long pipes of the company move simultaneously 'like the antennae of startled insects'; Mrs Crackenthorp, blinking and fidgeting continually with her ornaments, makes subdued noises 'very much like a guinea-pig that twitches its nose and soliloquises in all company indiscriminately'; as she dances, her turban-shaped cap with its perpendicular feather makes her appear to Ben Winthrop like 'a short-necked bottle wi' a long quill in it'; and a kitten, tantalized by Eppie during her meal, holds on with four claws to her shoulder 'like a design for a jug handle'. Priscilla Lammeter is an entertaining character; plain in looks and speech, and intended by God A'mighty (she says) for a single life, she is full of high spirits. To satisfy sister Nancy's idea of etiquette, she agrees that they shall wear the same kind of gown at the Red House dance, though it makes her 'yellow as a daffadil'. Preparations completed, she announces that she is 'as ready as a mawkin *can* be — there's nothing awanting to frighten the crows, now I've got my eardroppers in'. Kind-hearted Silas's adoption of Dolly Winthrop's coal-hole punitive treatment produces its unforgettable sequel, but for humour on a more extensive scale we turn to the village worthies at the Rainbow.

Though personally realized and far from types, the leading members of this group are distinguished by the predominance of occupational interest or of some leading peculiarity such as the landlord's tactful evasiveness in seeing the truth of both sides of a question. The comedy they provide is modified as well as generated by this consistency. Impressions are dramatically given of village life, with its proneness to superstition, and its unflinching frankness of humour at the recipient's expense. Reminiscences deepen our sense of parish community as we proceed. By gradations, too, the conversation leads with memorable art to the startling ghost-like appearance of Silas. In an original and varied manner George Eliot has given ampler and more diverting proportions to the chorus role with which she experimented in her first story; the wheelwright, and two anonymous members of the Raveloe choir, the bassoon, and the key-bugle, clearly have a 'Shepperton' origin (SCL1.i). The humour of the chorus is diversified with anecdote and memorable sayings: 'there'd be two pinions about a cracked bell, if the bell could hear itself'; 'it isn't the meaning, it's the glue'; 'a fly's a fly, though it may be a hoss-fly'. Few rustics show epigrammatic wit, and these examples all come from the knowledgeable, self-important parish-clerk Mr Macey. *The Saturday Review* gave the scene high praise: the characters are distinct and probable; the things they say are perfectly natural; and the quality is Shakespearian. To make the highly artistic seem natural is the mark of genius, and this was probably felt by Hardy, a regular reader of *The Saturday Review*, who developed all technical aspects of the Rainbow scene in his humorous rustic choruses, pre-eminently in the malthouse scenes of *Far from the Madding Crowd* and the bonfire scene of *The Return of the Native*.

Altogether *Silas Marner* gives a representative picture of Raveloe life as a whole. The Rainbow scene makes a major contribution to this; equally important, at a higher social level, is that supplied by the traditional New Year's dance at Squire Cass's. Though less genteel, it is, with the coming of the ladies, reminiscent of Jane Austen society; grander and in more splendid surroundings, it recalls, in the country-dancing and onlookers' remarks, the Christmas party at the tranter's in *Under the Greenwood Tree* (see p. 246). Mr Macey's comments differ in being more related to the story. In turning our attention away from these unclouded festivities, with Godfrey Cass 'taking draughts of forgetfulness from the sweet presence' of Nancy Lammeter, to the wintry scene where his wife dies in the snow from taking her habitual draught of oblivion, George Eliot provides the most striking, and the most damning, of all the contrasts in the novel. In search of a doctor, Silas Marner makes his second startling irruption among the Raveloe company he had shunned; again the effect is apparition-like, but only for Godfrey when he sees his child in Marner's arms, an apparition from his hidden life, which lies 'like a dark by-street, behind the goodly ornamented façade that meets the sunlight and the gaze of respectable admirers'.

We are in a real world, and it is this world which conditions Silas's recovery. Once it begins (in wintry darkness), his good fortune holds; his later years are bathed in autumn sunshine. The happiness of Eppie and Aaron when they marry in spring shines in the flowers of the garden at Stone-pits, the home they have chosen to share with Silas. All things seem to reflect the good luck which the Raveloe 'chorus' agrees Marner has deserved. Eppie has been a blessing to him, and the author explains why in a passage which recalls views she expressed in her essay on Riehl:

> The tender and pecular love with which Silas had reared her in almost inseparable companionship with himself, aided by the seclusion of their dwelling, had preserved her from the lowering influences of the village talk and habits, and had kept her mind in that freshness which is sometimes falsely supposed to be an invariable attribute of rusticity. Perfect love has a breath of poetry which can exalt the relations of the least-instructed human beings; and this breath of poetry had surrounded Eppie from the time when she had followed the bright gleam that beckoned her to Silas's hearth; so that it is not surprising if, in other things besides her delicate prettiness, she was not quite a common village maiden, but had a touch of refinement and fervour which came from no other teaching than that of tenderly-nurtured unvitiated feeling.

The story is rounded off realistically. Priscilla Lammeter's 'I could ha' wished Nancy had had the luck to find a child like that and bring her up' combines with Godfrey's absence from Eppie's wedding to recall a past he can never forget. At a more humorous level, we are reminded in a few words of the trials the good Dolly Winthrop has to live with: having attended his son's wedding, her husband Ben prefers not to accompany her and Silas and the young couple to Stone-pits, but to turn in at the Rainbow and receive the congratulations of his friends.

Another conclusion underscores the author's gospel. Silas takes Eppie in search of Lantern Yard, hoping to enlighten the minister about 'the religion' of the Raveloe countryside; but the old church is 'swep' away, and the town is a dark ugly place that hides the sky. The religion which condemned Silas remains 'dark to the last', but he has had 'light enough to trusten by' ever since 'the child was sent' to him. The poetry of 'the bright gleam', like that of the autumn sunshine and the garden in spring, is not adventitious but the poetry of experience; the true religion of Raveloe has its sanctum in the human heart.

ROMOLA

The idea of creating a historical romance from the career and martyrdom of Savonarola occurred to Lewes, and was enthusiastically taken up by George Eliot, during their first visit to Florence in May 1860. The following spring, after the completion of *Silas Marner*, they spent five weeks in Florence, 'foraging in old streets and old books', purchasing volumes for research at home, and becoming familiar with historic buildings and areas. For five days they worked in the Magliabecchian Library, where Lewes was most helpful in procuring books she needed for note-making on such period features as costume, fairs, common sayings, jests, and barbers. An enormous programme of reading followed, Italian works especially, with searches for rare books in London and reading at the British Museum. Over-exertion in scrupulous concern for historic detail inevitably hampered George Eliot's structuring of the novel, and she was so depressed at times that she almost gave it up. In August her plot emerged 'with new distinctness'. She began *Romola* on 7 October 1861, but was so despondent by the end of the month that she began to think of her next English novel; the next morning 'the Italian scenes returned . . . with fresh

attraction'. After completing the plot in December, she began
Romola again on New Year's Day. Her journal for Sunday, 26
January 1862, reads:

> Detained from writing by the necessity of gathering particulars:
> 1st, about Lorenzo de Medici's death; 2nd, about the possible
> retardation of Easter; 3rd, about Corpus Christi day; 4th, about
> Savonarola's preaching in the Quaresima of 1492. Finished 'La
> Mandragola' — second time reading for the sake of Florentine
> expressions — and began 'La Calandra'.

As a result of her ill-health and dislike of London air, frequent
visits to the country became necessary, but progress with the novel
continued. At the end of the year she was as despondent as ever
about her work, and by January 1863 it was clear that the twelve
contractual instalments would have to be increased to fourteen.
The twelfth was finished on 6 April (and read, as was customary,
to George, who was 'highly contented'); the thirteenth on 16 May,
when she 'killed Tito in great excitement'; the last on 9 June. She
found *Romola* more exhausting than any other of her books. After
reading it years later, she wrote: 'there is no book of mine about
which I more thoroughly feel that I could swear by every sentence
as having been written with my best blood, such as it is, and with
the most ardent care for veracity of which my nature is capable'
(30.i.77).

Reporting her depression of December 1861, Lewes told Blackwood that she knew more about her subject than any other writer
who had 'touched it', and urged him when he met her 'to dis-
countenance the idea of a Romance being the product of an
Encyclopaedia'. Undoubtedly prolonged historical research and
angst had a debilitating effect at times on George Eliot's creative
imagination, curtailing both opportunity and power to develop
character through psychological realism. The choice of Savonarola as one of the principal dramatis personae restricted her
freedom, and the historical pageantry of fairs and processions, in
conjunction with 'choric' conversations, led inevitably to a
reduction in dramatic presentation, the development of which,
particularly between Romola and Tito, might have made the
novel more imaginatively memorable. F. T. Palgrave was too
absolute when he complained that it was 'all mosaic-work, not
brushwork', for *Romola* contains vivid scenes and situations; it

tells a fascinating, even at times an exciting, story. It is artistically controlled and rarely disproportionate; historical colouring and analysis provide important elements, but they rarely cause the action to drag seriously, much less than in Scott. The most irritating exactitude is in the use of Italian terms with English synonyms, and occasionally without them. Background dialogue on fashionable interests such as literature suggests a short-sighted punctiliousness; usually its subject is politics, and it is enlightening rather than burdensome. 'I believe there is scarcely a phrase, an incident, an allusion, that did not gather its value to me from its supposed subservience to my main artistic objects. But it is likely enough that my mental constitution would always render the issue of my labour something excessive', George Eliot wrote humbly to one of her reviewers (8.viii.63). Yet, though the reader may at first be handicapped by its historical and foreign setting, the better *Romola* is known the more it will be appreciated. 'It is . . . hard for an author to make a sacrifice of present life and manners, by which she could more easily obtain an effect of reality for her scenes and of life for her characters, and to play at having been a living witness of past centuries', Viola Meynell wrote. 'She has to invite her readers to a tremendous and obvious pretence. A reader of *Romola* who is wise, and keen in the search for great qualities, will pretend with ease and spirit and friendliness.'

The difficulty of writing a historical romance may be seen in Scott's relative failures. When *Romola* appeared it was pronounced 'the greatest' and 'much the greatest' of George Eliot's first four novels. John Morley found it a 'wonderful book', and Henry James in 1866 thought it 'decidedly the most important' of her works, though not the most entertaining or readable. In 1885, with equivocation comparable to the oracular ambivalence of Oscar Browning's 'It remains perhaps, the best of all historical novels, but a warning that no more should ever be attempted', he declared that 'this magnificent romance' is 'on the whole the finest thing she wrote' and 'on the whole a failure'. It is fashionable today to accept the latter judgment with little qualification, but the vagaries of criticism throughout a century suggest that after all *Romola* has something to recommend it.

The subject was one of universal significance to George Eliot: 'The great river-courses which have shaped the lives of men have hardly changed; and those other streams, the life-currents that ebb and flow in human hearts, pulsate to the same great needs, the same great loves and terrors.' The old Florentine web of 'Epicurean levity and fetichistic dread', of 'pedantic impossible ethics uttered by rote' and 'crude passions acted out with childish impulsiveness', of self-indulgence and conscientious hope, is essentially the same in the modern world, where 'men still yearn for the reign of peace and righteousness – still own *that* life to be the highest which is a conscious voluntary sacrifice'. 'The finest effort to reanimate the past is of course only approximative – is always more or less an infusion of the modern spirit into the ancient form', the author had written in 'Silly Novels by Lady Novelists', adding that 'this form of imaginative power must always be among the very rarest, because it demands as much accurate and minute knowledge as creative vigour'. One reviewer concluded that 'the chief interest of *Romola* reposes on ideas of moral duty and of right' which are of such modern growth that they would be 'more appropriately displayed on a modern stage'; another, less debatably (his statement is equally applicable to *Silas Marner*), that 'we are in the hands of a thinker who has thought far down into the depths of the religious mind, and who has seriously and anxiously desired to ascertain what is the place of religious thought in the facts of life'.

The story is set in Florence from the death of Lorenzo the Magnificent on 9 April 1492 to the execution of Savonarola on 23 May 1498. The first of the three books presents the mysterious arrival of the handsome young Greek Tito, his swift rise to favour and influence, and his betrothal to Romola during the last week of Carnival. The second opens on 17 November 1494, more than eighteen months after their marriage at Easter; Romola's father Bardo has died. The Medici are driven from Florence, which is occupied for eleven days by the forces of Charles VIII of France. With them comes a prisoner, Baldassarre, the foster-father whom Tito has abandoned; he escapes, comes face to face with Tito, who disowns him and calls him a madman. His mind unhinged by hardship and suffering, Baldassarre can think only of revenge, but he is balked, and Tito prospers as an astute political agent and ambassador. He and Romola become estranged; her suspicions are heightened, and she leaves Florence after hearing that he has treacherously sold her father's library. Savonarola persuades her that her duty is at home, and she returns on Christmas Eve 1494. With the third book the story resumes at the end of October 1496. Tito has become more successful and important as a perfidious agent playing off one political faction against another in a triple game which involves the popular party inspired by Savonarola, the Mediceans, and the Arrabbiati or aristocrats, including the Compagnacci, a group of dissolute young men led by Dolfo Spini. Romola discovers that Tito has been married for years to Tessa, a simple contadina; she also learns the full story of his filial disloyalty to Baldassarre. After realizing, from his refusal to plead for the life of her uncle Bernardo, a leading Medicean, that Savonarola's high-minded principles are sullied by his own far-reaching ambition, she leaves Florence in despair, drifts out to sea, and lands on a plague-stricken coast, where her ministering to survivors becomes legendary. In the meantime Tito's duplicity has been discovered by Spini and, after escaping the vengeance of the Compagnacci, he meets his death at the hands of Baldassarre. Romola returns, hearing on the way of Tito's death and the arrest of Savonarola. The main action ends with the latter's execution, and an epilogue marks the eve of its anniversary eleven years later. The story has three clear phases, the first ending with Tito and Romola's betrothal, the second with the breakdown of their marriage, the third with the death of one whose higher self she can still admire. Like the end of *The Mill on the Floss*, the penultimate 'legendary' phase was conceived before the novel was planned as a whole, as George Eliot informed Sara Hennell (23.viii.63), when the latter wrote on the 'pure idealism' of the heroine: 'You are right . . . the various *strands* of thought I had to work out forced me into a more ideal treatment of Romola than I had foreseen at the outset − though the 'Drifting away' and the Village with the Plague belonged to my earliest vision of the story and were by deliberate forecast adopted as romantic and symbolical elements.'

The ending is the least satisfactory part of the novel. There are earlier weaknesses, particularly in the Tessa scenes; too unreal a character to excite pity, she trusts Tito, believing that he is good because he is beautiful (like the people entering Paradise), and gives the impression of being a simpleton to whom he turns for 'refuge' and solace in times of stress. Romola's role suffers from being rather passive before she breaks with Tito, and as they go their several ways he becomes less the individual than an agent of intrigue. With Romola's 'new baptism' in her Madonna role among the plague-stricken, we are in another world from Florence; yet, though idyllicized, it is more imaginatively real than the episode which follows. Savonarola's end produces spectacle, not drama; Romola can do no more than study the evidence against him, and we are presented with the author's own analysis of the case, with the minimum of fictional pretence. Leslie Stephen thought a historical character in a novel 'almost always a nuisance', and preferred to have George III 'just round the corner' and not 'in full front'. The risk is never more patent in *Romola* than at this point. All that remains for the heroine, with the assistance and companionship of Monna Brigida, is to help Tessa and her children. The epilogue emphasizes her veneration of Savonarola's humanistic virtues, and concludes with a homily, neatly setting forth the lessons to be derived from the novel, but much too adult and abstract for the boy Lillo to whom it is addressed. Described as 'lovely' in *The Westminster Review*, the epilogue is at best a pretty anticlimax, indicative of the straits to which the author was reduced when, as the action draws to an end, the principal dramatis personae disappear one by one, and only Romola is left.

Chance plays an important part in the plot. For Tito life becomes a game of chance, with check and counter-check. For the author chance is a convenient aid when Savonarola happens to be on the country road outside Florence, and the disguised Romola unfortunately lifts her cowl to look ahead just when he and another Dominican are approaching within a few yards of her. The process of chance whereby Baldassarre eventually reaches Florence to confront Tito is convincing, but it is remarkable that he should have spotted Tito's ring on the finger of a man at Genoa who remembered that he had bought it at Bratti's shop. When the noose, as it were, is tightening around Tito's neck, and all is in readiness for his escape, it is fitting that he should be trapped between armed bands of the Compagnacci; but that, after hood-winking them, he should be carried exhausted down the Arno and washed ashore two yards from Baldassarre, who has life left only to ensure his strangulation, is a contrivance which poetic justice hardly justifies. Revenge has been Baldassarre's constant com-panion, and he holds on till his last breath, intent on following Tito to hell 'that he might clutch him there'. (In his biography of George Eliot, Professor Haight gives the story she heard in Berlin during the winter of 1854–5 of a wealthy Roman whose adopted son cunningly secured his property and ordered him to leave his own house. The foster-father killed him on the spot, and refused to have a confessor, saying 'I wish to go to Hell, for *he* is there, and I want to follow out my revenge.')

Chance of a more artistic kind is seen in the dramatic irony of remarks by Bratti, barber Nello, and Bardo, which startle Tito and sharpen suspicion at intervals from the outset. Bardo's comment on the value of Tito's gems, 'Five hundred ducats! Ah, more than a man's ransom', is remembered when they are sold for five hundred florins, and Tito salves his stricken conscience with the thought of all the uncertainties that make it futile for him to attempt any rescue of his foster-father (whose message, in consequence of two chance meetings, reaches him from afar three weeks later, to the effect that the gems alone will serve to ransom him). Chance plays a more dramatic part with the painter Piero di Cosimo, a shrewd physiognomist who persistently casts suspicion on Tito, startling him 'as if at a sudden accusation' the first time they meet, when he suggests that Tito should sit for the face of Sinon (whose arch-treachery hints at further betrayals in a city state). Like Tessa, Romola at first deems Tito's beauty the expression of goodness; but Piero detects fear in his face, and the dramatic moment comes when the freed prisoner Baldassarre, rushing up the Duomo steps for sanctuary, stumbles and clutches one of the group of *signori* by the arm: it is Tito. When he turns and confronts the man he had hoped was dead, his face is bloodless with terror; and Piero sees at last the kind of ghost he needs for his unfinished picture of Tito, his face averted in fear from the wine-cup he holds up triumphantly in his right hand.

The wine-cup is symbolical; it is part of the picture commissioned by Tito for his betrothal. The first of Piero's pictures to which attention is drawn (iii) symbolizes the general conflict of spiritual forces in Florence, with Greek paganism opposed to Christianity, and Stoicism pursuing a middle course. The chief representatives of these life-philosophies are Tito, Savonarola and Romola's brother Bernardino (Dino), her father Bardo and Romola herself. Tito's betrothal picture combines with the crucifix she receives from her dying brother Dino to create perhaps the richest imaginative overtones of the novel. When Tito declares his love for Romola he has already 'sold himself to evil', turning his back on his foster-father 'to extract the utmost sum of pleasure' from life. For a time he acts in the role Romola's blind father had expected Dino to pursue for the glory of his family, instead of renouncing the world for cloisterdom. All three consider Dino's Christian creed superstitious and fanatical. Romola hears from his dying lips a vision which had come to him of her desolation after marrying one with the face of 'the Great Tempter'. Tito urges his 'golden-tressed Aurora' to forget these twilight monkish fantasies, and she sees in him all the Greek images of natural joyousness. The theme of the 'clashing deities' in *Romola* anticipates Hellenic–Victorian controversy in the writings of Pater, Arnold, Swinburne, and Hardy. For his betrothal to Romola, Tito requests, in their likeness and in tryptych form on a wooden shrine, a picture of the triumph of Bacchus and Ariadne with her golden crown. When he brings this to her, he takes the crucifix and locks it within the centre, where it is to remain hidden by images of youth and joy. Romola's dream, like Bardo's, is not fulfilled; 'the crowned Ariadne, under the snowing roses' feels 'more and more the presence of unexpected thorns'. When love fades, and Tito's selfish disregard of her father's wishes for the preservation of his library hardens Romola's suspicion of his treachery to Baldassarre, she is desolate but not submissive. She plans to escape. The dark wintry scene consorts with her mood, and emblematically she finds a grey serge cowled Franciscan habit in the chest which holds her wedding-clothes. She has hardly donned this in preparation for her departure on the morrow when the taper expires, and in complete darkness she remembers her brother's warning vision. The next morning she looks bitterly at 'the triumphant Bacchus with his clusters and his vine-clad spear, clasping the crowned Ariadne; the Loves showering roses, the wreathed vessel, the cunning-eyed dolphins, and the rippled sea: all encircled by a flowery border, like a bower of paradise'. Then she unlocks the shrine, and hangs the crucifix around her neck 'for Dino's sake'. Removing her betrothal ring with a sense that her life is rent in two, she encloses it in a letter to Tito announcing that her love is dead. When she returns to Florence, inspired by Savonarola, the shrine remains locked and empty, with the crucifix of self-renunciation and dedication to the needs of humanity placed outside it.

The ring is important as a symbol of personal loyalty. In selling Baldassarre's, Tito soon after his arrival in Florence registers his calculating disregard for the past, in contrast to his foster-father who continues to wear, as a relic of her love, the charm given him by his mother until, maddened by the thirst for revenge, he opens it in the hope of finding something he can sell to buy a poniard. The natural piety which roots one in the past is a foolish sentiment or superstitious scruple to Tito, especially if it leads to recognition;

and he forbids Tessa to wear a wedding-ring. He regards Romola's respect for her dead father's wishes as a 'futile devotion', an air-woven fetter which a little philosophy will soon dissolve. Only when her love for Tito is dead does Romola remove the ring from her finger, but not without a struggle of conscience: 'that force of outward symbols by which our active life is knit together so as to make an inexorable external identity for us, not to be shaken by our wavering consciousness, gave a strange effect to this simple movement towards taking off her ring . . . It brought a vague but arresting sense that she was somehow violently rending her life in two' (xxxvi). 'Our lives make a moral tradition for our individual selves, as the life of mankind at large makes a moral tradition for the race; and to have once acted nobly seems a reason why we should always be noble', George Eliot writes. Tito suffered from another tradition: 'he had won no memories of self-conquest and perfect faithfulness from which he could have a sense of falling' (xxxix). He gambles with chance. It is when he is elated with a sense of his adroitness in his party-political 'game', and with the conviviality of the supper party in the Rucellai Gardens, that he sings snatches from a Maenad chorus and suddenly finds Baldassarre confronting him with fierce dark eyes. The scene recalls the Bacchic triumph of Cosimo di Piero's picture and his association of Tito with treachery and fear.

Unlike her brother, Romola does not become a Christian; like Janet Dempster she devotes her life to others, setting an example consistent with the creed of George Eliot, who declares herself when she attributes Dino's prevision to 'the shadowy region where human souls seek wisdom apart from the human sympathies which are the very life and substance of our wisdom' (xv). In Florence, although Romola recoils in disgust from 'wearisome visions and allegories', Savonarola's preaching makes her life of sadness also 'a life of active love' during a period of widespread hunger and sickness. If she is the 'visible' Madonna, it is because the image of the Madonna remains unseen in the Church procession; only among superstitious country people is she mistaken for the Madonna herself. Yet superstitions are rife in Florence: according to popular rumour, the heavens blaze forth the death of Lorenzo the Magnificent; people hope that Savonarola will show greater command over lightning than will his enemy the Pope; and they lose faith in him when he refuses trial by fire. No angels come to cheer Romola in her gloom; then, as now, George Eliot writes, there were human beings who never saw angels, and had no other choice than to grasp the 'stumbling guidance' of other people, 'or else to pause in loneliness and disbelief, which is no path, but the arrest of inaction and death' (xxxvi). This alternative to a humanitarian faith for those 'unvisited by angels' recalls the vision of 'The Lifted Veil'.

Some incidental authorial reflections are made indirectly. Although he considers Romola unusually gifted among women, Bardo assumes that she cannot rise entirely above the lower category to which Nature has assigned her, and that the 'vagrant propensity of the feminine mind' incapacitates her for the work he had expected from his son. His reiterated emphasis on this score constitutes an ironical comment by the author of 'Woman in France' on the subjection of women. Likewise the wish for 'a new order of things' from Bernardo, who would prefer to say 'I belong to no party: I am a Florentine', and a gloss on the triumph of the people as the 'triumph of the fat popolani over the lean, which again means triumph of the fattest popolano over those who are less fat' (recalling George Orwell's 'All animals are equal but some animals are more equal than others') refer obliquely to the Victorian political scene.

The second of these political comments is made by an observer of one of the great Florentine processions; he is one of a group, members of which congregate from time to time, generally in barber Nello's shop. Chorus-wise they comment on personal and political developments in the action, lightening the author's task of background exegesis, and providing humorous relief. As the garrulous Nello is learned (drawn partly from Burchiello, the 'great predecessor' to whom he refers), and his clients include young *eruditi*, the humour is often too recherché to be effective; it is lively more often when the mercurial barber is operating and holding forth. Though farcical, the practical joke which he plays on a quack doctor, with the aid of the conjuror and his monkey, has all the marks of historical probability. Monna Brigida, the widow who believes in enjoying life, and whose loquacity is beyond her cousin Bardo's endurance, is staged mainly for entertainment. She succeeds chiefly, however, in giving greater reality, by contrast, to the Piagnoni, the self-denying followers of Savonarola. Her vanities − rouge, false black braided hair, pearl embroidery, and colourful adornments − are anathema to them. 'Holy Madonna! it seems as if widows had nothing to do now but to buy their coffins', she exclaims when recalling the exhortations she had received at a Piagnoni wedding, so gloomy that it might just as well have been 'put off till the next Quaresima for a penance'. During the Carnival celebrations organized by this sect to end all vanities, she suffers at the hands of over-zealous and mischievous juvenile proselytes, who delight in exposing her grey hair and unrouged face. When, after rescuing her, Romola (with a final over-earnestness that expresses the author rather than herself) attempts to comfort her by saying that 'all lines of the human face have something either touching or grand, unless they seem to come from low passions', Brigida answers wryly, 'it doesn't matter about being old, if one's a Piagnone'. She is fifty-two, and her reconciliation to age has not begun.

Novelty makes the ascetic Carnival with its huge pyramid of vanities for burning the most interesting of the crowd and procession spectacles; and empathy with Romola imparts a dramatic heightening to the public executions of her uncle Bernardo and Savonarola. No scene knits the action together more vividly than that in the Duomo, where Baldassarre, watched by Romola after realizing his rejection by Tito, looks amazedly at an alien interior, crowded with people looking up in breathless silence towards a pulpit where a Dominican friar preaches with crucifix in hand. When Savonarola announces that the day of vengeance is imminent, his voice is like a thunderous echo of Baldassarre's own vindictive passion. In manner, subject, and context, the sermon conveys a sense of drama and destiny which makes Dinah Morris's seem almost quotidian. Of the confrontations in Romola's life which are dramatically represented, the most tense and arresting are two with Tito and the encounter with Savonarola when she accuses him of self-interest in his refusal to plead for her uncle's life. The first (xxxii) occurs when Tito tells her that her father's library is sold; she accuses him of treachery and, 'driven to utter the words as men are driven to use the lash of the horsewhip', asks if he wears armour because he has robbed somebody who is *not* dead. The dramatic irony here is reversed when Tito counters with a reply which echoes his words when suddenly confronted by Baldassarre outside the Duomo. The second (xlviii) arises when Tito, after devious complicity with party against party, has secured his position in Florence and outside, and can appear friendly on Bernardo's behalf. Romola is not deceived; her marriage is a lie, and she now knows how basely he has betrayed his foster-father. Her subsequent disillusionment with Savonarola makes her leave Florence in despair.

The complexity of *Romola* lies in the narrative rather than in character, and the suspense which it engenders is centred principally in Tito's affairs. His pertness is obvious at a common level; at a higher, his 'lithe sleekness' is soon detected by Bernardo. Character, Mr Farebrother observes (M.lxxii), is not cut in marble; 'it is something living and changing, and may become diseased as our bodies do'. Morally tainted when he reaches Florence, and destitute of 'that awe of the Divine Nemesis which was felt by religious pagans', Tito is a crafty, hedonistic careerist whose engaging manners deceive right and left. The protective armour he wears in fear of Baldassarre locks his heart from Romola, until she learns that his self-seeking will is ruthless. His success in political circles increases in ratio to his unscrupulousness. As a suave and ingenious instrument he is serviceable to those who wish to preserve 'tolerably clean' hands in a world where there is 'much dirty work to be done'. With 'a sharp mind in a velvet sheath', he is considered more astute than Ulysses, and valued more highly than his acquaintance Machiavelli. 'Capable of treading the breath from a smiling child for the sake of his own safety', he belongs to the same species as Edmund in *King Lear*.

Bereft of father and brother, Romola needs her inherited fortitude and spirit to contend with Tito's shallowness, amoral indifference, and domineering intentions. She is young, but has strength to endure neglect and to translate her natural ardour into 'works of womanly sympathy'. By upbringing she is immune to Savonarola's supernatural pretensions, but her moral integrity is quickened by the largeness and nobility of soul which she found in his unequivocal response to the demand for self-subjection to 'the general good'. Not until he refuses to intervene for Bernardo's life does she realize his worldly ambition. With loss of faith in one who had represented 'the highest heroism' for her, her vision of 'any great purpose' which can 'exalt the common deeds of a dusty life with divine ardours' is 'utterly eclipsed'. At length, with growing awareness that her disillusionment is egoistic, she recovers; nothing 'could do away with the fact that there had been a great inspiration in him which had waked a new life in her'. Yet, though she had set up a legend in a coastal region, the conclusion suggests no epic life or far-resonant action in Romola's future; she has much in common with Dorothea Brooke.

FELIX HOLT

A statement by George Eliot on the inception of *Middlemarch* p. 179) raises the question whether the novel she began on 29 March 1865 owed anything to the English story she set aside in 1860 to write *Silas Marner*, or was a new development, arising partly from her interest in the contemporary campaign for electoral reform. After making little progress with it, she turned, with recollections of the rioting at Nuneaton in mind (p. 53), to *The Annual Register* for 1832 and *The Times* of 1832–3 for information on the elections which followed the Reform Bill of 1832. To give *Felix Holt, the Radical* further background validity, she read Samuel Bamford's *Passages in the Life of a Radical* and Daniel Neal's *History of the Puritans* (which gave her the idea of Mr Lyon's proposed public debate.* She also attempted a 'dim and perilous way' in Blackstone and other books of law to gain the assurance she needed on difficult points in the disputed Transome settlement. By the end of the year the first volume was incomplete, and in January 1866 she began consulting Frederic Harrison on the more complicated legal questions. Ill-health and depression continued to dog her, but the second volume (ending with the election riot) was finished by early April, and the novel by the end of May. At times she had been on the verge of abandoning it.

The opening which John Blackwood admired (22.iv.66) was the scene of expectation at Transome Court. When he received the 'author's introduction' is not known, but clearly it was not written until the conspectus of the novel was in view, for, after stressing the case for political reform, it takes the reader along an imaginary route (all the features of which were to be seen near Griff and Nuneaton) thirty-five years before the novel was first issued, pointing out the socio-economic conditions and church divisions which are inseparable from the politics of the story, and focusing attention finally on the tragic burden of the Transomes. The dominant motif in the changing scene, from the remote shepherd whose parish is his solar system to the trade unionism of disturbed industrial areas, is the ignorance or confused notions of the general public on many matters, particularly the question of Reform. This indicates the basis of the author's attitude towards her political subject, and furnishes the key to its fictional presentation, for,

---

* F. C. Thomson, 'The Genesis of *Felix Holt*', PMLA (1959), pp. 581–2.

though 'this history is chiefly concerned with the private lot of a few men and women', 'there is no private life which has not been determined by a wider public life' (iii).

Though carefully articulated, the plot of *Felix Holt* appears to be a curious amalgam, the centre of interest moving from character to character, not one being dominant. There are four related subjects: the tragic foreboding of Mrs Transome and its resolution, the fate of hero and heroine, electioneering and the election, and a network of proof which emerges piecemeal to establish rightful succession to the Transome estate. The clearest development in the novel as a whole is the critical antithesis between what may be termed the Transome world and the Felix Holt world, since they represent the class holding political power and the class demanding it; the contrast is sharply defined in two forms of Radicalism, and more dramatically and artistically through Esther Lyon's crucial rejection of Transome *mores* and affluence for the humanitarian idealism and relative poverty of life with Felix.

The unravelling of the sub-plot connected with the Transome succession serves two purposes. It creates curiosity and suspense, the disclosure of chicanery raising climactic expectations, of which some are eliminated by the ultimate nemesis of events. More than any other factor (the electioneering link being slight) it creates the inter-relatedness of the whole; without it the main climax could never have developed. In this, Esther Lyon, faced with uncompromising choice for her future, is more centrally placed than any other character throughout the book. Yet even here, as at the opening, dramatic interest centres in Mrs Transome. In the intervening chapters, where the hero is off and on the principal character, she is absent; she and Felix never meet. Increasingly she engages our tragic sympathy, but morally our sympathy is drawn to Felix and Esther. When Henry James dismisses Mrs Transome as 'unnatural, or rather, we should say, a superfluous figure', he registers the hasty uncritical impression of a confident young man; inherently it conveys his disapproval of an 'inartistic plot'. Stressing its vulgarity and lack of taste, he alludes, it seems, to George Eliot's one experiment in the fashionable adoption of a disputed inheritance as the mainspring for mystification. More valid is his comment on the inadequacy of the 'termination', for the most 'vulgar' features of the sub-plot are perfectly in keeping with the crude electioneering practices of the period.

Precisely when the study of Greek drama began to affect the shape of *Felix Holt* is unknown. Soon after she began the novel, George Eliot read Aeschylus and a book on the Greek theatre; five weeks later she made a second study of Aristotle's *Poetics* with renewed admiration. There is an obvious reference to the latter in 'the pity and terror' with which her introduction concludes; and a chapter epigraph (xlviii), recalling the 'hereditary, entailed Nemesis' of her notes on tragedy and *The Spanish Gypsy*, is taken from the *Agamemnon* of Aeschylus, which she read for the second time at the beginning of August 1865. By starting the Transome story near its end, where the tragic action begins, she followed Greek practice, and compressed the whole plot within a period of seven months (1 September 1832 to March, ignoring the happy ending of April–May which falls outside the Transome tragedy). Antecedent history is provided in flashbacks, the most notable, though not the most important, being the early life of Mr Lyon (vi). They function in the manner observed by Aristotle: 'Incidents extraneous to the action are frequently combined with a portion of the action proper, to form the Complication; the rest is the Unravelling. By the Complication I mean all that extends from the beginning of the action to the part which marks the turning-point to good or bad fortune' (*Poetics*, xviii; tr. S. H. Butcher). Two results follow: the necessity to speed the Felix Holt story after some preparatory chapters which are rather flaccid, and the impossibility of developing his character very markedly.

George Eliot, it seems, attached more importance to his role than to his development. He is an eccentric youth whose appearance (shaggy-haired, large-eyed, strong-limbed, without waistcoat or cravat) proclaims a pride or inverted snobbery which makes him obdurate against rising above cloth-cap status or living in a house 'with a high door-step and a brass knocker'. His contempt for cant and social veneer, and his experience as a Glaswegian student, recall Carlyle at times. After discovering the inefficacy and harmfulness of his father's medicaments, he annoys his widowed mother by refusing to continue a quack business, and becomes a watch-repairer, giving up his spare time to teach local boys in his home and uneducated non-electors in ale-houses. He had been converted, we are asked to believe, after six weeks' debauchery. Truth makes him speak out like a prophet, however bluntly and offensively. Though Esther Lyon's father takes him to task for rudeness and knows Felix has little time for preachers, he sympathizes with his radicalism. The sermon which he prepares (iv) casts light on the crux of the novel *vis-à-vis* electoral reform: 'Do you think there will ever be a great shout for the right — the shout of a nation as of one man . . . — if every Christian of you peeps round to see what his neighbours in good coats are doing, or else puts his hat before his face that he may shout and never be heard? But this is what you do . . .'. And this is what Felix Holt refuses to do.

The common assertion that his radicalism is moral and not political is untrue. Politics and public morality are indivisible, and the effect of the one on the other, for better or worse, has never been more manifest than it is today. Holt is endowed with George Eliot's prescience; he is too radical for political place-seekers and for the majority who are subject to propaganda. He wants 'the working men to have power', but insists that power for good depends on enlightenment; 'ignorant power comes in the end to the same thing as wicked power'. Three-quarters of the men in the country 'see nothing in an election but self-interest', and to assume that electoral reform will solve our ills is another example of the worship of 'machinery', the mistaking of means for ends which Arnold in *Culture and Anarchy* (1869) identified as the Englishman's 'besetting danger'. 'All the schemes about voting . . . and the rest, are engines', Holt argues; the water or steam to work them comes from public opinion, 'and while public opinion is what it is — while men have no better beliefs about public duty — while corruption is not felt to be a damning disgrace — while men are not ashamed in parliament and out of it to make public questions which concern the welfare of millions a mere screen for their own private ends, — . . . no fresh scheme of voting will much mend our condition' (xxx). George Eliot believed that a working, everyday religion of humanity was needed to subdue class and individual selfishness, and to promote general enlightenment, justice, and welfare. Everything depends on the prevalence of 'good feeling'. In short, until some deeper, more radical revolution takes place in the hearts and minds of the great majority, politicians will remain corrupt, and progress slow and uncertain. George Eliot may seem temperate or conservative, but she is radical at heart; she wants to see a more stable and assured progress, with sustained justice for all. The importance Felix Holt attaches to the education of the next generation (xi) has a genuine political significance.

Felix is a political idealist, a root-and-branch zealot to whom the spirit of innovation is a religion. Harold Transome, on the other hand, is averse to all forms of enthusiasm; he is a gentlemanly but snobbish opportunist who takes up Radicalism, not as a cause but as a career. A political place-seeker, with very little feeling for the working man ('O, I remember Jabez — he was a dolt. I'll have old Hickes. He was a neat little machine of a butler'), his 'very good nature' is 'unsympathetic'. He is a frank, clever egoist who wishes to live well, enjoying his estate and independence, though prepared for his own advantage to support 'all measures which the common sense of the country, and the increasing self-assertion of the majority, peremptorily' demand. His aim is to be 'a thorough Englishman', a supporter of the Constitution, and 'a Radical only in rooting out abuses', in substituting 'fresh oak' for the rot in Tory oaks. He may agree with Holt that the bribery of non-voters to use intimidation and force at the polls is repulsive, but he spends thousands to win the election, and cannot afford to be squeamish about electioneering practice; only after he has lost the election is his conscience activated on this score. There is much in his ambition and style of life which Felix would dismiss as 'rottenness'.

Ultimately Esher Lyon has to choose between them. When it is clear that she is the rightful heir to Transome Court, Harold and his mother behave graciously, Harold not without calculation that he can win Esther and retain the estate. Although attracted by him, she proves to be discerning; she finds dullness in a life of ease, and nothing above 'moral mediocrity' in the prospects of Harold's love. Like his kindness to his mother, his good nature never shows 'any thorough understanding or deep respect' for what is in the mind of people he obliges or indulges. She sees 'the same quality in his political views: the utmost enjoyment of his own advantages was the solvent that blended pride in his family and position' with any radicalism he was prepared to support. The comparison she makes between him and Felix is imaged in birch-stems. When Felix walks with her by the river, and they are falling in love (xxvii), the beauty of birches in the sunshine, by contrast with the old felled oak (not worth carrying away) on which they sit, suggests growth, purpose, the vision of the 'beyond' to which Felix unselfishly dedicates his life. After suddenly declaring that she is beautiful, he makes a tactless generalization which he finally elucidates when he announces his confidence that she will have the magnanimity which 'makes a great task easier to men instead of turning them away from it'. He cites Saint Theresa and Elizabeth Fry, and one thinks of Dorothea Brooke's choice of the wrong man and Lydgate's choice of the wrong woman. As if foreseeing her dilemma at Transome Court, he says, 'I want you to have such a vision of the future that you may never lose your best self. Some charm or other may be flung about you — some of your atta-of-rose fascinations — and nothing but a good strong terrible vision will save you.' It saves her from Harold Transome. On the fateful illumination that comes to her, George Eliot writes, 'It is terrible — the keen bright eye of a woman when it has once been turned with admiration on what is severely true; but then, the severely true rarely comes within its range of vision' (xliii). Harold has begun to wonder whether the view can be improved by thinning the distant trees to reveal the oaks beyond, and Esther, who has grown to like a 'beyond' everywhere, expresses surprise that a man so habitually sure of himself can have any uncertainty. Still hoping to win her, he asks what she supposes he would do if he were unable to have what he wanted, and she answers carelessly, 'as if she were considering the distant birch-stems', that he would bear it quite easily as he had done his election failure. His admission that he never longed for anything out of his reach recalls Andrea del Sarto's 'Ah, but a man's reach should exceed his grasp,/Or what's a heaven for?' in Browning's *Men and Women* (1855).

Harold has hopes of a peerage, but Holt abhors the scramble for wealth and position. He wants to be a new sort of demagogue, for he believes (as George Eliot showed she did in *Adam Bede*) that the lot of the handicraftsman is good, and that such a worker 'may be better trained to all the best functions of his nature than if he belonged to the grimacing set who have visiting-cards'. He is indifferent to refinements such as wax instead of tallow candles, and despises Esther's 'fine-ladyism', her romantic escape in Byron's poems or in *René*, and the discontentedness which arises in her, not because the world is full of people who are 'ground by wrong and misery, and tainted with pollution' but egoistically, simply because she cannot get the *small* things that suit her pleasure. Harold Transome, with his distinguished appearance and polished manners, suggests 'that brighter and more luxurious life on which her imagination dwelt', yet 'the first religious experience of her life — the first self-questioning, the first voluntary subjection, the first longing to acquire the strength of greater motives and obey the more strenuous rule — had come to her through Felix Holt'. She had never known nobility of character before she knew him, a man who renounced 'all small selfish motives for the sake of a great and unselfish one'. The revelation of her step-father's example in choosing to live in poverty 'like a working man' for the sake of her mother had made her realize that 'the best life' is gained when all is borne and done 'because of some great and strong feeling'. When she comes to 'the first and last parting of the ways' and chooses Felix, she gives unity to a life without 'atta-of-rose fascinations', making her memory 'a temple where all relics and all votive offerings, all worship and all grateful joy, are an unbroken history sanctified by one religion'. She is true to her best self.

Mr Lyon's apparent inability at times to distinguish Esther's inheritance from 'a story in ancient history' is not an accident, for her parents are dead, and she is the author's 'light-footed, sweet-voiced Queen Esther' of the dingy house in Malthouse Yard. Harold looks forward from the start to the improvement of the Transome estate during his 'reign', and when the inheritance falls to Esther, and he hopes to share it with her, tells her that she is the empress of her own fortunes, and more besides; she hardly knows what to do with her empire, she answers, as she leans back on the cushions. Allusion to the Old Testament parallel seems to be maintained when Mrs Holt arrives suddenly to invoke Harold's intervention for her son's pardon; she insists that, 'whatever Miss Lyon may be now, in the way of being lifted up among great people, she's our minister's daughter', and tells Harold that if he had been king himself she would have 'made free' to tell him her opinion. The meeting occurs when life at Transome Court has made Esther feel that 'the higher ambition which had begun to spring in her was for ever nullified'. Her final decision to abdicate occurs when, after discovering with horror the tragedy of Mrs Transome's reign, she does all in her power to end its 'dreary waste of years empty of sweet trust and affection'. George Eliot's radicalism did not allow Esther to remain a queen.

The main theme of the novel, reaching its climax with Esther's 'revolutionary' decision at the end, makes the author's radicalism most evident. It may be seen in the first flashback, on the education of Miss Lingon, the girl whose unhappy lot was to become the 'imperious' but lonely, guilt-ridden Mrs Transome. Clever, accomplished, and 'rather ambitious of intellectual superiority', she had secretly read 'the lighter parts of dangerous French authors', laughed at *Lyrical Ballads* and biblical characters, but 'believed all the while that truth and safety lay in due attendance on prayers and sermons, in the admirable doctrines and ritual of the Church of England, equally remote from Puritanism and Popery; in fact, in such a view of this world and the next as would preserve the existing arrangements of English society quite unshaken, keeping down the obtrusiveness of the vulgar and the discontent of the poor'. Institutionalized Christianity spelt civilization; 'and the providential government of the world, though a little confused and entangled in foreign countries, in our favoured land was clearly seen to be carried forward on Tory and Church of England principles, sustained by the succession of the House of Brunswick, and by sound English divines'. When the Benedictines ceased to control the church at Treby Magna, the Debarrys, as lords of the manor, 'naturally came next to Providence and took the place of the saints'. Their appearance generally ensures some good satirical entertainment at the expense of their class. Sir Maximus speaks for them when he says, 'All we have to ask is, whether a man's a Tory, and will make a stand for the good of the country', and the implication is that only the Tory will make a stand for his country's good. He is one of those aristocrats whom it 'pleased Providence to call' to vast estates (vii), and whose religion promises the poor their reward in heaven (xxx). Elsewhere, in one of those egotistical intrusions which are all the more noticeable from their comparative rarity (the pressure of plot complexity, like the pressure of material in *Romola*, admitting little room for them), George Eliot cannot resist observing, 'No system, religious or political, I believe, has laid it down as a principle that all men are alike virtuous, or even that all the people rated for £80 houses are an honour to their species.'

Sir Maximus Debarry, under pressure from his son Philip (a successful election candidate, now detained in London, who has never forgotten his obligation to Mr Lyon), attends the trial of Felix. Before the proceedings, he observes Esther with curiosity 'owing to the report of her inheritance, and her probable marriage to his once welcome but now exasperating neighbour, Harold Transome'. 'A fine girl! something thoroughbred in the look of her. Too good for a Radical', he remarks. He had been severely critical of the prisoner, but her speech in his defence moves him to tears, and reverses his opinion. 'She's a modest, brave, beautiful woman. I'd ride a steeplechase, old as I am, to gratify her feelings. Hang it! the fellow's a good fellow if she thinks so.' Like two representatives of the Church, his brother Augustus and jolly, cock-fighting John Lingon (who is easily persuaded to support his nephew Harold's candidature), he is one of the minor characters who give life and variety to many scenes. They include the publican Chubb, Sproxton miners, farmers such as Mr Goffe who do not know how to vote, Sir Maximus's steward Mr Scales, Philip's factotum Christian, Rufus Lyon's servant Lyddy, Mrs Transome's devoted maid Mrs Denner, the children Job and Harry, and, above all, Mrs Holt. Her strong-mindedness, volubility, and recurring tactlessness suggest hereditary characteristics in her son, though his father had been a preacher (who did better than preach to the blacks, Mrs Holt tells Mr Lyon, 'for he married me'). There is humour in her irrelevance, and a peculiar logic:

'. . . Felix never meant to harm anybody but himself and his mother, which he certainly did in respect of his clothes, and taking to be a low working man, and stopping my living respectable, more particular by the pills, which had a sale, as you may be sure they suited people's insides. And what folks can never have boxes enough of to swallow, I should think you have a right to sell. And there's many and many a text for it, as I've opened on without ever thinking; for if it's true, "Ask, and you shall have", I should think it's truer when you're willing to pay for what you have.'

George Eliot's social range exceeds Jane Austen's, and it is reflected as much in the principal characters, the more idealistic Felix, Rufus Lyon, and Esther on the one hand, and Mrs Transome, Jermyn, and Harold on the other. Mr Lyon's learned tediousness is sweetened with gentleness and wisdom. The portrait of Felix is clear, and he is prominent in such scenes as the election riot and his trial, but Esher by her charm, intelligence, and adaptability, and by the conflict of choice which she experiences at Transome Court, creates a deeper and more attractive impression. Harold is precisely defined from first to last and, like Jermyn, indelibly sketched in certain scenes. Yet it is the tragic figure of Mrs Transome who makes the most memorable impact.

Mrs Transome's unfortunate marriage and the birth of a half-witted son had led to her affair with Jermyn, and her knowledge of his legal malpractice to preserve the Durfey–Transome succession had strengthened his hold on her, with consequent maladministration and neglect of the estate for his own greedy ends. With the death of her elder son, hope of its improvement and of a reciprocal affection revives in Mrs Transome as she awaits the arrival of the new heir, her wealthy son Harold, from the Levant. Proud and imperious though she is, and however sorry one may be for her nervous imbecile husband, her presentation continually excites pity and awe. The failure of one who has 'no ultimate analysis of things . . . beyond blood and family' (the Herons of Fenshore or the Badgers of Hillbury) to understand a son who announces that he is a Radical is a slight ordeal compared with the tragic burden of her fears. Physical hints quickly suggest the Jermyn–Harold relationship, as does an unsavoury glimpse of Jermyn when the sight of his daughter (whom he does not recognise) recalls a distant passion which led him and 'another bright-eyed person' to think they could 'determine for themselves how their lives should be made delightful in spite of unalterable external conditions' (xxi). Harold's determination, despite his mother's protest, to settle old scores with Jermyn leads to two painful scenes, the first when Jermyn tries to force Mrs Transome to save him by telling Harold his paternity ('To such uses may tender relations come when they have ceased to be tender! . . . There is heroism even in the circles of hell for fellow-sinners who cling to each other in the fiery whirlwind and never recriminate'). The second occurs when Jermyn, left to fend for himself, enters the White Hart and asks to speak to Harold privately. Galled by the veiled threat in 'You will repent else − for your mother's sake', Harold strikes the lawyer across the face with his whip and, as Jermyn clutches him hard by the clothes immediately under this throat, tells him to let go or he'll be the death of him. 'Do', says Jermyn in a grating voice; 'I am your father.' Both are white; Harold turns his eyes from Jermyn's face, and sees the same face in the adjacent mirror with his own beside it, and 'the hated fatherhood reasserted'. He can show no pity towards his mother, and it is left to Esther to comfort her in a scene (xlix–l) which so impressed Thomas Hardy by its tragic power that he adapted it in *Desperate Remedies*. Mrs Transome's bitterness against her son is expressed in egoistical self-pity. She is not penitent; 'always the edge of calamity had fallen on her . . . God had no pity'; for her 'the great story of this world' has been reduced to 'the narrow track of her own lot, wide only for a woman's anguish' (xxxiv), but it makes her grief more natural and poignant.

Nowhere is the mirror image used with more startling dramatic effect in *Felix Holt* than in the White Hart scene. Two mirror reflections of Mrs Transome in her 'joyless', embittered age' convince her that she is a hag, and contrast with the 'youthful brilliancy' of her smiling full-length portrait in the evening costume of 1800 (with a garden for background), which is twice seen in her drawing-room. Other images function poetically with more pervasive effect in the Transome drama, imparting a tonal design which makes many scenes in the novel prosaically grey or bare in comparison.

An unusually evocative image makes its first appearance at the end of the introduction, with reference to an enchanted forest in the underworld, where (as in Dante's *Inferno*, xiii) the souls of the damned suffer torments in stunted trees or bushes, fractures of which result in bleeding and 'dolorous speech'. George Eliot's image concentrates on the 'unuttered cries' of the branches, the 'pain that is quite noiseless'; and it is felt almost at once in the grand trees, near and far, around Transome Court, all motionless and 'seeming to add to the stillness'. In general features, detail, and tenor, this tragic setting is comparable to the opening scene of Keats's *Hyperion*. We are reminded of it when Jermyn walks with Mrs Transome under the tall trees, 'treading noiselessly on fallen leaves'. 'For years there had been a deep silence about the past between them: on her side, because she remembered; on his, because he more and more forgot.' Aware of the dangers confronting both of them from Harold's penetration and 'assertion of mastery', she is inclined to blame him for what has happened; immediately the thought that she had brought it on herself checks her, and she tremulously asks leave to take his arm. She wishes him to vow that he will never quarrel with his son. He refuses to be bound, and when they part she stands shivering alone on the gravel where they met; where all had been brightness and warmth in the trees, there were 'white ashes', and 'the sunshine looked dreary as it fell on them' (ix). Here as elsewhere subordinate images such as the fallen leaves and the gravel have metaphorical significance. The sunshine generally lacks warmth; it is autumnal or wintry. Mrs Transome's hopes are woven of sunbeams and annihilated by a shadow soon after Harold's return from the Levant. When he learns the truth from his father and rides home through the park, the March sun throws a long shadow of himself and his groom across the grass; the gleaming of the sun through the trees seems almost 'as odious as an artificial smile', and he wishes he had never come back to 'this pale English sunshine'.

Harold believes in warmth and comfort, and has spent much on refurnishing the home where his mother had lived among 'desecrated sanctities' and honours that, like the gilding in her room, 'looked tarnished in the light of monotonous and weary suns'. He can give her satin cushions, but she can never enjoy them while she lives in fear; and when her fears are realized she buries her head in their deafening down and hears no sound of comfort. What future is there for her? She looks out into the dim night; and 'the black boundary of trees and the long line of the river' seem 'only part of the loneliness and monotony of her life'. At this very time, Esther, realizing that life at Transome Court is 'a silken bondage' which arrests all motive and is 'nothing better than a well-cushioned despair', draws up her blinds and, seeing 'veiled glimmerings of moonlight, and the lines of the for-ever flowing river', desires 'the largeness of the world to help her thought'. It is with this larger world that she feels her destiny rest in marrying Felix. So, as we learn when they take their first walk by the river, 'our lives glide on; the river ends we don't know where' (xxvii).

Such imagery contributes cohesiveness to the Transome scenes, and endows them with an imaginative power and a maturity of style which recur in George Eliot's later novels, but never more consistently than here. It is doubtful whether any other English novel is more subtly charged with the Greek spirit of tragedy than *Felix Holt*.

*   *   *

The 'Address to Working Men, by Felix Holt' was suggested by John Blackwood (7.xi.67) after hearing Disraeli speak on the new Reform Bill to workers in Edinburgh. It was completed on 4 December, and appeared in the January number of *Blackwood's Magazine*. *Felix Holt* shows that George Eliot had already considered her subject carefully. Her sympathies were with the victims of injustice, but she was sufficiently intelligent and conversant with human nature and history, to realize that enlightened progress was far from assured, even though the working-class had been enfranchised. A large proportion had received no education, and very few of them had advanced beyond basic literacy or a readiness to consider any needs but their own. Such were their deprivation and ignorance that they were a ready prey to political exploitation. George Eliot's problem was not merely to organize her argument fairly, but to convey it in simple language; she does so, but the implications have a wide-reaching comprehensiveness and profundity more appropriate to statesmen and philosophers than to the majority or to self-seeking politicans.

It begins with the assumption that the workers have no more virtue or wisdom than any other section of the community, and that a nation with a wise and virtuous majority would already have 'better members of Parliament, better religious teachers, honester tradesmen, fewer foolish demagogues', a higher standard of right and wrong, less belief in falsehood, and a less degrading notion of pleasure 'or of what justly raises a man above his fellows'.

Indignation against injustices is excellent if it is wisely directed. The franchise has given the working-class a heavy responsibility; to ensure the furtherance of sensible reforms, they need knowledge, ability, and honesty. Many of the inherited evils are the consequence of folly, neglect, or self-seeking. We must beware lest impatience for immediate ends make things worse for future generations. If a man cares only for himself, and is prepared to let others suffer, 'he is defending the very worst doings that have brought about his discontent'. Society is held together by the dependence of men on each other, and the working-class can least of all afford to ignore this; to prosper, a society must consist of people who consider the general good as well as their own.

Society is not composed of a single class; it is like a body with parts that are interdependent. So long as men are selfish, one class will try to gain advantage at the expense of others. This is one danger. Another is the desire to make sweeping changes, destroying what is operative before something better can be created. The only acceptable change for all parties is one that promotes the common good. This will not be secured by extending the franchise, but only by using it with knowledge, foresight, and integrity.

Observing that there can be no assured progress or sanity without law, George Eliot stresses the danger of giving power to dishonest or ignorant men. Great reforms need to be made, but by consent and not by coercion, lest we injure our inheritance, and deny our children its benefits. If we demand more leisure, let us use it 'for the rational exercise of the faculties which make us men'. Education for all is a prerequisite; political change in itself cannot alter ignorance, 'or hinder it from producing vice and misery'. 'There is a low sense of parental duties in the nation at large', with insufficient concern for children's welfare; and this is especially true of the poor. Without their enlightenment, we breed 'a moral pestilence'. Wrong everywhere must be resisted, in low places as well as high. Wisdom does not belong to one class, nor can we blame others for our evils. There are evils in human nature which no change in institutions can remove; and the difference between manliness and childishness, between good sense and folly, lies in discerning the evils that can be removed and those that must be borne.

More than a century has passed since this general statement was written, and England has yet to learn its wisdom. Paradoxically, it is far more thorough and radical by implication than all that has subsequently been achieved in a country that mistakes political maleducation, chicanery, expediency, and divisiveness for freedom. Every word of Felix Holt's address is as true today as ever. It is little read; by some it is regarded as fiction or the utterings of an eccentric; to others it is little more than a string of platitudes. Newfangled sophistries, ready-made views, and the fomenting of partisan abuse and hatred will always obscure and devalue perennial truth.

'THE SPANISH GYPSY' AND OTHER POEMS

Perhaps Robert Browning encouraged George Eliot to think of writing verse when, on 2 August 1863, after reading the greater part of *Romola*, he wrote enthusiastically to express gratitude for 'the noblest and most heroic prose-poem' he had ever read; although the later chapters disappointed him, his views on 'the great style and high tone' remained unimpaired. The idea of *The Spanish Gypsy* came in Venice the following year, Titian's *Annunciation* suggesting a theme reminiscent of Greek drama, 'a subject grander than that of Iphigenia' which had never been used: that of a maiden, full of young hope on the brink of marriage, being suddenly called to fulfil a great destiny which would entail 'a terribly different experience from that of ordinary womanhood'. The problem was not just to invent a story but to clothe it 'in some suitable set of historical and local conditions'. Nothing finally seemed more appropriate than the period of Spanish history when the struggle with the Moors was reaching its climax, and 'the gypsy race' was involved in a way which would create a 'hereditary claim' on the heroine; the opposition of race was necessary to make the renunciation of marriage imperative.

Fascinated by her subject, George Eliot began to study Spanish history and grammar. By 6 September 1864 she had written her prologue and begun the first act; it was her first serious attempt at blank verse. During November, after she had completed the second act, the structuring of the sequel posed continual problems. Eventually, as she informed Frederic Harrison (15.viii.66), she had to put it aside 'after writing four acts, precisely because it was in that stage of Creation or "Werden", in which the idea of the characters predominates over the incarnation'. The problem had been to give dramatic life to her theme. After writing *Felix Holt*, she was eager to recast her play. Her Spanish studies were continued, and she began the work a second time in March 1867 after visiting Spain. It was now designed as a poem in many scenes, the majority dramatic in form. Progress was slow but, benefiting from a summer holiday in northern Germany, she finished the first book at the end of October and the whole work on 29 April 1868. The end was shorter and less tragic than she had 'threatened', Lewes having persuaded her to return to her original conception; Oscar Browning concluded that she had intended a catastrophe turning on the death of the hero Don Silva. *The Spanish Gypsy* sold well, especially in America; and it is interesting to find that John Addington Symonds could find no woman in modern fiction like Sophocles' Antigone 'except perhaps the Fedalma of George Eliot'. Lewes thought that 'no one thoroughly acquainted with the stage *and* the poem would fail to see that it was eminently suited for an opera' and 'as eminently unsuited for an *acting* play'.

With songs and romantic phases, *The Spanish Gypsy* is at least as opera-like as dramatic; and failure to resolve the plot satisfactorily after its first crisis seems to be responsible for its final form, a succession of dramatic scenes, combined with narrative and descriptive verse. The story is unconvincing at certain crucial points, though the poetic medium and a high heroic plane of sentiment and action tend to tranquillize scepticism. Fedalma, daughter of Zarca, chieftain of the Zincali gipsy tribe, had been captured by the Spaniards in her childhood, but does not know her origin and is about to marry Don Silva, Duke of Bedmár, a fortress town near the Moorish border. His uncle Isidor, a rabid representative of the Inquisition, is highly suspicious and, with the war against the Moors suspended, accuses his nephew of disloyalty. More fiercely than *Romola*, the story presents the fifteenth-century clash of Hellenism and Christian fanaticism:

The maimed form
Of calmly-joyous beauty, marble-limbed,
Yet breathing with the thought that shaped its lips,
Looks mild reproach from out its opened grave
At creeds of terror; and the vine-wreathed god
Fronts the pierced Image with the crown of thorns.

Don Silva plans to wed Fedalma secretly the next day, but the prisoner Zarca, who had recognized his daughter when she was dancing in the plaza, confronts her in the castle, where he and other gipsies have planned their escape; finally, he convinces her that she is bound, as his successor, to join them. She accepts her doom. Rather than lose her, Don Silva abandons his duty, follows her to Moorish territory, and pledges allegiance to Zarca and his Zincali band. On condition that they will settle his gipsies in northern Africa, Zarca and his warriors help the Moors to capture Bedmár by night, the Duke ignorantly assisting in the darkness. Furious on discovering his dishonour, he protests at the execution of Isidor and stabs Zarca; before dying, the gipsy chieftain charges that Silva shall remain free, accursed with two opposing crimes, against his own people and against the Zincali. Fedalma sorrowfully departs with her tribe for Africa, and her doubly-fated lover is left intending to redeem his name in knightly deeds for Rome. Fedalma speaks for both:

Our dear young love — its breath was happiness!
But it had grown upon a larger life
Which tore its roots asunder. We rebelled —
The larger life subdued us. Yet we are wed;
For we shall carry each the pressure deep
Of the other's soul.

In *Felix Holt* love and the larger life for Esther Lyon are found to coincide; here circumstances have forced them into ineluctable opposition.

George Eliot's notes on *The Spanish Gypsy* (Appendix 2, p. 254) stress the 'irreparable collision between the individual and the general' in tragedy (cf. p. 70, on her review of Sophocles' *Antigone*). For Mrs Transome the 'general' is moral tradition; for Maggie Tulliver it is a conjunction of moral tradition, hereditary nature, and loyalties; with Fedalma and Don Silva it turns on hereditary obligations. 'Silva presents the tragedy of entire rebellion: Fedalma of a grand submission, which is rendered vain by the effects of Silva's rebellion', George Eliot writes. Although she finds tragedy in Zarca's 'struggle for a great end, rendered vain by the surrounding conditions of life', it makes little dramatic impact on the reader; he is an inspiring and intractable power which Fedalma finds irresistible in his presence, but which she can hardly sustain when he is dead. Yet, in conjunction with symbolism, the struggle between the individual and the general creates the most dramatic tragic scene in the whole work. Fedalma, whose gipsy instinct makes her yearn for the open air and join in the dancing, is stirred by 'old imperious memories' when, ignorant of her origin, she is fascinated by her father's necklace. Late on the eve of her expected marriage, a bird falls dead at her feet; it carries the message that her father comes. When he reveals himself, it is clear that the gold necklace symbolizes the fate which binds her to Zarca and to her past and future. He snatches the circlet of rubies from her brow, and asks her, as he grasps her hand and shoulder, if she chooses to be forgetful. She believes she can show her loyalty to him by securing his freedom after her marriage; she has divided loyalties and memories:

> Look at these hands! You say when they were little
> They played about the gold upon your neck.
> I do believe it, for their tiny pulse
> Made record of it in the inmost coil
> Of growing memory. But see them now!
> Oh, they have made fresh record; twined themselves
> With other throbbing hands whose pulses feed
> Not memories only but a blended life —
> Life that will bleed to death if it be severed.

Zarca insists that she has a higher compulsion; hers is no ordinary lot. As his successor, queen of the gipsies, she is expected to perform royally. She consents unwillingly, 'an unslain sacrifice', removes her bridal gems, and accepts her fate, to wed her people. Her 'young joy' dies like the bird which announced Zarca's coming.

Don Silva's conflict is not externalized. It occurs in the black solitude of night after he has joined the Zincali unconditionally. In this inner drama thought is weaker and less trustworthy than feeling; he defends his action reflectively but 'the universe/Looks down inhospitable' and 'the human heart/Finds nowhere shelter but in human kind'. There are no specifically Positivist overtones here or elsewhere in the work, although Dr Congreve ascribed 'a mass of Positivism' to it (cf. 16.xii.68), and Edmund Gosse more than half a century later described it as 'a Comtist tragedy'. Silva's 'larger soul' cannot scorn those memories from ancestral homes, that 'hereditary right' which troubles his conscience as if it were 'the voice divine of human loyalty'. The great trust he has broken turns reproach on him from those human and divine faces which had witnessed his knightly pledges as a champion of the Cross. Such is the revenge 'wrought by the long travail of mankind/On him who scorns it, and would shape his life/Without obedience'. Significantly, at the end, when Silva is intent on redeeming his honour with his 'knightly sword', the blackness he sees with Fedalma's departure is 'overhung by stars'. Taking her cue perhaps from Matthew Arnold's preface to the 1853 edition of his poems, George Eliot expressed the view that 'art which leaves the soul in despair is laming to the soul', and attributed the fostering of nobler sentiments in her tragedy to individual deeds and 'the all-sufficiency of the soul's passions in determining sympathetic action'. The critical weakness of *The Spanish Gypsy* is that, although the tragic conflict is clear in Fedalma and Silva, it rarely succeeds in lifting the passions to tragic heights.

The introduction is leisurely; like the proem of *Romola* it begins with a descriptive approach which is cinematic in technique, taking the reader by stages from an aerial view of Spain 'leaning with equal love/On the Mid Sea that moans with memories,/And on the untravelled Ocean's restless tides' (before Columbus's voyage to America) to Bedmár and a tavern courtyard. Here a group of characters provides a chorus, commenting on events which introduce the main action. The individualization of this group in description and action is justified by the sequel, for all play minor stage roles, none more importantly than the minstrel Juan and the juggler Roldan, with the lame boy Pablo (another singer). The first dramatic note is sounded by the booming bell which calls to prayer and ends the dancing in the plaza, where Fedalma's joy is quelled by the rebuking gaze of the prisoner gipsy chief. With the confrontation between the prior Isidor and Silva, and events leading to Zarca's winning of Fedalma, the remainder of the first book (which comprises almost half the work) reaches a level of dramatic tension which is rarely equalled and never long sustained in the sequel. The most imaginative of the incidents and episodes which follow occurs in the third book, and acquires its power when a brief climactic action is almost suspended with tableau effect to give symbolic concentration to the tragic dilemma at the heart of the work. Silva has found Fedalma; they embrace; she starts back with a look of terror, still holding him by the hand, and says:

> Silva, if now between us came a sword,
> Severed my arm, and left our two hands clasped,
> This poor maimed arm would feel the clasp till death.
> What parts us is a sword . . .

Her speech is cut short: Zarca, after approaching from the background, has drawn his sword and thrust the naked blade between them.

George Eliot recognised the supremacy of the feelings in making great moral decisions but, unlike Emily Brontë, lacked the imaginative power to express feelings with sustained dramatic life and intensity. She shows that she can engineer dramatic situations, and indeed achieve some lively vigour in dramatic scenes; but thought and noble sentiments tend to predominate over feeling. Even so, it would be a mistake to regard the verse as a failure. The songs, however, are not inherently lyrical, and seem to have been composed to imaginary music; Juan's 'Day is dying! Float, O song' (which conveys an admirable picture) and his song to Pepita are two of the more successful. With the exception of two short lighter scenes in prose, the remainder of the work is in blank verse, which everywhere bears the mark of careful composition, even in such detail as the astrologer Sephardo's mouth:

> shut firm, with curves
> So subtly turned to meanings exquisite,
> You seem to read them as you read a word
> Full-vowelled, long-descended, pregnant — rich
> With legacies from long, laborious lives.

The monkey Annibal, left with Pablo in Sephardo's care, while his master, the juggler Roldan, seeks Fedalma for Silva,

keeps a neutral air
As aiming at a metaphysic state
'Twixt 'is' and 'is not'; lets his chain be loosed
By sage Sephardo's hands, sits still at first,
Then trembles out of his neutrality,
Looks up and leaps into Sephardo's lap,
And chatters forth his agitated soul,
Turning to peep at Pablo on the floor.

The style suits the action in movement, as in the description of Roldan's juggling or of Silva's hurried search for Fedalma, after hearing that she has been seen dancing in the plaza. As she dances, the admiring tension of the spectators finds relief which is exquisitely expressed in 'Sighs of delight, applausive murmurs low,/And stirrings gentle as of earéd corn/Or seed-bent grasses, when the ocean's breath/Spreads landward'. Pictorial effects are equally fine. The verse is often dramatic and clear-cut; elsewhere (deliberately with the minstrel Juan), without being lavishly rich or superfluous, it is over-poetic in texture, tending to express thought in imagery. It is no wonder that Henry James found *The Spanish Gypsy* 'much more of a poem than was to be expected', though his admiration of 'its extraordinary rhetorical energy and elegance', 'its splendid generosity of diction', and 'its marvellous power of expression' is probably rather overpitched. By comparison, however, Elizabeth Barrett Browning's *Aurora Leigh* seems improvized, prolix, and prosaic.

* * *

Unable to make progress with her first version of *The Spanish Gypsy*, George Eliot continued the writing of verse in 'My Vegetarian Friend' (which she had sketched in prose three or four years earlier) and in 'Utopias', both being completed in January 1865. They were combined, it seems, to form 'A Minor Prophet' as it appeared in *The Legend of Jubal and Other Poems* (1874). The first part, the prophecy of Elias Baptist Butterworth, is satirical and witty, the opening lines resembling a parody of Wordsworthian matter-of-factness; it glances at contemporary spiritualism, and entertains the idea that rappings come from the Thought-atmosphere, to which people will have unimpeded recourse in the vegetarian era, when all will be ideal. The poet, however, prefers an imperfect world where amelioration is bought with sacrifice. In a world that moves to smiles and tears, the 'twists and cracks in our poor earthenware' (an allusion to the main image of Browning's 'Rabbi Ben Ezra', which had appeared in 1864) touch her to 'more conscious fellowship' with her coevals. She believes in progress towards the ideal, but her faith springs from the past, from noble and gentle deeds, heroic love, and even (a Browning thought) from failure and yearning. When she adds that it comes from 'every force that stirs our souls/To admiration, self-renouncing love', her Positivist sympathies are clear.

'Two Lovers', a lyric composed in September 1866, communicates deep feeling in excellent form, rounded to give a sense of life's wholeness. 'O May I Join the Choir Invisible' expresses a Positivist view of immortality, the hope that the author's 'better self' will always be remembered and become a source of strength to others. For many it is the only poem by which George Eliot is remembered as a poet. It was written in Germany during the summer of 1867.

The following summer, after completing *The Spanish Gypsy*, she made a further study of English verse. It had been a principle with her, which she found supported in practice by 'all the finest writers', occasionally to use lines of irregular length, especially of twelve syllables, in blank verse. She was impressed by Milton's example ('such listening for new melodies and harmonies with *instructed* ears'); and it is significant that her August reading included *Samson Agonistes* and Guest's *English Rhythms*. Among the projects she listed for 1869 were *Middlemarch*, a long poem on Timoleon, and several shorter ones, including '(Tubalcain) Vision of Jubal', 'Agatha', 'Stradivarius', and 'Arion'.

'Agatha' was finished in January. It is a sketch based on recollections of a visit George Eliot and Lewes made the previous July with the Gräfin von Baudissin (the countess) and her daughter to a peasant's cottage among the mountains of south-western Germany. Description of the scenery is followed by the dialogue of Countess Linda and Agatha ('sweet antiphony of young and old'); and the poem concludes with a song, purportedly by Hans the tailor in honour of Agatha and her cousins Kate and Nell, whom she houses because, though younger, they are 'feeble, with small withered wits'. The influence of Agatha's piety, even on the young, makes her a link between 'faulty folk and God'. Tennyson did this sort of thing better, Swinburne wrote; he also did worse. The subject has no pretensions to profundity, but it is tactfully observed and gracefully composed. *The Atlantic Monthly* paid £300 for it, and the author probably never made money more easily.

Three weeks later she had finished 'How Lisa Loved the King', a greater achievement which alone would make George Eliot worthy to be remembered. It is an amplification of a Boccaccio story (*Il Decamerone*, X.vii), and its rhymed verse suggests the influence of *The Canterbury Tales*, familiarity with which is to be seen among the epigraphs of *Middlemarch*. With excellent judgment she frequently uses alexandrines to bring paragraphs to a close. It is creative work, a free translation, notable as much for the originality and delicacy of its imagery as for the technical mastery which is often displayed in variety and ease of movement within the regular insistencies of its medium.

The last of the 'Brother and Sister' sonnets was written at the end of July, just before the original opening of *Middlemarch* was begun. Initially entitled 'Sonnets on Childhood', they suggest that incidents in *The Mill on the Floss* which are commonly regarded as autobiographical have been modified for fictional ends. The recollections have a twofold significance. Like Wordsworth's 'spots of time' they record memories which have enriching or renovating virtues:

> The firmaments of daisies since to me
> Have had those mornings in their opening eyes,
> The bunchèd cowslip's pale transparency
> Carries that sunshine of sweet memories.

George Eliot's soul, like Wordsworth's, had its 'fair seed-time'; those early hours were 'seed' to all her 'after good', and she ascribes her moral development to childhood experiences fostering love and fear, 'the primal passionate store,/Whose shaping impulses make manhood whole'. They were her 'root of piety'.* The sonnets also show how brother and sister helped to enlarge each other's world, the author describing them (21.iv.73) as 'little descriptive bits on the mutual influences in their small lives'. Through him she became more aware of reality, and found less satisfaction in the world of dreams. With school their shared life came to an end. The subsequent rift between Mrs Lewes and her brother Isaac is

---

* For the Wordsworthian correspondences, see *The Prelude*, XII.208ff., I.301–414, and 'My heart leaps up'.

alluded to in the 'Change' that is 'pitiless'. Another Shakespearian
sonnet, written subsequently as an epigraph (M.lvii) does not
belong to this sequence; it is made to fit the fiction but it recalls the
author's love of Scott's *Waverley* in her childhood, and how she
wrote out the story when the book had to be returned before she
could finish it.

'The Legend of Jubal' was begun when *Middlemarch* was interrupted by Thornton Lewes's fatal illness, and finished 'about
Christmas' (1869). The passage on Death was written under the
shadow of great grief when he passed away, Lewes told Alexander
Main (21.x.71). The thought that life must end imparts 'new
dearness' to everything, 'finer tenderness' to love, and ambition to
achieve something that will abide:

> Come, let us fashion acts that are to be,
> When we shall lie in darkness silently,
> As our young brother doth, whom yet we see
> Fallen and slain, but reigning in our will
> By that one image of him pale and still.

The poem returns to the rhymed couplet form of 'How Lisa Loved
the King' with occasional alexandrine variations. The legend is
imaginary, starting from Genesis and *Paradise Lost* (XI.558–63).
After inventing the lyre and discovering the power of music over
his own race, Jubal seeks inspiration in new lands. When from a
mountain peak he sees the ocean, and hears 'its multitudinous
roar,/Its plunge and hiss upon the pebbled shore', he can no
longer respond to new voices, and turns back to rejoin his
brethren, hoping that 'fresh-voiced youth' will express all that is in
his soul. He travels far, losing his way and his ancient lyre. When
at length he returns white-haired, 'the rune-writ story of a man',
he sees 'dread Change' around. Utterly exhausted and near death,
he lies watching an approaching procession and hears it chanting
to many instruments in praise of Jubal. At this his joy revives,
giving him strength to run and meet them. When he tells them
that he is Jubal, the inventor of the lyre, he is greeted with derision,
beaten, and left to find refuge among thorny thickets. 'The immortal name of Jubal filled the sky,/While Jubal lonely laid him
down to die.' He feels shadowy wings enclose him, sees the loving
face of his dedication in the past, and hears praise of the glorious
heritage he has left melt into symphony as he is upborne. There is a

Positivist inspiration in this heroic theme, but the poem, like so much of George Eliot's poetry, though it contains much that is impressive and exquisite, suggests a finished composition rather than the living voice and passion of the highest art.

'Armgart' is a rather slight dramatic sketch in five scenes which was begun 'under much depression' in August 1870; the subject had engaged George Eliot's interest a few weeks earlier at Harrogate. In one respect she was like the singer Armgart, who is asked how she can bear 'the poise of eminence' with 'dread of sliding'; in another, she was more fortunate, for Armgart is expected to renounce her art when she marries. She refuses, but a year later loses her voice, and vents her bitterness in proud anger. Her outbursts bring the verse to life, but her haughty egoism is pricked with surprising suddenness by the lame cousin who has waited on her for years:

> Now, then, you are lame –
> Maimed, as you said, and levelled with the crowd:
> Call it new birth – birth from that monstrous Self
> Which, smiling down upon a race oppressed,
> Says, 'All is good, for I am throned at ease.'

Armgart admits that she has been blind, and that true vision comes only, it seems, with sorrow. She will make amends to her cousin, and become a teacher of music and singing (a career she has despised). She is confirmed in her resolution when she learns that her master had suffered the same disappointment.

Two shorter poems belong to 1873. 'Arion', written in the stanza of Marvell's Horatian ode on Cromwell's return from Ireland, is a splendid composition until it falters at the very end. 'Stradivarius' is admirable from start to finish. Mainly a duologue, it is dramatic throughout and influenced by Browning's style. The painter Naldo, a believer in the inspiration derived from 'drinking, gambling, talk turned wild' or 'moody misery and lack of food', with 'every dithyrambic fine excess', speaks slightingly of the 'painful nicety' with which Stradivari works. Stradivari contends that he will be appreciated by master violinists of the future, that the 'fullest good' one gives is God, and that 'not God Himself can make man's best/Without best men to help Him'. Naldo ends his excuses for not finishing his latest picture with 'A great idea is an eagle's egg,/Craves time for hatching'; and the poem closes with Stradivari's rejoinder:

If thou wilt call thy pictures eggs
I call the hatching, Work. 'Tis God gives skill,
But not without men's hands: He could not make
Antonio Stradivari's violins
Without Antonio. Get thee to thy easel.

'A College Breakfast-Party' provides very different fare. Written in April 1874, it developed from talks with Trinity men during George Eliot's visit to Cambridge the previous May. A metaphysician may enjoy it, but most readers probably wish the author had persisted in her intention never to publish it. Lewes arranged for its publication in *Macmillan's Magazine* for a £250 fee, and it was added to the *Legend of Jubal* volume when Blackwood asked if she had more poems to 'swell it out to the required length' in the Cabinet Edition. To satirize without tedium the prolixity, non sequiturs, and inconclusiveness of philosophical discussion presents an artistic dilemma which was beyond George Eliot's invention. The verse copes admirably with the eloquence of academic sophistry, but such a subject needs either a structural idea which can quintessentialize it or the continual relief of witty comment and amusing incident. The device of a dialogue between selected *Hamlet* characters, with the indecisive prince left to form his own conclusions, is promising; but a long succession of argument in which 'None said, "Let Darkness be", but Darkness was' is inevitably tedious. The high debate oscillates from abstract to real, from absolute to relative, and from the scientifically explicable to the unknown of religion. After hearing that analogies in reasoning have as much significance as a crow and a bar to a crowbar, the priest, trying to supply an imperative to Hamlet's thronging doubts, discourses learnedly and, after proving by analogy to his own satisfaction that everything said supports belief in a Presence, leaves for another appointment. Discussion on the relative leads to taste, and taste to the ideal beauty which is seen in art and poetry, and which exists independently of all human turmoil and philosophical change. Guildenstern insists that beauty and taste develop in accordance with human evolution, but Hamlet, uncertain to the last, thinks that poetry could belong to 'a transfigured realm' which is free from our grosser world.

And then he dreamed a dream so luminous
He woke (he says) convinced; but what it taught

Withholds as yet. Perhaps those graver shades
Admonished him that visions told in haste
Part with their virtues to the squandering lips
And leave the soul in wider emptiness.

No uncertainty on George Eliot's attitude to transcendentalism in philosophy and aesthetic theory can remain after this conclusion.

'Stradivarius' suggests that George Eliot's poetic gifts were not inconsiderable. With *Daniel Deronda* in hand she could do no more in verse than continue the practice she had begun in *Felix Holt* of supplying her own chapter epigraphs where nothing more suitable came to mind. They can be lyrical or humorous; but the gravely philosophical tend to be more impressive, as when Gwendolen Harleth, her murderous thought making her feel guilty of her husband's death, experiences 'that new terrible life lying on the other side of the deed which fulfils a criminal desire' (DD.lvii):

Deeds are the pulse of Time, his beating life,
And righteous or unrighteous, being done,
Must throb in after-throbs till Time itself
Be laid in stillness, and the universe
Quiver and breathe upon no mirror more.

They are often dramatic, one of the most apt and poetical referring to that 'moment of naturalness' between Lydgate and Rosamond which 'shook flirtation into love' (M.xxxi):

How will you know the pitch of that great bell
Too large for you to stir? Let but a flute
Play 'neath the fine-mixed metal: listen close
Till the right note flows forth, a silvery rill:
Then shall the huge bell tremble — then the mass
With myriad waves concurrent shall respond
In low soft unison.

Later Novels

MIDDLEMARCH

George Eliot had considered *Middlemarch* at various times before she made it one of her projects for 1869. In February she informed John Blackwood that she intended beginning it 'at once, having already sketched the plan'. 'The various elements . . . have been soliciting my mind for years', she added, after stating that 'between the beginning and middle of a book' she was like the lazy Scheldt but 'between the middle and end' like the arrowy Rhone. The hero was a physician, and the 'Introduction' which she wrote in July almost certainly presented Lydgate's early history and background much as it appears in the fifteenth chapter.* Her Journal for 2 August 1869 reads: 'Began "Middlemarch" (the Vincy and Featherstone parts)'. Soon afterwards, busily engaged with medical books (including copies of *The Lancet* for 1830–31), she was afraid that she could not 'make anything satisfactory' of the novel. She asked Mrs Congreve to procure information she needed about provincial hospitals for 'imagining the conditions' of her hero. After a long interval the 'Miss Brooke' story was begun early in November 1870, and a month later she decided to make it part of *Middlemarch*. By March she had made good progress with this enlarged work and hoped to complete it in November; her problem was that she had 'too much matter – too many *momenti*'.

The 'Miss Brooke' story, as far as it was independently written, takes up the first nine chapters and the opening of the tenth. Professor Beaty has shown that the bridging which took place between it and the original opening of *Middlemarch* occurs from the tenth (where it is most evident) to the beginning of the twelfth chapter; that the section which follows to the end of the sixteenth

---

* Jerome Beaty, *'Middlemarch' from Notebook to Novel* (Urbana, Ill., 1960).

chapter is a revision from the early *Middlemarch*; that, though the seventeenth and eighteenth were considerably revised, there is nothing from the seventeenth chapter onwards which appears to have been written for the first *Middlemarch* or for 'Miss Brooke' as a separate story; and that the much revised twenty-third chapter was originally the nineteenth and the last of the work completed by 19 March 1871. As there were 'too many *momenti*', Lewes persuaded Blackwood that a four-volume publication would be required, and that he could more successfully compete with the circulating libraries by following the example of Hugo's *Les Misérables* and publishing at intervals in eight half-volume parts. No major aspect of the story was to be overlooked in any issue. From December 1871 publication in parts continued every two months, and such was their reception that the author wondered how she could maintain the standards expected of her. When the second appeared, only half of *Middlemarch* had been completed. The concluding two books were written rapidly, enabling Blackwood to issue the last three numbers at monthly intervals, the publication of the final almost coinciding with that of the four-volume novel in December 1872.

'Miss Brooke', as George Eliot noted in her Journal (2.xii.70) was begun 'without any very serious intention of carrying it out lengthily', but the present work abundantly indicates that the original *Middlemarch* was conceived as a full-length novel. From 'the Vincy and Featherstone parts' grew three related stories: that of Fred Vincy, presented at intervals in scenes of considerable Middlemarch detail, its moral emphases underscored by the Garths; that of the banker Bulstrode, which develops powerfully after Casaubon's death; and, equal in importance with 'Miss Brooke', that of Lydgate and Rosamond Vincy. These two stories are of dominant interest in the work as a whole, for they are complementary in theme, the balked idealism of the hero offering a parallel to that of the heroine. Narrative interlinking arises in several minor ways, through Vincy–Featherstone–Bulstrode family ties, and more importantly through Lydgate's attendance on Casaubon, Dorothea's visits to Lydgate and Rosamond, Ladislaw's involvement with Rosamond, and the not overcomplicated relationship of a melodramatic subplot which emerges from a murky past to establish a connection between Ladislaw and Bulstrode. The author's sketch-map shows Lowick two miles north-west, and Freshitt and Tipton three miles south-east, of Middlemarch.

The amalgamation of two independently conceived works of fiction broadened the basis of *Middlemarch* as 'A Study of Provincial Life'. Some of the 'Miss Brooke' characters become involved in municipal affairs, Mr Brooke as a governor of the hospital and a prospective parliamentary candidate, with Ladislaw as his agent; Dorothea supports Lydgate's hospital work. Conversely, strengthening the links between Middlemarch and its neighbourhood, the Garths live in the country, and Stone Court, the setting for memorable Featherstone and Bustrode scenes, is in Lowick parish. Yet the idiosyncrasies of 'Miss Brooke' differentiate it from most of the Middlemarch scenes. The Brookes of Tipton Grange, the Chettams of Freshitt Hall, the Reverend Edward Casaubon of Lowick Manor, all belong to the landed gentry; Mrs Cadwallader, a parson's wife, is of aristocratic lineage. The opening chapters in which they appear have a Jane Austen tincture which recurs in some of the concluding scenes. By and large these county representatives, unlike Lydgate and Bulstrode, are not controlled or endangered by Middlemarch affairs or Middlemarch opinion. Mr Brooke suffers a speedy extinction of his political hopes, but he and his position remain virtually unchanged. Neither do the comments of Celia, the Chettams, and Mrs Cadwallader, have any effect on Dorothea and Ladislaw. Conscience is their arbiter, and they possess sufficient strength of character to act irrespectively of others' views after Casaubon's death.

George Eliot agrees with Novalis that 'character is destiny' but additionally affirms the influence of circumstances on individual lives (MF.VI.vi). 'Our deeds are fetters that we forge ourselves', says the first gentleman, and the second replies, 'Ay, truly: but I think it is the world/That brings the iron' (ep.iv). The Garths may seem too exemplary, but *Middlemarch* in its major aspects illustrates the grip of circumstances arising from human weakness and error on the one hand, and on the other, with special reference to Lydgate and Bulstrode, from the weight of public opinion. 'There is no private life which has not been determined by a wider public life', George Eliot wrote in *Felix Holt*. *Middlemarch* continues the study of provincial life she began in that novel, but the interest is broader and much more social, the political issue being far less prominent than medical practice or the state of the clergy. The period is only fractionally earlier; excluding the finale, it extends from the end of September 1829 to the early summer of 1832. Mr and Mrs Casaubon return to England in January 1830 (xxviii);

Raffles' first visit to Stone Court coincides with the death of Huskisson in September 1830 (end xli); Brooke begins his electioneering soon after the dissolution of Parliament in April 1831 (li); and Dorothea and Ladislaw are married soon after the rejection of the Reform Bill by the House of Lords in May 1832.

Everything in the novel is related, and there are no loose ends. In this sense it comprises a whole, though it does not create an unequivocal sense of unity. Nowhere is this more evident than in the prelude, which can apply only to the 'Miss Brooke' story. Three stories are linked thematically, for the failure of Lydgate and Dorothea to fulfil their ideals has its qualified parallelism in Bulstrode's public welfare enterprise and his final disgrace; Fred Vincy's success story supplies some eventual sunshine in the greyness of sobriety and disillusionment. Many scenes provide backgrounds to dramatic crises in the lives of individuals; paradoxically the shift of interest from group to group gives a greater air of reality to the general picture, for one cannot expect to follow a number of lives closely without leaving much untold. In this way we miss, for example, the marriage of Dorothea and Casaubon, of Celia Brooke and Sir James Chettam, and of Lydgate and Rosamond. Enrichment in one direction has a curtailing effect in another but, if 'parts are much more striking than the whole', the same is true of novels with more obvious unity. A. V. Dicey, who made this complaint in January 1873, reinforced it with the argument that 'the form of the story' made it 'impossible to centre the interest fixedly on any one character'. The criticism is rather unreasonable, though many readers must have wished that more in the life of Lydgate and Rosamond had been presented. All that we have is sharply focused, but the author told John Cross that she had found Rosamond the most difficult of all her characters to sustain.

Hints of her design in the presentation of provincial life are to be found in the novel and elsewhere. Middlemarch may indicate simply a town in the Midlands or Mercia rather than a typical 'march' or debatable tract of territory behind the frontier of enlightenment and progress. It may also imply the avoidance of extremes, the *via media* of mixed humanity and compromised ideals; George Eliot told Blackwood that she wished 'to show the gradual action of ordinary causes rather than exceptional', and to do this 'in some directions which have not been from time immemorial the beaten path − the Cremorne walks and shows of

fiction' (24.vii.71). As she states in the finale, 'the growing good of
the world is partly dependent on unhistoric acts'. Here, as in the
prelude, she has in mind the Dorotheas of this world. The medium
in which the ardent deeds of Theresa and Antigone took place 'is
for ever gone. But we insignificant people with our daily words and
acts are preparing the lives of many Dorotheas', for 'there is no
creature whose inward being is so strong that it is not greatly determined by what lies outside it'. And the opposite is true: 'if we had
been greater, circumstance would have been less strong against us'
(lviii). Human lots are both woven and interwoven (xv); as Farebrother tells Lydgate, 'You have not only got the old Adam in
yourself against you, but you have got all those descendants of the
original Adam who form the society around you' (xvii). Progress is
denied or retarded by common occurrences, as George Eliot
stresses, first when Lydgate considers Dorothea an inferior woman
to Rosamond (xi):

> any one watching keenly the stealthy convergence of human
> lots, sees a slow preparation of effects from one life on another,
> which tells like a calculated irony on the indifference or the
> frozen stare with which we look at our unintroduced neighbour.
> Destiny stands by sarcastic with our *dramatis personae* folded in
> her hand.

Again, thinking of those who like Lydgate 'once meant to shape
their own deeds and alter the world a little' but in the end came to
be 'shapen after the average', she remarks (xv):

> Nothing in the world more subtle than the process of their
> gradual change. In the beginning they inhaled it unknowingly:
> you and I may have sent some of our breath towards infecting
> them, when we uttered our conforming falsities or drew our silly
> conclusions: or perhaps it came with the vibrations from a
> woman's glance.

The slow, unremitting effect of one individual on another is seen
in the changes which Dorothea and Lydgate suffer as a result of
imprudent marriages; nowhere is the effect of public opinion
better illustrated than in the spread of scandal against Bulstrode
and Lydgate and its first impact on the former (lxxi).

With many *momenti* and a wealth of illustrative material, George

Eliot achieves extensive imaginative integration through parallels and contrast. The thwarting of philanthropic aims becomes more impressively real when they are presented in three widely different forms: the ardent but generally undefined and groping, the highly intelligent and practical, and the penitential masquerading in public benefaction. Inexperience, unpracticality, weakness, error, and evil are so enmeshed with good that it is often difficult to discern where sympathy should end and condemnation begin with Dorothea, Lydgate, and Bulstrode. Co-ordination is recurrent in the subject themes of all eight books except the first. 'Waiting for Death' applies more imminently and dramatically to Featherstone, but quite ominously for Casaubon. 'The Dead Hand' clearly refers to the restrictions of Casaubon's will, but the phrase is used first in connection with Featherstone's, the 'rigid clutch of his dead hand' (xxxiv) ultimately bringing Raffles to Stone Court, to ruin Bulstrode's career and give the final stroke to Lydgate's failing reputation and resolution. Contrasts are more numerous, and some of them underline the irony of chance. When Lydgate, heavily in debt, seeks his wife's co-operation and gains no response, he thinks first of Laure who killed her husband because she was weary of him; then he remembers Dorothea's suffering and desire to help her husband when he first attended him. The thin neutrality and self-centred indifference of Rosamond's 'What can *I* do, Tertius?' recalls the sarcasm of Time initiated by Lydgate when, after a single conversation with Dorothea, he concluded that she 'did not look at things from the proper feminine angle'. When he has lost face in Middlemarch, she is the first person to express confidence in his integrity and future, and for the first time he experiences 'the exquisite sense of leaning entirely on a generous sympathy, without any check of a proud reserve'. Her love might help a man more than her money, he reflects (lxxvi). An early passage (xii) suggests that Mary Garth was intended as the foil to Rosamond in the first plan of the novel. Most men in Middlemarch thought the fair Rosamond 'the best girl in the world'; some called her an angel. Plain and brown, Mary Garth was handicapped in complexion like Maggie Tulliver, but she had the shrewd practical sense, patience, and kindness which would have ensured Lydgate's happiness and success. The wide gap between Mrs Bulstrode's self-conquest and magnanimity and Rosamond's repugnance when their husbands are disgraced needs no demonstration. There are interesting comparative links in the pattern of *Middlemarch* which are free from tragic overtones: Mary Garth's practical integrity is far removed from Dorothea's altruistic zeal; Caleb's principles clash with Bulstrode's self-interest and self-deception; and his efficiency contrasts admirably with Mr Brooke's inadequacies as a landed proprietor. His remark 'What people do who go into politics I can't think: it drives me almost mad to see mismanagement over only a few hundred acres' is indissociable from Brooke's dramatic encounter with his tenant Dagley and his collapse as a parliamentary candidate before his first public speech is under way.

Surveying the whole novel, one can see incidental ironies flashing backwards and forwards. Just after Featherstone's funeral service, Dorothea remarks that she cannot bear to think that anyone should die and leave no love behind; she would have said more but for the entrance of her husband at this point. Called in to give medical advice, and ignorant of the terms of Casaubon's will, Lydgate recommends that Dorothea should do whatever gives her repose of mind, and adds, 'That repose will not always come from being forbidden to act.' When Lydgate's 'bird of paradise' is confronted with the disenchanting prospect of economies, Trumbull holds an auction which causes some excitement in Middlemarch, and rouses interest in a collection of riddles by sample and comment: ' "How must you spell honey to make it catch lady-birds? Answer – money." You hear? – lady-birds – honey – money. This is an amusement to sharpen the intellect; it has a sting – it has what we call satire . . .'. Time's sarcasm is implied more gravely when Bulstrode, assuming that his past has been divulged to no one but the discreet Caleb Garth (by Raffles, then lying ill at Stone Court), interprets his hope of secrecy as 'a sort of earnest that Providence intended his rescue from worse consequences'.

The backwardness and superficiality of English attitudes to women is ridiculed with admirable artistic discipline in *Middlemarch*, and the author's irony is heightened when the common upper-class view is expressed by the thoroughly muddle-minded and incompetent Mr Brooke. His patronizing attitude to women and their abilities is reminiscent of Bardo's towards his daughter Romola. 'But there is a lightness about the feminine mind', he says, 'a touch and go – music, the fine arts, that kind of thing – they should study those up to a certain point, women should; but in a light way, you know. A woman should be able to sit down and play you or sing you a good old English tune.' Rosamond Vincy has all these accomplishments; she had been 'the flower of Mrs Lemon's school, the chief school in the country, where the teaching included all that was demanded in the accomplished female – even to extras, such as the getting in and out of a carriage'. She is one of the most self-willed and heartless of accomplished females outside the pages of Jane Austen. T. S. Eliot found her far more frightening than Goneril or Regan. It is hardly surprising (though Jane Austen would not have been entirely in agreement) that George Eliot puts the emphasis on feeling when Dorothea chooses to marry Ladislaw. The comedy of men's attachment to female glamour is voiced most pointedly by the bachelor Chichely (x):

> 'Ay, to be sure, there should be a little devil in a woman', said Mr Chichely, whose study of the fair sex seemed to have been detrimental to his theology. 'And I like them blond, with a certain gait, and a swan neck. Between ourselves, the mayor's daughter is more to my taste than Miss Brooke or Miss Celia either. If I were a marrying man I should choose Miss Vincy before either of them.'

The spotlight in *Middlemarch* is on people rather than setting; little attention is given to physical features of the town, and where they occur they are slight and incidental. Several scenes take place at the Vincys' and the Lydgates', but the surroundings with which we become most familiar (though much is left to the imagination) are at Stone Court and Lowick Manor. Chichely, a coursing celebrity and coroner, is one of the dramatically sketched individuals whose brief appearances help to create impressions of relevant sections of Middlemarch society at large. Among them are Bambridge the horse-dealer, once one of Fred Vincy's associates, whose lot is to bring the scandalous story of Bulstrode to Middlemarch. Mr Hawley, lawyer and town-clerk, a man of action and strong feelings, makes the most of it; in opposition to Bulstrode on the hospital chaplaincy appointment, he rudely silences the eloquent rich tanner Mr Hackbutt. Blinded by prejudice, he is a great force in Middlemarch as a vigorous opponent of change and progress; his anti-reforming zeal makes him brand Ladislaw a foreign agent or spy (of 'any cursed alien blood, Jew, Corsican, or Gypsy'), and organize the opposition which quickly reduces Mr Brooke to an electioneering butt. The grocer Mr Mawmsey expresses the typical elector's point of view when he tells Mr Brooke that he must consider the effect of Reform on his till and ledger. Some of the more humble citizens meet, and comment in choric style on the main action, at the Tankard in Slaughter Lane, where the high-spirited landlady Mrs Dollop persists in believing that Lydgate had been all for 'cutting up everybody before the breath was well out o' their body'. Her blood has been 'set a-creeping' at the sight of Bulstrode ever since he came to buy her house: 'folks don't look the colour o' the dough-tub and stare at you as if they wanted to see into your backbone for nothingk'. The group of ladies which dis-cusses him and Mrs Bulstrode at the time of his disgrace consists of Mrs Hackbutt, Mrs Sprague, Mrs Tom Toller, and Mrs Plymdale. A sidelight on the social emphasis of the novel is afforded by the view of Featherstone's funeral from an upper window at Lowick Manor. As the mourners come out of the church, Sir James Chettam, with a foxhunter's disgust, describes Vincy the Mayor, whom Brooke has just spotted, as 'a coursing fellow'. 'And one of those who suck the life out of the wretched handloom weavers in Tipton and Freshitt. That is how his family look so fair and sleek', adds Mrs Cadwallader.

The state of medicine in Middlemarch is of critical consequence to the action. To acquire the best preparation for his career, Lyd-gate had followed his more advanced medical courses outside England. He knew that his profession needed reform, and had come to the conclusion that his best course was to 'settle in some provincial town as a general practitioner, and resist the irrational severance between medical and surgical knowledge in the interest of his own scientific pursuits, as well as of the general advance; he would keep away from the range of London intrigues, jealousies, and social truckling, and win celebrity, however slowly, as Jenner had done, by the independent value of his work'. In this way he hoped to do 'good small work for Middlemarch, and great work for the world'. Quackery and excessive drug-prescription being common, his policy was to prescribe and not dispense drugs or take a percentage commission from druggists. Inevitably this innovation would be regarded as a criticism of his fellow-practitioners. Nor could he expect his new methods of treatment to win ready favour in oppos-ition to current practice and prejudice. The position is summarized with reference to two surgeon-apothecaries and two physicians or consultants. Middlemarch assessments of doctors were reached in-tuitively, mainly by lady patients. One group supported Wrench and 'the strengthening treatment', another Toller and 'the lowering system'; and nobody believed that 'Mr Lydgate could know as much as Dr Sprague and Dr Minchin, the two physicians, who alone could offer any hope when danger was extreme, and when the smallest hope was worth a guinea'. Dr Sprague, as senior physician in the town, was thought to have more 'weight', Dr Minchin more 'penetration'. The former was believed to be irreligious, but this belief made his 'weight' more credible. 'They enjoyed about equally the mysterious privilege of medical reputation', and concealed their mutual contempt 'with much etiquette'. When Lydgate was given the unsalaried post of medical director at the new hospital, all the Middlemarch doctors set themselves resolutely against it, even trying 'to blacken the whole affair and hinder subscriptions'. It was 'a dark period', George Eliot tells us. Lydgate's use of the stethoscope indicates how far ahead he was of lagging practice, and it is ironical that he is suspected of collusion with Bulstrode in the death of Raffles after his instructions have been ignored in favour of the treatment usually prescribed.

The limitation of church representatives in Middlemarch to Anglicans emphasizes the small part played as yet by Catholics and Dissenters in public affairs (see p. 54). Prejudice against the former was widespread; it is voiced by the aristocratic Mrs Cadwallader and the shoemaker Mr Limp, who remembers how Wellington 'turned his coat and went over to the Romans' when the Catholic Emancipation Act was passed in 1829; Mrs Cadwallader dismisses Dorothea's charitable schemes as 'Methodistical'. The political bias of the Church was still Tory, though the Evangelical movement often connoted a more liberal outlook. Middlemarch clergymen do not suggest a great power for enlightenment and reform, and the expectation that a young man like Fred Vincy will enter the Church is significant, as is Mary Garth's forthright comment: 'His being a clergyman would be only for gentility's sake, and I think there is nothing more contemptible than such imbecile gentility.' Cadwallader exemplifies the gentleman parson; his main interest is trout-fishing, and Casaubon, even though he took an unexpected line on the Catholic question, is a fine fellow because he has a trout stream. Casaubon has a curate to do his duties while he pursues his moribund research. Mr Thesiger of St Peter's is a moderate Evangelical who strongly supports the application of Mr Tyke, the curate of a chapel of ease in his parish, for the hospital chaplaincy. He regards Mr Tyke as 'a zealous able man', and Mr Powderell thinks he is 'a real Gospel preacher'; his opponents have nothing to say against him, except that they cannot bear him and suspect him of cant. Mr Farebrother judges him to be not very learned or wise, and Lydgate considers the 'apostolic' zeal of his hospital preaching 'a sort of pinching hard to make people uncomfortably aware of him'. Mr Farebrother is no enthusiast. Having cultivated scientific hobbies, he finds he has 'got into the wrong profession'; but he is shrewd, honest, a thorough gentleman, and an excellent preacher. To some degree he satisfies Dorothea's (and the author's) requirements of Christianity, the betterment of as many people as possible. He is a friend and counsellor to Fred Vincy and Lydgate at critical points in their lives, and does his best to help his parishioners. He admires Mary Garth, but sacrifices his heartfelt interest magnanimously when he discovers her long attachment to Fred. Like Mr Irwine, he helps to support his mother and sister (his aunt Miss Noble also), but he is not well-off, and plays at cards and billiards for money; his main interest as a candidate for the hospital chaplaincy is financial.

Bulstrode's religion is a strange mixture of good and evil. As a young bank-clerk in London he had been a Calvinist; he had then joined a pawnbroking business which made huge profits from distress and corruption. The owner died, and Bulstrode married his widow; her daugher ran away. By concealing her place of abode, he inherited a fortune, the retention of which he justified in the conviction that he had been chosen to use it for God's purposes. At Middlemarch he had enjoyed respectability for nearly thirty years when Raffles' arrival threatened to shatter his prospects. He had become a Churchman of evangelical zeal, a banker who administered town charities, a public benefactor, and also a 'sleeping partner' in profitable businesses which drew on his ability to effect economies in their raw materials. Mr Vincy, reproached by Bulstrode for bringing up Fred in idleness and expectation of Featherstone's property, reminds him that one of these partnerships produced silk-rotting dyes, adding 'Perhaps if other people knew so much of the profit went to the glory of God, they might like it better.' Bulstrode enjoyed power, made the most of it in directing hospital affairs, and thereby increased hatred and opposition in 'an evil generation'. His predominance made some people call him a Methodist or a hypocrite. He made numerous private charities, and they were bestowed, like his public bene-factions, for the glory of God and the increase of his power. Even the egoistic terrors which afflicted him when Raffles appeared were 'clad . . . in doctrinal reference to superhuman ends'; and his failure to oppose Mrs Abel's wish to follow the usual treatment (thereby ignoring Lydgate's strict instructions) when Raffles was sinking was prompted by the hope that his consequent death would be another of those 'remarkable providences' with which he had been favoured, freeing him for 'the rest of his days here below' from 'the threat of an ignominy which would break him utterly as an instrument of God's service'.

Though neither a villain nor a Pecksniff, Bulstrode contributes with ominous subtlety to the depressing picture of English life in *Middlemarch*. The counterbalancing forces are rather light in the scale. Fred Vincy's intrinsic honesty earns admiration, though occasionally he needs the Garths and Farebrother to keep him on the right course. Mary Garth's love of Fred is deep-rooted; it shows 'l'incorruptible adhérence de ceux qui se sont aimés dès l'aube de la vie' (ep.lxxxvi), and her steadfastness until he has recovered from the follies which education and parental indulgence have bred is matched by her resolution not to marry him if he enters the Church against his will, merely for a life of ease and gentility. Her adamant refusal to be implicated in Featherstone's disposal of his property, lest she should be party to some rash irrevocable decision (possibly to Fred's advantage), contrasts dramatically with the guilt that generates self-justification in Bulstrode, and creates a more favourable impression than her father's sudden termination of his agreement, on hearing Raffles' story, to manage Stone Court for Bulstrode. In the circumstances most people would have sought corroboration before acting; Caleb's action suggests a certain inhumanity or excess of virtue. At times the Garths are too exemplary to enlist the full sympathy their author accorded them. Nevertheless they elicit admiration, and none more than Caleb, whose best qualities (like Adam Bede's) were drawn from Robert Evans. His sense of the right relationship between industrial production and the welfare of 'the social body' is like poetry or religion to him, making him support railway development despite the resistance stirred up among ignorant workers by proprietors with private interests at stake; 'his virtual divinities were good practical schemes, accurate work, and the faithful completion of undertakings: his prince of darkness was a slack workman'. Nothing can be more honourable for him than 'getting a bit of the country into good fettle', and he is delighted to find that Mrs Casaubon's ambition is to improve 'a great piece of land' and build 'a great many good cottages' because the work is healthy and people benefit from it after it is done. The diffusive value of her 'beneficient activity' as Ladislaw's wife strengthens the note of optimism with which the novel ends.

Fortunately *Middlemarch* has its humorous relief, though it is never as copious as in *Adam Bede* or as comical as in *The Mill on the Floss*. Initially it is directed against Dorothea and Casaubon; and it proceeds directly from the author as well as through intermediaries. The incidental irony of Dorothea's readiness in spirit to accept Hooker or Milton or 'any other of the great men whose odd habits it would have been glorious piety to endure' is typical, and the comic sense which creates Casaubon's amatory style is akin to Jane Austen's. There is an amusing dramatic quality in his 'frigid rhetoric', which, at the end of his most eloquent speech, is said to have the sincerity of a dog's bark or 'the cawing of an amorous rook'. Celia's 'naïve malice' shows more perception than her sister's intuitions, but the sharpest attacks on the 'Lowick Cicero' express Mrs Cadwallader's disgust when she learns that Dorothea is engaged to him. Miss Brooke's belief that he is 'a great soul' is dismissed with withering contempt when Mrs Cadwallader brings the news to the rejected Sir James Chettam. 'A great bladder for dried peas to rattle in', she comments; Dorothea, she tells her husband, might have been sensible had she married Sir James, but now she wishes her joy of her 'hair shirt'. Mrs Cadwallader's mind is as active as phosphorus; her tongue is unbridled. She can make the liberal-minded Mr Brooke feel very uncomfortable. Her suspicion of Ladislaw hardens into antipathy when he edits *The Pioneer* for Brooke's political campaign: 'a sort of Byronic hero − an amorous conspirator, it strikes me. And Thomas Aquinas is not fond of him.' With a reputation for speaking her mind (a blackamoor who cannot smirch herself), she comes over to Freshitt Hall at the instigation of Sir James, hoping to save Dorothea from a second bad marriage, engages in conversation with the two of them by referring to a rumour that *The Pioneer* will turn all political colours when Ladislaw is gone, and reveals that 'Mr Orlando Ladislaw is making a sad dark-blue scandal by warbling continually with your Mr Lydgate's wife, who they tell me is as pretty as pretty can be' (lxii).

The most dramatic figure for unintentional humour is Mr Brooke; his bumbling conversation reflects a glib, reminiscential, superficially cultured, slipshod mind. 'Your sex are not thinkers, you know — *varium et mutabile semper* — that kind of thing. You don't know Virgil', he tells Mrs Cadwallader, and he is about to claim 'the personal acquaintance of the Augustan poet' (so accustomed is he to claim familiarity with anyone or anything of consequence) when a return of chronological intelligence saves him from absurdity. One never suspects him of mastering any subject, though he is prepared to talk on whatever arises. He over-studied once, he says, and thinks Casaubon could have done so in Rome. Speaking from experience, he conveys authorial irony when he continues, 'You may go any length in that sort of thing, and nothing may come of it, you know.' He recommends that Casaubon should get Dorothea to read 'light things, Smollett — "Roderick Random", "Humphrey Clinker": they are a little broad, but she may read anything now she's married, you know'. The bland, confiding affability of his characteristic 'you know' goes far to convey the assurance with which he is accustomed to air his views in polite conversation. Discussing political matters, he tells Ladislaw that he has the ideas, but lacks Burke's way of expressing them, and he proves his ineptitude in both respects when he attempts his first and last electioneering speech. Brooke is an unfailing source of humour, and one of the finest portraits in the novel. Perhaps he is at his best when, talking of game and poaching, he tells what happened to the Methodist preacher Flavell, after the latter had knocked down a hare when he was out walking with his wife (xxxix). In the unforgettable scene which follows, the landlord 'who had gone into everything, especially fine art and social improvement', but had parsimoniously neglected his farms, hears some unpalatable hometruths from one of his tenants. His tongue loosened by political talk and excess of drinking on market-day, Dagley clutches his pitchfork and tells Brooke, who had regarded himself as rather a favourite with his tenants since he had dispensed with Caleb Garth's services, what such landlords as he can expect with the coming of 'Rinform'. Discussions such as that in which coroner Chichely airs his view of Rosamond Vincy, and that with Mrs Dollop at the Tankard, provide further relief while extending or deepening interest in the main action; no scene does this more entertainingly than the auction conducted by that 'amateur of superior phrases', Borthrop Trumbull (lx). Nor should the rather grotesque comedy of Featherstone be forgotten, and the remarks and suspicious fears of all the predatory relatives who meet at Stone Court both before and after his death. The most dramatic moment comes when, despite his orders, two of these 'Christian Carnivora' enter his bedroom, and the sight of their 'funereal figures' enrages him, giving him strength to seize his gold-headed stick and wave it backwards and forwards in as wide a sweep as possible as he hoarsely screeches, 'Back, back, Mrs Waule! Back, Solomon!'

The interrelationships of *Middlemarch*, and the effect of character and circumstance on lives and careers constitute a 'web' (xv, Finale), but the image also applies to the troubles Lydgate creates for himself by flirting with Rosamond (xxxi), to their romantic illusions (xxxvi), Casaubon's jealous suspicions of Ladislaw (xlii), and (thickening with the years) the religious justification with which Bulstrode has padded his moral sensibility (lxi). The most dramatically presented image is the chain. The fear that she is losing Lydgate brings tears naturally to Rosamond, and they are the 'crystallizing feather-touch' which shakes flirtation into love. As he rises from picking up the chainwork she had nervously dropped, and catches sight of her tears, he does not know the extent of the chain; but, completely mastered by tenderness, he kisses her, leaving the house 'an engaged man, whose soul was not his own, but the woman's to whom he had bound himself' (xxxi). When he is the victim of Middlemarch calumny, he wonders what its effect on Rosamond will be. 'Here was another weight of chain to drag, and poor Lydgate was in a bad mood for bearing her dumb mastery' (lxxiii). The judgments of individuals by ordinary people are imaged as reflections in small mirrors; they may distort like a spoon (x) or be far from flattering, as when Bulstrode hears uncomfortable hometruths from Vincy (xiii). The most interesting mirror image relates to egoistic illusions (xxvii); it could well be applied to Dorothea, Lydgate, and Bulstrode, but the reference is to Rosamond:

Your pier-glass or extensive surface of polished steel made to be rubbed by a housemaid, will be minutely and multitudinously scratched in all directions; but place now against it a lighted candle as a centre of illumination, and lo! the scratches will seem to arrange themselves in a fine series of concentric circles round that little sun. It is demonstrable that the scratches are going everywhere impartially, and it is only your candle which produces the flattering illusion of a concentric arrangement, its light falling with an exclusive optical selection. These things are a parable. The scratches are events, and the candle is the egoism of any person now absent — of Miss Vincy, for example. Rosamond had a providence of her own who had kindly made her more charming than other girls, and who seemed to have arranged Fred's illness and Mr Wrench's mistake in order to bring her and Lydgate within effective proximity.

Unlike this 'parable', the contrasting imagery associated with Ladislaw and Casaubon is part of the imaginative texture of the novel. It is related to Dorothea: Ladislaw brings brightness and sunshine; in conjunction with her almost unrelieved disappointment and frustration, Casaubon's declining vitality and growing sense of failure in research are conveyed in seasonal impressions and varied metaphor. Dorothea's first impression of Lowick Manor is small-windowed and melancholy on a sunless November day. During her honeymoon in Rome she feels with 'stifling depression' that 'the large vistas and wide fresh air' which she had dreamed of are replaced by 'anterooms and winding passages' which seem to lead nowhere. As if unable to find his way among small closets and winding stairs, Casaubon has lost sight of whatever purpose directed his studies; 'his taper stuck before him', he forgets 'the absence of windows' and becomes 'indifferent to the sunlight'. They enter their home in January when snow is falling; and the shrinking of the land around, as the 'uniform whiteness' combines with 'low-hanging uniformity of cloud' to create a 'white vapour-walled landscape', images the shrinking prospect of those marriage duties, and the loss of those 'clear heights' of communion, to which Dorothea had once looked forward with fervour. Casaubon's languid soul, instead of flying, flutters in the swampy ground where it was hatched. So it continues, his longings clinging 'low and mist-like in very shady places'. The mere chance of seeing Ladislaw occasionally is like a lunette opened in the wall of her prison, 'giving her a glimpse of the sunny air' (for the development of the image, see p. 116, on a similar relationship between Maggie Tulliver and Philip Wakem). Premonitions of her husband's death follow, and they are reinforced with the watching of Featherstone's funeral from an upper window. Another autumn comes, and Casaubon carries 'his taper among the tombs of the past' more fitfully; as he looks into the eyes of death for the first time, the dark yew trees give him 'a mute companionship in melancholy'. Just before his death,

after catching sight of Ladislaw in church, Dorothea finds everything dreary though it is spring; it seems that she is 'to live more
and more in a virtual tomb'. Reversing the Orpheus–Eurydice
climax, it is as if 'she had stood at the door of the tomb and seen
Will Ladislaw receding into the distant world of warm activity and
fellowship – turning his face towards her as he went'.

George Eliot's attitude to Casaubon is inconsistent rather than
ambivalent. Satirical irony (such as that at the opening of vii) is
followed by awkward expressions of sympathy and pity until full
empathetic realization communicates his alarm lest Dorothea's intense interest lead to critical awareness of his failure. The contrast
between actuality and the apparent assurance of his magisterial
utterance is striking. Nevertheless, George Eliot's intervention on
behalf of this proud secretive man continues, and its redundance
and relative superficiality are proved when Dorothea turns from
indignant self-commiseration to 'a resolved submission' which in-
stantly produces gratitude and mutual relief. The dramatic
climax (xlii) is brief, but it exemplifies George Eliot's strength as a
novelist. The psychological insight and profound humanity on
which it depends are even more evident in her presentation of
Bulstrode. His self-delusive reasoning is 'essentially no more
peculiar to evangelical belief than the use of wide phrases for
narrow motives is peculiar to Englishmen. There is no general
doctrine which is not capable of eating out our morality if un-
checked by the deep-seated habit of direct fellow-feeling with
individual fellow-men.' His critical aversion to Lydgate's financial
troubles forfeits our sympathy, yet when fate catches up with him
('Our deeds still travel with us from afar,/And what we have been
makes us what we are') the author's fellow-feeling makes her write
with noble imaginative sympathy and regard for justice:

> Strange, piteous conflict in the soul of this unhappy man, who
> had longed for years to be better than he was – who had taken
> his selfish passions into discipline and clad them in severe robes,
> so that he had walked with them as a devout quire, till now that
> a terror had risen among them, and they could chant no longer,
> but threw out their common cries for safety.

Her pity is expressed most through the experience of Mrs Bulstrode,
who, like Dorothea after Ladislaw's fall from grace, has first to
conquer her own unhappiness. Her misery and conflict are greater.

So too is her forgiveness; it creates the most dramatic impact in the novel, and one of the great moments in English literature.

Rosamond deserves, and receives, little sympathy. Educated as a lady, she contrasts notably with Esther Lyon in *Felix Holt*. Lydgate, it seems, offers her the rank which is her 'middle-class heaven'; by enslaving him she can 'associate with relatives quite equal to the county people who looked down on the Middlemarchers'. Such snobbishness inspires the hope that Lydgate will get 'some first-class position' elsewhere, away from her inferior parents. She can play the coquette after marriage, and becomes more interested in Ladislaw than in her husband's work. Flirting with Lydgate's cousin, a baron's son, and horse-riding against her husband's advice, she loses her baby. Everything she wants is her right, and she goes her own way, behaving injudiciously when debts are mounting. When Lydgate is disgraced, the feeling that no lot is as cruel as hers makes her think of him with repugnance; his failure and abandonment of research are her triumph. He acquires a lucrative practice which alternates, according to the season, between London and a continental seaside resort. The story he tells of the Belgian anatomist Vesalius, who was maligned by Galenists, shipwrecked, and fated to die miserably (xlv) is proleptic; so too is the story he heard from Laure (xv): Rosamond becomes his basil, 'a plant which had flourished wonderfully on a murdered man's brains'. The influence of women on men for better or worse is an important theme in *Middlemarch*; and one of George Eliot's distinct achievements is the clear-cut quality of her dramatic scenes between Lydgate and this vain, self-willed woman, 'this veritably mulish domestic flower', as Henry James described her.

Lydgate's professional distinction and altruistic aims are offset by 'unreflecting egoism' and 'spots of commonness' which lead to his undoing. His 'chivalrous kindness' makes him vulnerable to women. How shallow his judgment of them can be is shown at the outset, when he finds Dorothea wanting, and Rosamond his ideal; with her he expects the kind of happiness 'known in the Arabian Nights, in which you are invited to step from the labour and discord of the street into a paradise where everything is given to you and nothing claimed'. He is overconfident, and his sense of social superiority is reflected in his taste for most expensive furniture. Farebrother's advice is lost on him; he has not noticed Mary Garth, and is certain that he will not go the way of his perfectibilian friend

Trawley, now practising at a German bath, after marrying a rich patient. Flirtation leads to an engagement he sought to avoid, circumstance proving to be on Rosamond's side, and Lydgate's intentions like 'a jelly-fish which gets melted without knowing it'. Romance dies as he repeatedly learns that he has no power over his 'bird of paradise'; extravagance leads to debts; and borrowing to the scandal which links him with Bulstrode and the death of Raffles. Had he known all the attendant facts, he could never have been certain that this could have been prevented; but his professional integrity is vitiated by his failure to investigate, having 'got into the debasing company of money obligation and selfish respects'. Despite Dorothea's encouragement, his will is sapped, and unpleasantness at home and in Middlemarch makes him renounce his ambition: 'I must do as other men do, and think what will please the world and bring in money; look for a little opening in the London crowd, and push myself; set up in a watering-place, or go to some southern town where there are plenty of idle English, and get myself puffed, — that is the sort of shell I must creep into and try to keep my soul alive in.' Mr Farebrother, with reference to his own weakness against the world, had once reminded him of the story of Hercules: how 'he came to hold the distaff, and at last wore the Nessus shirt' (xviii).

The supreme irony of *Middlemarch* inheres in Dorothea's illusion that it is possible 'to lead a grand life here — now — in England'. Her unworldliness is manifest in indifference to all jewels except those which have a spiritual meaning for her. Her idealism is destined to suffer from 'meanness of opportunity', and its unpracticality is matched by her physical short-sightedness. She has 'very childlike ideas about marriage', her ideal husband being 'a sort of father' who can teach you Hebrew if necessary. The 'dried bookworm' Casaubon seems to have greatness of soul; he is like a Protestant Pope, a Bossuet, or Augustine, to whom she can turn for understanding, sympathy, and guidance. Her ardent nature seeks principles in all knowledge, and she imagines that luminous correspondences in Casaubon's 'attractively labyrinthine' researches will deliver her from the ignorance and confusion which have resulted from her narrow education, hemmed in by the labyrinthine courses of social life. The reference to Milton's 'affable archangel' (iii) suggests that George Eliot had not forgotten similar illusions in the company of the 'archangel' Dr Brabant (20.xi.43), who (as Professor Haight has pointed out) made no headway in a work which aspired to be the key to all theologies. Believing that Latin and Greek enabled one to see 'all truth' more truly, Dorothea is perplexed to find that Casaubon is indifferent to her plans for cottage improvement; Hebrew, she therefore thinks, may be necessary 'to arrive at the core of things, and judge soundly on the social duties of the Christian'. When she is weighed down by the unintelligibility of Rome's masquerade of the ages, Casaubon provides no illumination or comfort. The difference between the imagined and the real in marriage deepens her depression. Each suffers, but remains blind to the other's inner troubles. 'We are all of us born in moral stupidity, taking the world as an udder to feed our supreme selves', the author comments (adapting one of the emblems of Francis Quarles). Dorothea rises above self and devotes herself to Casaubon, but during the brief remainder of his life she is blind to many things, his attitude to Ladislaw especially. Her real self emerges at the prospect of improvements for the community, when Garth is re-engaged as her uncle's land-agent, and (ironically) when Brooke plans to enter Parliament. At such times she can speak with a lively, characteristic directness, expressing feelings with an enthusiasm which Casaubon had suppressed. The 'grand purpose' which she sees in Lydgate's researches for medical improvement enlists her ready support.

The evidence shows that Dorothea (not the author, as is sometimes said) fell in love with Ladislaw. He inherits an artistic temperament and rebellious blood, his religion being a love of the good and beautiful and a refusal to submit to whatever he dislikes. He holds that genius is 'necessarily intolerant of fetters', that it can confidently await inspiration from the universe, and (like the painter in 'Stradivarius') that receptivity can be furthered by 'every dithyrambic fine excess', in wine, for example, or fasting, or opium. The best way 'to try and take care of all the world', he tells the altruistic Dorothea, is to enjoy life when you can, in art or anything else. He is 'a bright creature, abundant in uncertain promises', and very impressionable; the bow of a violin drawn near him cleverly would 'at one stroke change the aspect of the world for him'. Dorothea had 'the ardent woman's need to rule beneficently by making the joy of another soul', and Ladislaw's apparent readiness 'to see more in what she said than she herself saw' (xxxvii) was like sunshine to her in her tomb-like imprisonment with Casaubon. Ladislaw's dislike of Casaubon is intensified by this marriage; she is divine, her voice like that of 'a soul that

had once lived in an Aeolian harp', and he is her slave, ready
to guard her from 'whatever fire-breathing dragons might hiss
around her'. George Eliot's ironical attitude towards his romantic-
ism could hardly be more patent. His willingness to criticize Casaubon and meet Dorothea secretly reveals neither in a very favourable
light. As Brooke's political editor, he shows the talents of a
dilettante, but Dorothea believes he is concerned with justice for all
when he talks of taking up politics 'by-and-by'. He is at his best
when he scornfully rejects Bulstrode's generous offer of compensation. Fascinated by Rosamond, however, he is in danger of becoming her slave. Dorothea sees him as a man who enters everyone's
feelings, and her feelings towards him are stirred by Casaubon's
testamentary interdiction. The emphasis in her second marriage is
on feeling.

The ending is soberly realistic rather than anticlimactic. There
was a current in Dorothea's mind 'into which all thought and
feeling were apt sooner or later to flow – the reaching forward of
the whole consciousness towards the fullest truth, the least partial
good' (xx). At a time when the 'grand' or noble life was far less
possible for women than for men, Dorothea's compromise was inevitable. 'Her full nature, like that river of which Cyrus broke the
strength, spent itself in channels which had no great name on the
earth'; and many thought it a pity that 'so substantive and rare a
creature' should be known only 'in a certain circle as a wife and
mother'. In 'an imperfect social state' great feelings often take
'the aspect of error' and great faith 'the aspect of illusion'.
Ladislaw became 'an ardent public man', and a member of
Parliament; and it is a fair inference that he was inspired by
Dorothea, who took vicarious pleasure in his work. 'No life would
have been possible' for her 'which was not filled with emotion,
and she had now a life filled also with a beneficent activity'. The
novel ends in the belief that idealism is not lost: 'the effect of her
being on those around her was incalculably diffusive . . .; and
that things are not so ill with you and me as they might have
been, is half owing to the number who lived faithfully a hidden
life, and rest in unvisited tombs'. The thought which inspired the
'Miss Brooke' story is identical with that of 'O May I Join the
Choir Invisible'.

Middlemarch is as impressive as it is massive; it is memorable for
scenes of dramatic intensity and power. Differences of quality and
tone in those relative to Bulstrode, Lydgate and Rosamond,

Dorothea and Casaubon, testify to the wide range of George Eliot's sympathy. The Featherstone scenes are vividly dramatized. The picture of Dorothea in the Vatican, with the shaft of sunlight of which she is unaware, and the two artists who see her in grey drapery offset by the marble voluptuousness of the reclining Ariadne (xix), is in a different key and, particularly in retrospect, more subtle in its imaginative appeal, since it not only brings into focal relationship a critical juncture in the lives of three of the principal characters but (less obviously than the January scene outside Lowick Manor) has the extra-dimensional power of metaphor, if not of symbolism. At the other extreme there are occasional pages of prolix narrative description or pedestrian conversation on issues of little moment. More irritating are some of the authorial intrusions in the first half of the novel; it is as if George Eliot had difficulty in recovering the art of self-concealment she had markedly acquired in *Felix Holt*. Few writers can equal her ability to share relevant reflections unobtrusively with the reader or to express them in impressive figurative epigram. One of the finest examples of the latter ('If we had a keen vision and feeling of all ordinary human life, it would be like hearing the grass grow and the squirel's heart beat, and we should die of that roar which lies on the other side of the silence') is somewhat spoilt, like other reflective passages, by the author's lack of restraint. Expressions of pity for Casaubon are applied externally when his character is not livingly realized. The sarcasm of 'Let any lady who is inclined to be hard on Mrs Cadwallader inquire into the comprehensiveness of her own beautiful views' is cheap and superfluous. A satirical intervention which is unegotistical and acceptable, though of greater length, occurs in the Brooke–Dagley scene; as a realistic comment on the picturesqueness of rustic deprivation and hardship in art from the author of 'The Natural History of German Life' it reinforces Dorothea's uninhibited remarks on the unreality of her uncle's simpering drawing-room pictures in the same chapter, and illustrates in a minor way the constructive radicalism of George Eliot's approach to forces which counteract progress in the Middlemarch community. The glimpse of optimism which the end of the novel affords prompts the question which concludes *Saint Joan*: 'How long, O Lord, how long?' The inherent and wide-ranging appeal of *Middlemarch* to a higher morality than the actual makes it, in Virginia Woolf's words, 'one of the few English novels written for grown-up people'.

DANIEL DERONDA

Hardly was *Middlemarch* finished when, at the end of September 1872, George Eliot became absorbed in a spectacle which proved to be the germ of her next novel. She thought that burglary was more heroic than the gambling she saw in the hellish Kursaal at Homburg, and was distressed to see Miss Leigh, Byron's grand-niece, 'completely in the grasp of this mean, money-raking demon'. The sight of 'her young fresh face among the hags and brutally stupid men around her' brought tears to her eyes. Ironic-ally she found little dramatic 'Stoff' at the time in what she saw and heard, yet out of it developed her greatest character and scenes of arresting tragic intensity. Her reading soon after returning to England suggests that the fusion of the Gwendolen Harleth story with a Zionist theme was an early development. The following July Lewes noted that books on Jewish subjects were bought 'for Polly's novel' at Frankfurt; here and at Mainz they attended synagogue services.

The success of *Middlemarch* made George Eliot approach her next novel with great caution, and the 'simmering' towards 'another big book' was slow (5.xi.73). Preparatory research filled her with nervous fear and depression; 'she simmers and simmers, despairs and despairs, believes she can never do anything again worth doing', Lewes wrote (17.i.74). He read the opening chapters in June, but the sixteenth was not begun until January 1875. Plans for publication were on the same lines as for *Middlemarch*, and the first four monthly parts were ready early in October. On Christmas Day, after making less progress with her sixth book than she had hoped, George Eliot recorded that she had 'thought very poorly' of the work throughout, and that each part *im Werden* seemed 'less likely to be anything else than a failure'; she remembered that she had felt similarly during the writing of *Romola* and *Middlemarch*. Lewes's delight at 'seeing her free from the terrible strain' when she completed *Daniel Deronda* in June 1876 was inexpressible. The eight monthly parts were published from February to September that year, and the four-volume edition appeared shortly afterwards.

The early success of *Daniel Deronda* was even greater than that of *Middlemarch*, but George Eliot was afraid that 'the Jewish element' was 'likely to satisfy nobody'. Writing to Harriet Beecher Stowe (29.x.76), she said she had expected greater resistance 'and even repulsion'. She did not know, 'in the light of their professed principles', whether the usual attitude of Christians to Jews was 'more impious or more stupid', and thought the arrogance of the English towards all Oriental peoples 'a national disgrace'. Conscious of the great debt of western civilization to the Jews, she felt she must treat them with as much sympathy and understanding as possible. In consequence she received many expressions of gratitude; a 'highly accomplished' Christian thanked her for 'embodying the principles by which Christ wrought and will conquer'. This, she informed Madame Bodichon, was 'better than the laudation of readers who cut the book into scraps, and talk of nothing in it but Gwendolen. I meant everything in the book to be related to everything else there' (2.x.76).

Although Daniel Deronda, Mordecai, and Mirah are idealized, George Eliot ensures that her presentation of the Jews is mixed; her most repulsive character is a Jew. In an illustrated article (*Nineteenth-Century Fiction*, March 1976) Hugh Witemeyer has shown how she uses Italian paintings to ennoble and spiritualize her Jewish leaders in contrast to the more worldly English. Titian's *Tribute Money* (xl) provides 'another sort of contrast' than that between Mordecai and Deronda but, if any comparison with Christ (suggested by 'a man little over thirty') is intended, it relates to the more spiritual visionary and not to Deronda, who combines refinement with strength such as may be found in Titian's *The Young Man with a Glove* (xvii). English society is represented in the Mallinger family portraits (xvi), and the difference between Deronda and a portrait of Sir Hugo is noticed by Gwendolen; to her mother the former is a striking young man, reminiscent of Italian paintings (xxix). Gwendolen's pride and vanity are suggested by her posing after the style of famous actresses in fashionable pictures of St Cecilia (iii) and Hermione (vi). Sir Joshua Reynolds would have been glad to take her portrait, we are told; and Hans Meyrick is engaged to paint Sir Hugo's daughters in the Gainsborough style. (His reference to Gwendolen as 'the Vandyke duchess' and to Grandcourt as 'the duke' prompts the question whether the character and role of Grandcourt were in any way influenced by Browning's 'My Last Duchess'.) The pictorial dichotomy illustrates the two worlds of which Deronda becomes more and more aware, and they are as dissimilar as 'a portico with lights and lacqueys' and the door of a tent where 'the only splendour' comes from 'the mysterious inaccessible stars' (lxi).

Daniel Deronda differs most obviously from George Eliot's previous novels in presenting a distinctly higher social range of life and in reflecting the contemporary world with which she had become more familiar. Pointers to such events as the American Civil War (ending in April 1865), the culminating victory in the Austro–Prussian War (1866), and the Church Rate Abolition Bill, show that the period of the story extends little over two years from October 1864. Grandcourt first encounters Gwendolen at the Archery Meeting in July 1865; she is observed gambling at Leubronn in September; the dance at Abbot's Topping takes place on New Year's Eve, seven weeks after her marriage; and Deronda meets her for the last time the following October. Settings are drawn from London, Germany, and Italy, but they belong chiefly to 'Wessex', which, though it takes its general features from downland country in southern England, is composite, including for example a coal-mining area and impressions derived from Lacock Abbey. Comparison with *Adam Bede* accentuates the lack of emphasis on the community, the minimizing of landscape description, and the author's expert economy in producing scenic effects. Daniel Deronda is central to the novel; only through him are the complicated narrative strands knitted together. Yet the main drama concerns Gwendolen. In concentrating on the life of the heroine for about a year, and revealing the rift between her outer and inner worlds, George Eliot was able to develop a single tragedy more fully than she had chosen to do in *Felix Holt* and *Middlemarch*, thereby achieving her greatest triumph in psychological presentation and in dramatic crises of highly imaginative power.

Adopting classical precedents, she begins her story *in medias res* with the gambling observed by Deronda, and his restoration of Gwendolen's necklace. The hall is gas-poisoned; the equality to which the European gamblers are reduced is vulturine; it is as if they had 'eaten on the insane root/That takes the reason prisoner'. Gwendolen plays recklessly because she is 'bored to death'. 'Faites votre jeu, mesdames et messieurs', speaks 'the automatic voice of destiny', as if from *Vanity Fair*. The scene succeeds in its two ulterior purposes: it excites curiosity in the flashbacks which follow, and it is prefigurative. The heroine will watch 'chances' before she accepts Grandcourt; on the morning of her wedding she is as wrought up as when Deronda watched her critically and she began to lose at the gambling-table; the 'ambitious vanity and desire for luxury within her which it would take a great deal of slow poisoning to kill' makes her stand 'at the game of life with many eyes upon her, daring everything to win much'. The 'great gambling loss' she sustains in marriage is far beyond her reckoning. She had resented Daniel's interference, but he reflects her conscience, and she cannot forget him; she has no one else to whom she can turn for spiritual guidance. The question for him as he tries to assess her beauty in the gaming-hall is whether good or evil is dominant in her expression. Her dress gives her 'the ensemble du serpent' (reminiscent of Bertha in 'The Lifted Veil'), and the sinuosity of a Lamia is seen again in her figure and drapery when she is on her way to sell the necklace with reckless intent to continue her gambling. Balked by Deronda's intervention, she obeys her mother's call to return home after the family's ruin through the commercial gambling of Grapnell & Co. She enters the 'long Satanic masquerade' of her Grandcourt marriage 'with an intoxicated belief in its disguises', and does not escape before being filled with 'shrieking fear lest she herself had become one of the evil spirits who were dropping their human mummery and hissing around her with serpent tongues' (lxiv).

Childhood uprootedness is a significant, but not equal, factor in the development of both hero and heroine; it combines with upbringing to produce notably different results. Deronda knows nothing of his origin; he does not know that his mother, a beautiful and ambitious singer and actress, did not wish to marry or have a child, that he had lost his father at an early age, and that Sir Hugo Mallinger, who had wished to marry his mother, had been his guardian since he was little more than two years old. Much turns on Deronda's ignorance of his Jewish blood; his mother had insisted that he should be brought up as an Englishman, and that Sir Hugo should never divulge his parentage. The mystery of his birth had made Daniel assume that he was illegitimate, and the apparent confirmation of his illegitimacy arising from the prospective inheritance of Sir Hugo's estates by his nephew Grandcourt had increased his sympathies towards the wrongs and sufferings of others. His affectionate nature owes much to his guardian's genuine love and friendship. Gwendolen Harleth loves no one but her widowed mother; subject to fears, she turns to her for affection, and is treated like 'a princess in exile'; she is 'the spoiled child'. Her father, whose family was 'so high as to take no notice of her mamma', died when she was a babe. She had disliked her stepfather. Having hurt her mother by asking why she remarried, she had never dared to inquire about her father again. Except for two years at 'a showy school', where she had been given pride of place on all occasions of display, she had been debarred by a roving life from all opportunity of making herself important; and the lack of a home around which memories 'inwrought with affection' might have grown had been a further handicap in her emotional development. She was completely unsympathetic to her four half-sisters, and determined to have her way in life. Though her conscience was retarded, she was not remorseless, having a disagreeable recollection of strangling her sister's canary 'in a final fit of exasperation' because its shrill singing had continually interrupted her own. (This incident in the life of a child indulged by her mother has its counterpart in the boyhood of Zeluco, a hero who does not learn the folly of his ways until he is at death's door.)

No change for the better takes place in Gwendolen before her marriage. Egoistic desire and habitual command make her assume that she can 'manage her own destiny'. Mamma is obedient to her bidding, and the housekeeper refers to her as 'her Royal Highness'. She has the ability both to charm and inspire fear; mirrors continually indulge her vanity, and she loves to pose in *tableaux vivants*. Twice during such acting she is terrified when a hinged panel opens to disclose the picture of an upturned dead face and a figure fleeing. Although, by anticipating her recollections of Grandcourt's death, this may appear a bold prolepsis, it is given artistic validity in its context as a foreshadowing of Gwendolen's need after marriage to pose in public and masquerade a torment of murderous intent and fear. She is a strange mixture of strength and weakness; she rules in a petty world, and her experience is limited; she has no religion but suffers 'fits of spiritual dread', is afraid of solitude, and senses 'immeasurable existence aloof from her', in the midst of which she is 'helplessly incapable of asserting herself'. Though being 'sued or hopelessly sighed for as a bride' is 'an indispensable and agreeable guarantee of womanly power' to her, her ambition is not in marriage but beyond it; she is afraid of matrimony and domestic fetters. Rex Gascoigne's callow love provides an episode which stresses her 'fierceness of maidenhood', a sexual frowardness or repulsion which augurs ill for her marriage with anyone. The perception that he wishes to be tender to her makes her 'curl up and harden like a sea-anemone at the touch of a finger'; she cannot bear anyone to be near her except her mother.

'There is nothing worth living for', she sobs; she can't love people; she hates them. The thought is repeated when she refuses to marry Grandcourt, after discovering how basely he has treated Mrs Glasher. Far more mature than Gwendolen, Mrs Glasher has no physical inhibitions; even in an interview in which she suffers torture, she has a power of persuasion over Grandcourt which is beyond Gwendolen's nature.

When Gwendolen is invited to join the Archery Club, she claims to enjoy nothing more than taking aim and hitting; she can't help hitting, she says, when Grandcourt is expected. He would not have the slightest power over her, she thinks. Handsome and superficially polished, this creature of 'refined negations' speaks with a languid drawl; if he is animated, it is not by feeling or wide interests but by will, and when his will is peremptory he speaks in subdued, distinct tones. He had hunted tigers, and regarded human beings, male and female, as odious brutes by and large. He is determined to marry, and have the mastery over, Gwendolen, knowing that she consents from straitened circumstances and in full cognizance of his previous de facto marriage. The sudden, rather startling appearance by the Whispering Stones of Mrs Glasher and two of his children, at the meeting arranged by Lush between her and Gwendolen, suggests an incongruous evocation faintly reminiscent of Scott. Grandcourt visits his mistress at Gadsmere in the hope of recovering his mother's diamonds, which long ago he had confided to her and which now he has promised Gwendolen; and a moving picture shows Mrs Glasher, after he had applied 'the thumbscrew' by telling her of his imminent marriage, pressing her face against the hard cold window, causing her children, who think she wants them, to run from their play and stand in front of her, their faces upturned expectantly. Mrs Glasher recovers and persuasively insists that she will send the diamonds in accordance with her wishes. Gwendolen receives them on the evening after her wedding. She has broken the pledge she made at the Whispering Stones not to marry Grandcourt, and is afraid that Deronda will now be as critical as he had been of her gambling. Opening in feverish excitement the packet containing the diamonds, she finds a letter which tells her that Grandcourt has 'a withered heart', and that her chance of happiness will be buried in the same grave as the writer's. 'You took him with your eyes open. The willing wrong you have done me will be your curse.' Gwendolen leans towards the fire; the letter is caught in a great draught of flame, the casket falls, and the diamonds roll out on the floor. She cannot discern herself in the mirror, only reflections of 'many women petrified white'. The poison imagery associated with gambling at Leubronn recurs: 'here were poisoned gems, and the poison had entered into this poor young creature'. Grandcourt appears, dressed for dinner; the sight of him brings on a new nervous shock, and Gwendolen screams 'again and again with hysterical violence'. 'The Furies had crossed his threshold', the author adds; and they do so with more convincing power than in T. S. Eliot's plays. In a few weeks she can no more resist her husband's mastery than she could 'the benumbing effect from the touch of a torpedo' (an image found in the opening pages of Dr Moore's *Zeluco*); her own will dissipated by fear, she finds herself in the grip of 'a will like that of a crab or a boa-constrictor which goes on pinching or crushing without alarm at thunder'. Later, as Gwendolen rides with Grandcourt in Rotten Row, she is shocked to see him ignore Mrs Glasher and two of his children; only his death can be her deliverance, but she foresees him always living in domination over her. In the end she knows, as Mrs Glasher has known, that Grandcourt's words have 'the power of thumbscrews and the cold touch of the rack'.

At the time of her engagement, when she expected to be the dominant partner, Grandcourt's 'strongest wish was to be completely master of this creature'. The two horses on which they ride are 'the symbols of command and luxury', and George Eliot uses this metaphor to vivify and emphasize relationships in scene and action. In some important respects (as may be seen in the final paragraph of FH.i) Gwendolen resembles Mrs Transome before marriage. A propos of the marriage expected between her son and Esther Lyon, Mrs Transome says (xxxix): 'This girl has a fine spirit – plenty of fire and pride and wit. Men like such captives, as they like horses that champ the bit and paw the ground.' The first statement is appropriate to Gwendolen during her engagement, and the second to Grandcourt from first to last. Riding as an extended metaphor is used when she accompanies Rex Gascoigne with the hounds and, confident that no ill-luck will befall her, leaves him behind while she keeps 'up with the best'; Rex falls and is injured, but not irremediably, and Gwendolen is amused. Her second outing is with Grandcourt when she is not prepared to sacrifice her freedom; she refuses to take a leap, checks her horse as she counters his prelude to a proposal, and brings him and his horse to a halt as he damns her to himself (xiii). Her rejection of him, after meeting Mrs Glasher, follows, but when she returns from Leubronn the thought that she can avoid demeaning employment, help her mother, and persuade Grandcourt to make a liberal restitution to Mrs Glasher, overcomes principle; Grandcourt's two horses are beautiful in contrast with 'the ugliness of poverty and humiliation at which she had been looking close'. She is conscience-racked and vaguely alive to the existence of 'avenging powers'. The next morning a diamond ring and a large cheque from Grandcourt, with his assurance that her mother will stay at Offendene, restore her spirits, and she resolves to act courageously as if she were on horseback. She and Grandcourt have a glorious gallop, and the wedding-day is fixed. Checked or confident, the riding parallels states of mind, as is seen again when Gwendolen, after feeling that she has deprived not only Mrs Glasher and her children but also Deronda of their inheritance, shakes off depression and rides, enjoying the hunt until conscience returns and she reins to be overtaken by Deronda, whose general views on her dilemma she learns through reference to gambling (xxix). When there is nothing more to conceal between her and her jealous husband, she is indifferent to the terms of his will, and rides with him as if nothing had happened, intent on showing that she could match him 'in ignoring any ground for excitement'. Just before his death he is 'perfectly satisfied' that he holds his wife 'with bit and bridle', and she is certain that he will have the mastery as long as he lives.

The metaphor has occasional variants, the most interesting being that of a chariot with two riders. Gwendolen's first thought is that she will 'mount the chariot and drive the plunging horses herself', her husband giving countenance with folded arms. When, before marriage, she is hampered by her knowledge of Mrs Glasher's claims, it is 'as if she had consented to mount a chariot where another held the reins', but she ignores her fears, and finds the horses in the chariot she has mounted going at full speed.

With wider reference music also reflects attitudes and states of mind. Its general pattern accentuates the difference between self-centred ambition and self-subjugation to art, to interest in others, or to great causes. In conjunction with singing, it helps to link the main parts of a complicated story. Daniel, like Mirah, has 'a fine musical instinct' but no wish to be a great singer and appear before the public as if he were 'a wonderful toy'; in her girlhood she had found it painful 'to sing for show at any minute' as if she were 'a musical box'. Daniel meets her one July evening, as Grandcourt does Gwendolen, but in sadly contrasting circumstances. Nothing expresses them better than the words from Dante he sings as he guides his boat to the side of the Thames to avoid an oncoming barge, and catches sight of Mirah in despair; later he rescues her when she is about to drown herself. As a singer she has acquired an excellence which earns Klesmer's high approval. The 'subdued but searching pathos' of her 'Per pietà non dirmi addio' shows 'that essential of perfect singing, the making one oblivious of art or manner, and only possessing one with the song'. Deronda is listening, and the author's intention is clear when she writes, 'It was the sort of voice that gives the impression of being meant like a bird's wooing for an audience near and beloved' (xxxii). When Mirah sings the song again, Gwendolen is present, and Deronda knows that her rescue will be 'much more difficult than that of the wanderer by the river'. 'It was as if he had a vision of himself besought with outstretched arms and cries, while he was caught by the waves and compelled to mount the vessel bound for a far-off coast' (xlv – another proleptic image).

Unlike his father, who was 'all lovingness and affection', Deronda's mother, a great singer and actress, is an ambitious egoist. All men except her father had been subject to her. In reaction to his insistence on her marriage, she had been opposed to love and subjection to any man. She did not desire a child and, contrary to her father's wishes, determined that Daniel should never know that he was a Jew. Similarly, though antithetically cast in many ways to this proud princess, Lapidoth brings up his daughter Mirah 'in disregard – even in dislike of her Jewish origin'. In self-centred ambition and love of admiration and command, the princess clearly resembles Gwendolen before she suffers; and music, one of those young ladies' accomplishments in which the latter is thought to excel, is used to illustrate her character in scenes resonant with metaphorical overtones. Gwendolen does not hesitate to sing before Herr Klesmer at the Arrowpoints', or to insist on his frank appraisal. He has to tell her that her note-production is poor, and that her song shows 'a puerile state of culture', with no depth or 'sense of the universal'. Gwendolen is not irredeemable, and it is significant that she has 'fulness of nature enough to feel the power' of Klesmer's playing. When intent on taking up a career, she seeks his advice on becoming a singer and actress, thinking she can 'achieve substantiality for herself and know gratified ambition' without the ties of marriage. Klesmer is sorry for the girl; she must submit to sustained discipline without guarantee of success; above all she must forget self and thoughts of celebrity, making artistic excellence her sole aim. Tormented by wrong-doing, she believes that Deronda does not think highly of her. He encourages her to practise her music. Life would be poor, he says, 'if we were reduced for all our pleasure to our own performances', and did not aim privately at 'what is good'. 'Excellence encourages one about life generally; it shows the spiritual wealth of the world.' Here we approach the main theme of the novel, and it becomes more specific when he says, 'Lives are enlarged in different ways. I daresay some would never get their eyes opened if it were not for a violent shock from the consequences of their own actions.' Metaphorical meaning is dramatized as Gwendolen slips on to the music-stool, and looks up at him with pain in her eyes, 'like a wounded animal asking help'. Later, when he returns to her refusal to cultivate music 'for the sake of a private joy in it', the parallelism is reinforced: there is no spiritual wealth for 'souls pauperised by inaction'; the refuge she needs is 'the higher, the religious life . . . something more than our own appetites and vanities'.

Gwendolen grew up with 'a naïve delight in her fortunate self' which she frequently indulged before a mirror. Just before Klesmer's arrival for consultation on her career, she advances slowly towards her mirrored image and thinks, 'I *am* beautiful'. The effect of her disappointment when he leaves, is that all memories, all music, and even the reflection of herself in the glass seem 'no better than the packed-up shows of a departing fair', despite an assertion of her better self. Seven weeks after her marriage she is no longer inclined 'to kiss her fortunate image in the glass'. Grandcourt's innuendo on Deronda's relations with Mirah is so disturbing that she does not recognise herself in the glass panels before she sets out to discover the truth. Her remark 'Ah! I must be changed. I have not looked at myself', when she is recovering from shock and self-incrimination after Grandcourt's death, confirms the process of regeneration, the spiritual salvation 'as by fire' to which George Eliot refers (18.xi.75).

When Catherine Arrowpoint, a pianist of some distinction, defies her parents and risks the loss of a fortune by choosing to marry her tutor Herr Klesmer, she affords a delightful contrast to

Gwendolen in every way. She can distinguish the true from the trappings. Mr Arrowpoint is marked by 'nullity of face and perfect tailoring' (of *Sartor Resartus* extraction); his wife, 'the heiress of a fortune gained by some moist or dry business in the city', is a lady of literary pretensions, whose patronage of Klesmer provides cultural éclat to impress neighbouring families. His eccentricities are thoroughly acceptable until Mrs Arrowpoint learns that he is her prospective son-in-law, when she tells Catherine that her father will horsewhip him off the premises. Removing his cigar from his mouth, Mr Arrowpoint rises to the occasion by saying 'This will never do, Cath.' Disgust raises racial antipathy as it does with Ladislaw in *Middlemarch*; the great musician becomes 'nobody knows what — a gypsy, a Jew, a mere bubble of the earth' to Mrs Arrowpoint. Her husband expects Catherine to marry a gentleman like himself; they must do as other people do, and 'think of the nation and the public good'. When the Arrowpoints accept the marriage, Lady Pentreath remarks, 'As to *mésalliance*, there's no blood on any side. Old Admiral Arrowpoint was one of Nelson's men, you know — a doctor's son. And we all know how the mother's money came.' The satire could have come from Jane Austen. The contrast between Klesmer's genius and Arrowpoint's conventional insignificance is amusing but less important than that with Gwendolen's elegant, torpid, arrogantly superior, sadistic husband. Klesmer's liveliest encounter is with one of the Arrowpoints' guests, Mr Bolt, a politician and Philistine with 'the general solidity and suffusive pinkness of a healthy Briton on the central table-land of life'. Surprised by Klesmer's outburst on 'the lack of idealism in English politics, which left all mutuality between distant races to be determined simply by the need of a market', Bolt assumes that he is a political refugee, a Panslavist. Klesmer replies sarcastically, 'No; my name is Elijah. I am the wandering Jew', thereby touching on the theme of the book, which offsets a self-centred, privileged, and even haughty form of English provincialism against enthusiasm for any larger, nobler cause. When Catherine, trying to make the most of the situation, tells Bolt that Klesmer 'looks forward to a fusion of the races', the politician answers blandly, 'I was sure he had too much talent to be a mere musician.' Klesmer's reply that creative artists are not ingenious puppets 'who live in a box and look out on the world only when it is gaping for amusement' recalls the standpoint of Deronda and Mirah; his claim that they 'make the age' as much as do legislators or any other public men echoes Shelley's peroration in *A Defence of Poetry*. The worldliness of the Church is seen in Mr Gascoigne, who does all in his power to persuade Gwendolen to marry Grandcourt, 'aristocratic heirship' excepting the latter from 'the ordinary standards of moral judgments'. Mrs Gascoigne stops short in counting all that Grandcourt is heir to, and the author wittily adds, 'It seemed a pity there was nothing for the fifth finger.' Another piquant observation (based, no doubt, on memories of Thornton Lewes's papers) relates to an examination which might disclose a link between 'the welfare of our Indian Empire' and 'a quotable knowledge of Browne's Pastorals'. Generally, however, George Eliot is more satirically successful in dramatization than in direct comment.

If Klesmer represents art on one side of *Daniel Deronda*, Hans Meyrick, a lesser light, represents it on the other. Both are eccentric, and Hans supplies some comic relief, though his fanciful exuberance is inflated to tedious lengths. It is no accident that the 'fusion of races' motif is seen in the Klesmer–Arrowpoint marriage and in the unstinted kindness of Mrs Meyrick towards both Mirah and her brother Mordecai. Deronda and Hans fall in love with Mirah: Hans is confident of success despite her Jewish loyalties; Deronda is less sanguine, and needs Hans's disclosure that she is jealous of Gwendolen before venturing to declare his love. The happy ending is too easily engineered; fortunately it is not prolonged, for idealization of character brings it dangerously near the edge of sentimentality. Even so, George Eliot has taken care not to present an unbalanced picture of the Jews. Mirah's father is a despicable wretch, with no genuine thought for anyone but himself; at the end of the novel he dramatically illustrates the dehumanizing motif which is to be found in the opening scene at Leubronn, his gambling appetite appearing in a 'final, imperious stage' of degradation evocative of 'the unjoyous dissipation of demons, seeking diversion on the burning marl of perdition' (lxvi). Deronda had come to the conclusion that the Jews retained 'the virtues and vices of a long-oppressed race'. Frankfort presents glimpses of them which are less flattering than the Cohen family, who are worthy in many respects but very mercenary. Little Jacob has acquired the appetite for money at an early age, and his tricks are amusing for a while; George Eliot has him performing while the visionary Mordecai reads religious poetry. Suddenly he catches sight of the lad on his hands, his feet in the air, mountebank style, while he picks up a bright farthing with his lips; the sight is like 'a Satanic grin' upon Mordecai's prayer, and provokes a remonstrance against Jews who worship Mammon. A working men's club debate which enables the author to present the pros and cons of the Zionist movement (xlii) is a further indication of her anxiety not to appear partial on a controversial subject, but history has given a savage double irony to Mordecai's forecast that 'there will be a land set for a halting-place of enmities, a neutral ground for the East as Belgium is for the West'.

Improbabilities verging on the miraculous occur in the Deronda story. The meeting of the hero and his father's friend in Frankfort is a remarkable coincidence; and it is more amazing that Deronda's search for Mirah's brother soon leads him to Mordecai. Thereafter the ultimate discovery that the latter is Mirah's brother is predictable. What is special to Mordecai is his intuitive conviction from the first that Deronda is the Jewish leader for whom he has long been waiting. We are not in Francis Thompson's world of spiritual wonder where 'the many-splendoured thing' is seen as 'Christ walking on the water,/Not of Genesareth, but Thames' but in a London where a Jewish visionary with the prescience of a Samuel or of Jesus himself may be found in a second-hand bookshop. A hint of a resemblance between Mordecai and Christ has already been indicated with reference to Titian's *Tribute Money*; and it is notable that George Eliot emphasizes the poetry of the real and ordinary in connection, not with the world of Gwendolen (which is associated with hell and purgatory) but with the first meetings of Deronda and Mirah (xix) and of Deronda and Mordecai (xxxiii). As a result of watching sunrise and sunset from its bridges, Mordecai, who is keenly alive to the poetry of London views, has come to expect that 'the Being answering to his need' will appear as one approaching, back turned towards him, and 'darkly painted against a golden sky'. This is how, after waiting five years for the realization of his dream, he sees 'the prefigured friend' rowing towards Blackfriars Bridge, then looking up at him and signalling. Deronda has paused to draw his cape over him, and as he does so he recognises his friend above the parapet, the 'spiritual eagerness' of his emaciated face illuminated by the western light 'into startling distinctness and brilliancy' (xl). As evening initiates the Jewish Sabbath, so the poetry of this climactic scene proclaims the arrival of Mordecai's 'new life'. For him the bridge is a place where spiritual messengers meet. He himself is a bridge, hearing the prayers of past and future generations; when he dies, his soul will join Deronda's, and 'its work will be perfected' (xliii). After the final meeting with his mother, Deronda thinks that his grandfather must have been 'almost as exceptional a Jew as Mordecai', one of those men whose visions mould the world, 'feeding the more passive life which without them would dwindle and shrivel into the narrow tenacity of insects, unshaken by thoughts beyond the reaches of their antennae'. Kinship makes Deronda aware of the fulfilling mission for which he has long been searching, and he espouses Zionism, with the aim of establishing a national centre in the Levant.

Lacking the dramatic tension and psychological depth which characterize the Gwendolen story, the Jewish sections of the novel (from which the Meyrick scenes are inseparable) inevitably suffer; they have the disadvantage too of not promoting the main action for considerable periods. Their occasional liveliness rarely rises above the mediocre, though some of the Cohen scenes are colourfully presented; apart from Mordecai, they show little imaginative development. Subjectively expressed, Mirah's jealousy of Gwendolen rouses empathetic response, but a long narrative summary of her rather melodramatic youth, in monologue with minimal interruptions (xx), contrasts unfavourably in flashback technique with the dramatic presentation of Deronda's two interviews with his mother. George Eliot, one feels, was too shackled by Jewish researches to give some of the scenes adequate time for both imaginative emergence and critical appraisal. Her anxiety to appear impartial on the Zionist question leads to an interesting debate, but it is never fictionally alive until Mordecai, inspired by Deronda's presence, finally speaks with impassioned faith. The previous chapter (xli), giving Deronda's musings on Mordecai's conviction that he is a Jew, moves from 'negative whisperings' to uncertainty, but much of it falls flat because it consists of authorial reasoning, assertion, and illustration ('And since the unemotional intellect may carry us into a mathematical dreamland where nothing is but what is not, perhaps an emotional intellect may have absorbed into its passionate vision of possibilities some truth of what will be . . .'). Paragraphs of this kind invade consecutive chapters (xxxvii, xxxviii), as if they had spilled over from chapter epigraphs, the excessive length of some of which suggests a growing habit rather than a critical creativeness.

The wider and deeper psychological penetration of the Gwendolen–Grandcourt story shows the author's greater rapport with her subject. It spreads to minor characters such as Mr Gascoigne and Mrs Davilow, to Rex when he allows his hopes of Gwendolen to revive briefly after Grandcourt's death, and pre-eminently to the tragic Mrs Glasher. It can create sympathy even for Mr Lush.

The part assigned to Deronda would not be easy for any author, but to regard him as a failure is uncharitable. R. L. Stevenson's condemnation ('that melancholy puppy and humbug', 'the literary abomination of desolation in the way of manhood') suggests unbridled feeling. Deronda's relationship with his guardian Sir Hugo Mallinger is engagingly drawn, and does much to explain his general happiness and refinement. George Eliot shows both a delicate sympathy and a subtle psychological insight in communicating a sensitive adolescent's brooding over the mystery of his parentage and the fear of illegitimacy which it arouses. 'The sense of an entailed disadvantage', rather like Byron's susceptibility about his deformed foot, makes the imagination of such a youth tender (xvi). The private sufferings of one brought up with many advantages creates a natural sympathy for others, which combines with inherited inclinations (defined ultimately by discovery of his Jewish kinship) to make him respond wholeheartedly to a particular cause, 'his judgment no longer wandering in the mazes of impartial sympathy, but choosing, with the noble partiality which is man's best strength, the closer fellowship that makes sympathy practical'; and the author has not failed 'to thread the hidden pathways of feeling and thought' leading to the action she envisages in the Promethean references of epigraphs xvi and xxxviii. Daniel's sacrifice of self-interest for his relatively indigent friend Hans Meyrick reveals a rare but not improbable nobility; Sir Hugo warns him not to be too 'unselfish and generous'. His first view of Mirah makes him think of girl-tragedies throughout the world, hidden 'as if they were but tragedies of the copse or hedgerow, where the helpless drag wounded wings forsakenly, and streak the shadowed moss with the red moment-hand of their own death'. His willingness to rescue, to 'draw strongly at any thread in the hopelessly entangled scheme of things' at this juncture (xvii), recalls contrastingly the self-seeking designs of Gwendolen at about the same time, after her first triumphal meeting and dance with Grandcourt (xi): 'Could there be a slenderer, more insignificant thread in human history than this consciousness of a girl, busy with her small inferences', excited by 'blind visions' and unaware of the 'universal kinship' of mourners in the United

States with families on the edge of starvation in Lancashire? Unlike Mirah's, her rescue will be moral and spiritual.

Deronda regards Grandcourt as 'that remnant of a human being', and their facial contrast, the one richly tinted and expressing 'calm intensity of life', the other colourless and inanimate, accentuates Daniel's humanity. Gwendolen, afflicted with guilt, can turn only to him for guidance; he becomes part of her conscience, and her hunger to consult him makes him her confessor or 'priest'. Daniel is embarrassed, thinks at first that she is coquettish, and finds it difficult to help her; he dreads 'the weight of this woman's soul flung upon his own' when she is intent on confessing the extremity of her guilt. At times he is indeed reduced to the role of 'the Prince of Prigs', as Stevenson describes him. This occurs when the author, making him her mouthpiece, is unequal to the crisis: 'Try to care about something in this vast world besides the gratification of small selfish desires'; 'Turn your fear into a safeguard. . . . It may make consequences passionately present to you. Try to take hold of your sensibility, and use it as if it were a faculty, a vision.' It is little wonder that Deronda wishes 'to escape standing as a critic outside the activities of men'. His final advice is that the vision of 'injurious, selfish action' which has come to Gwendolen in the springtime of her life should be turned into a preparation for the future. She has not thought of it without him; 'we are all apt to fall into this passionate egoism of imagination, not only towards our fellow-men, but towards God', George Eliot adds, with a daring appendage to the relevant generalization. Gwendolen's dependence on Deronda is wholly spiritual, and when she realizes that separation is inevitable she proves more equal to it than he. Her 'recoverable nature' has been tried by purgatorial fire; she rises above self, ready to face a new life, the better for having known him.

'But for complete enjoyment the outward and the inner must concur' (x); they did so when Gwendolen moved confidently in the narrow 'sphere of fashion' before she gambled foolishly in marriage. How they will concur in her new life is left to the imagination. The expiatory consequences of her rashness are reiterated; they are the subject of the epigraph to the book. Unlike Madonna Mia's (liv), her 'process of purgatory' is on earth. She does not suffer so much from Grandcourt's mastery and 'refined negations' as from a sense of her own guilt and nemesis; her 'fatal meshes' are 'woven within more closely than without', and the climax is reached when she is prisoned with Grandcourt on a yacht in the Mediterranean. Just when Deronda is about to discover his altruistic mission in the wider world, the last reduction of an egoist who knows that by selling 'her truthfulness and sense of justice' to a man whose absolutism is so complete that he holds them 'throttled into silence' is imaged in the 'tiny plank-island' which they share, mainly in well-bred silence; so she is borne along, 'gliding on and no help — always into solitude with *him*, always from deliverance'. The immediate contrast is between her outer and inner worlds: 'the glory of sea and sky softening as if with boundless love around her', the luxury of the yacht, and boredom, oppression, despair, murderous thoughts, terror. 'What sort of Moslem paradise would quiet the terrible fury of moral repulsion and cowed resistance which, like an eating pain intensifying into torture, concentrates the mind in that poisonous misery?' Thoughts 'like furies preparing the deed that they would straightway avenge' come 'quick, quick', just as recollections of Grandcourt, mingling horror with triumph, agitated Gwendolen when the drift towards her engagement began (xxvi). She overcomes the temptation to murder, but her guilt is compounded, and she can never forget that she has killed him in her thoughts. The 'evil prayers' are with her when he is struck overboard; she sees her wish outside her, and her heart leaps. When, after hesitating, she jumps in to rescue him, it is as if she is leaping against both herself and her crime, acting against the demon which possessed her.

Unlike Rosamond Lydgate, who never ceases to exert her hard egocentric will for a superior life of ease and comfort, Gwendolen conquers self and becomes indifferent to the life of affluence and command which had once been her ambition. Through suffering and the influence of Deronda her character is strengthened. It is true that his adoption of the Zionist cause makes her feel more solitary and helpless in a widening world, and that remorse transforms her into 'a melancholy statue of the Gwendolen whose laughter had once been so ready when others were grave'. The recurring statue image (from *The Winter's Tale*) augurs a new life; and the shock of separation proves that 'the struggling regenerative process' enables Gwendolen to welcome dislodgment from 'supremacy in her own world'. The manner in which she accepts the loss of Deronda confirms the assurance she gives her mother that she is 'going to live'. The conclusion is open-ended, but decidedly truer to life (and more modern) than that of *The Mill on the Floss*:

it is more hopeful than that of *Middlemarch*. In the one, George Eliot presents a full-length portrayal of her heroine from childhood; in the other, memorable dramatic scenes in the lives of several characters. Showing greater confidence, it seems, she concentrated in *Daniel Deronda* as never before on a relatively brief critical period in the life of a single person. If one wishes that she had concentrated on it even more, and made less of the Jewish story, it is because Gwendolen is her supreme creation, the central figure in her greatest tragic fiction.

Later Essays and Notes

Towards the end of the sixteenth century Isaac Casaubon, editor of Theophrastus's *Charactères*, was Professor of Greek at Geneva; and here, during the winter of 1849–50, Mary Ann Evans became acquainted with his edition of the Greek philosopher's sketches. Her characters in *Impressions of Theophrastus Such* (1879) are also types, as their names indicate, but they are presented in more extended form, and are based on her own observations. The success of these essays was due more to her prestige as a novelist than to their intrinsic merit. They are finished compositions, and the relevance of some of them a century later has probably increased, but imaginative vitality seems rather a spent force, and the confident aggressiveness and trenchant wit which had made George Eliot a formidable reviewer have given way to tactful timidity and reasonable persuasiveness. There may be wisdom in this, but she would have profited had she followed the example of *The Spectator* or Charles Lamb more consistently, by giving colour and substance to her views through imagined or recollected experience. She writes too readily in the abstract, and the Theophrastian characters she introduces are with few exceptions rather too incorporeal to make a lasting impression.

At the outset an allusion to an accident in the Alps and to other 'items' that shaped the semi-fictitious author's life makes one realize how much vividness is lost behind a philosophical screen which reminds George Eliot that in self-presentation she could appear like one with 'solemn face and ridiculous legs' dancing a hornpipe as in youth and imagining a high place for herself in the beholders' estimation. When a writer is famous, it is archly nugatory of her in a book she means to be published under her familiar pen-name to question whether it is to the advantage of an opinion if she is known to hold it. This fictional diffidence or affectation does not preclude the piquant satire of

It is to be borne in mind that I am not rich, have neither stud nor cellar, and no very high connections such as give to a look of imbecility a certain prestige of inheritance through a titled line; just as 'the Austrian lip' confers a grandeur of historical associations on a kind of feature which might make us reject an advertising footman.

Yet the general tone is fastidiously serious and modest. The circumstances of George Eliot's life made her averse to autobiography, and Rousseau's *Confessions* had taught her the illusoriness of self-revelation; 'half our impressions of his character come not from what he means to convey, but from what he unconsciously enables us to discern'. She therefore adopts the humble stance of one whose realization of her shortcomings, and of the certainty that she is unaware of many of them, places her in the ranks of her fellow-men. There could be 'at least half the truth' in the supposition that 'a gratified sense of superiority is at the root of barbarous laughter', and she accordingly commends 'a loving laughter in which the only recognised superiority is that of the ideal self, the God within, holding the mirror and the scourge for our own pettiness as well as our neighbours' '.

The general tendency of these moral essays is towards 'that surpassing subtilty' of abstract argument which, as the author realizes, invites popular neglect. Nowhere does she avoid it more than in 'Looking Backward'. The style is smooth rather than arresting, and the fiction is extended, the author posing as the son of a rural rector. From Theophrastus he has learned that he is 'the better off for possessing Athenian life solely as an inodorous fragment of antiquity'; he is detached enough to acknowledge that every age has its ugliness as well as its beauty. There is not much enchantment in looking back three-quarters of a century, but the period it recalls, 'the time of my father's youth', can never be prosaic, 'for it came to my imagination first through his memories'. In this veiled autobiography one sees the girl Mary Evans riding with her father on his outdoor business, or learning to read the alphabet of England 'among the midland villages and markets, along by the tree-studded hedgerows, and where the heavy barges seem in the distance to float mysteriously among the rushes and the feathered grass'. In his dismissal of 'noisy teachers of revolutionary doctrine' as 'a variable mixture of the fool and the scoundrel', Robert Evans is unmistakable; equally so, in his ability to consort with miners, weavers, field-labourers, and aristocrats.

George Eliot finds a correspondence between the national life of England and the scenery she 'early learned to love'; it is 'not subject to great convulsions' but susceptible to minor changes. In the Midland plains she sees the direction of labour creating new features such as canals and railways which are all part of 'our social history in pictorial writing'. Yet the familiar remains: the delicate ivy-leaved toadflax on a crumbling wall, grey thatch with 'a troop of grass-stems on its ridge', 'broad-shouldered barns where the old-fashioned flail once made resonant music, while the watch-dog barked at the timidly venturesome fowls making pecking raids on the outflying grain', and roofs among elm and walnut trees, or by stacks of hay and corn, or below a square stone steeple, 'gathering their grey or ochre-tinted lichens and their olive-green mosses under all ministries'. All these give 'sober harmonies' to our landscape, and link us pleasantly with former generations.

Sentiment does not blind her to contemporary work and achievement; we must preserve 'some affection and fairness for those who are doing the actual work of the world':

> Otherwise, the looking before and after, which is our grand human privilege, is in danger of turning to a sort of other-worldliness, breeding a more illogical indifference or bitterness than was ever bred by the ascetic's contemplation of heaven. Except on the ground of a primitive golden age and continuous degeneracy, I see no rational footing for scorning the whole present population of the globe, unless I scorn every previous generation from whom they have inherited their diseases of mind and body, and by consequence scorn my own scorn, which is equally an inheritance of mixed ideas and feelings concocted for me in the boiling caldron of this universally contemptible life . . .

The impetus in this passage comes from a positive humanism which recalls the values proclaimed twenty years earlier by the author in her essay on Edward Young.

The satirical irony of 'How We Encourage Research' is devastatingly complete. Discoverers of truth are no longer physically tortured, but they suffer 'plenty of controversial bruising, laceration, and even life-long maiming', as is illustrated in the story of

Merman, who dared to challenge the conclusions of the accepted authority Grampus. The immediate reaction was to prove that his 'pretended facts' were 'chimeras of that remarkably hideous kind begotten by imperfect learning on the more feminine element of original incapacity'. The narrative is lightened with humour, but the Cetacean analogy loses its sparkle by over-use. Ultimately what Merman feared comes to pass; his main idea is adopted by Grampus and accepted by the public. Even his friends, after hearing the story, are unwilling to believe that Grampus is to blame. The introduction states the conclusion: 'so long as this sort of truth-worship has the sanction of a public that can often understand nothing in a controversy except personal sarcasm or slanderous ridicule, it is likely to continue'.

In 'A Man Surprised at his Originality' Lentulus is presented in too generalized a style to create a vivid impression. His appearance, reserve, and unwillingness to praise, suggest hidden genius; close acquaintance uncovers the egoistic conviction that he knows how to reform society. Yet his taste proves to be inferior and uncertain; he has faith in the miraculous and spiritualistic (human media and mahogany tables). Fortunately he lacks the gift of expression; otherwise, 'instead of being astonished at his inspiration in private, he might have clad his addled originalities, disjointed commonplaces, blind denials, and balloon-like conclusions, in that mighty sort of language which would have made a new Koran for a knot of followers'. This irony gives momentary life to a subject which calls for brief dramatic representation in a comic light. The essay concludes with 'Blessed is the man who, having nothing to say, abstains from giving us wordy evidence of the fact − from calling on us to look through a heap of millet-seed in order to be sure that there is no pearl in it.' The preamble, which contains one of La Rochefoucauld's pearls, is forgotten; read again, it seems as great a stumbling-block as ever. By contrast the opening sentence of 'A Too Deferential Man' is admirably direct; there can be no mistaking the subject. Dramatic illustrations increase interest, though the portrait of Hinze is less memorable than the image describing the mind of one he admires: 'Tulpian, with reverence be it said, has some rather absurd notions, such as a mind of large discourse often finds room for: they slip about among his higher conceptions and multitudinous acquirements like disreputable characters at a national celebration in some vast cathedral, where to the ardent soul all is glorified by rainbow light and grand associations.'

George Eliot's types are perennially recognisable, but they demand sustained concentration to yield their excellence. In 'Only Temper' she doubts whether 'a high order of character' can coexist with irascibility like Touchwood's, for it interrupts 'the formation of healthy mental habits, which depend on a growing harmony between perception, conviction, and impulse'. Temper should be overlooked only in people who are a benefit to society. The satire of 'A Political Molecule' is not very subtle. Spike, with his mind 'well glazed by nature against the admission of knowledge', becomes a representative of other people's interests simply because they are his own; he becomes 'public-spirited in spite of himself'. Born a little later, he might have been an eligible member of the post-Reform parliament; 'if he had belonged to a high family he might have done for a member of the Government'. 'The Watch-Dog of Knowledge' is rather more imaginative. Mordax has excellent gifts, combined unhappily with such 'arrogant egoism' that he is never prepared to give credit to others or to admit his own errors. There are 'fierce beasts' within us which we should chain until they 'learn to cower before the creature with wider reason'. Mordax's heart and mind should 'restrain the outleap' of his 'roar and talons'. Victims such as Laniger deserve sympathy even if Mordax alleges that the preservation of Truth is the motive for his attacks, and is 'pictured with a halo in consequence'. In general 'the action by which we can do the best for future ages is of the sort which has a certain beneficence and grace for contemporaries':

> The deed of Judas has been attributed to far-reaching views, and the wish to hasten his Master's declaration of himself as the Messiah. Perhaps — I will not maintain the contrary — Judas represented his motive in this way, and felt justified in his traitorous kiss; but my belief that he deserved, metaphorically speaking, to be where Dante saw him, at the bottom of the Malebolge, would not be the less strong because he was not convinced that his action was detestable. I refuse to accept a man who has the stomach for such treachery, as a hero impatient for the redemption of mankind and for the beginning of a reign when the kisses shall be those of peace and righteousness.

'A Half-Breed' has a special interest. Hardly any of his acquaintance knows what Mixtus really is; he himself doesn't know. A capitalist married to Scintilla, he has changed his priorities. He can still regard 'the spread of Christianity as a great result of our commercial intercourse with black, brown, and yellow populations'; but now he puts commerce first, 'not excluding a little war if that also should prove needful as a pioneer of Christianity'. Satire notwithstanding, the author is moved 'pathetically' by his lot: 'This involuntary renegade has his character hopelessly jangled and out of tune. He is like an organ with its stops in the lawless condition of obtruding themselves without method, so that hearers are amazed by the most unexpected transitions – the trumpet breaking in on the flute, and the oböe confounding both.' The reason for this sympathy is not far to seek. George Eliot also has nostalgic memories of a youthful period of unworldly idealism, when her 'chosen associates were men and women whose only distinction was a religious, a philanthropic, or an intellectual enthusiasm', when she also hung on the words of writers of 'minor religious literature', visited and exhorted the poor 'in the alleys of a great provincial town', and heard 'liberal advanced views' of Germanic origin which were far beyond 'the ordinary teaching' of her sect.

Among these essays none is more pertinent to our media-addicted world than 'Debasing the Moral Currency', with its premonitions of 'a hideous millennium, in which the lion will have to lie down with the lascivious monkeys whom (if we may trust Pliny) his soul naturally abhors'. The genuinely ridiculous is always with us; 'wit and humour may play as harmlessly or beneficiently round the changing facets of egoism, absurdity, and vice, as the sunshine over the rippling sea or the dewy meadows'. But why should it flourish 'like a brigand on the robbery of our mental wealth', degrading 'healthy appetites and affections', and 'lowering the value of every inspiring fact and tradition so that it will command less and less of the spiritual products, the generous motives which sustain the charm and elevation of our social existence – the something besides bread by which man saves his soul alive'? Civilization cannot be preserved without ideal feelings; our posterity is threatened with 'a new Famine, a meagre fiend with lewd grin and clumsy hoof', which 'is breathing a moral mildew over the harvest of our human sentiments'. It is not a long step from this to 'The Second Coming' of W. B. Yeats.

The egoisms of George Eliot's representative characters are recognisably universal, but her presentations have the authenticity of reflected observation or experience, as may be seen in her discussion of plagiarism. A Euphorion takes the view that any form of originality must be infinitesimal compared with 'the massive inheritance of thought on which every new generation enters'. In a world where criticism correlates to the prestige of the performer rather than to his performance, the appropriation of fine ideas is commonly found among astute speakers like Aquila. The author of 'How We Encourage Research' re-affirms the effectiveness with which the plagiarist carries the public with him, 'so that the poor Columbus is found to be a very faulty adventurer and the continent is named after Amerigo'. This truth is amusingly illustrated in an apologue: only after a series of false attributions and claims did a sweet-toothed majority discover that honey was produced by the wasp. When the evidence was seen to be irrefutable, 'there was a murmur the reverse of delighted, and the feelings of some eminent animals were too strong for them: the Orang-outang's jaw dropped so as seriously to impair the vigour of his expression, the edifying Pelican screamed and flapped her wings, the Owl hissed again, the Macaw became loudly incoherent, and the Gibbon gave his hysterical laugh; while the Hyaena, after indulging in a more splenetic guffaw, agitated the question whether it would not be better to hush up the whole affair, instead of giving public recognition to an insect whose produce, it was now plain, had been much over-estimated'.

A lighter piece describes the dilemma of Ganymede, who enjoyed the flattering unction of being 'so young' in his precocious youth, and fostered the illusion in his plump midde-age, not realizing what a handicap a label could be which suggested immaturity of judgment. The related subject of 'How We Come to Give Ourselves False Testimonials' leads to nothing remarkable (apart from the thought that judging oneself by what one observes in others may weaken 'the energies of indignation and scorn' which 'should continually feed the wholesome restraining power of public opinion') until we reach the distinction between self-deception and high imagination, the latter arising from a keen vision of reality. 'Witness Dante, who is at once the most precise and homely in his reproduction of actual objects, and the most soaringly at large in his imaginative combinations.' The creative energy is 'constantly fed by susceptibility to the veriest minutiae of experience, which it reproduces and constructs in fresh and fresh wholes'. Dante is quoted (*Purgatorio*, xv) in support of the conclusion that 'the strongest seer' is he 'who can support the stress of creative energy and yet keep that sanity of expectation which consists in distinguishing . . . between the *cose che son vere* outside the individual mind, and the *non falsi errori* which are the revelations of true imaginative power'.

'The Too Ready Writer' recalls youthful self-confidence, and prompts the question whether 'mixing our own flavour' with every great subject by every great writer may not have the effect of Spanish wineskins, 'which impress the innocent stranger with the notion that the Spanish grape has naturally a taste of leather'. The excessive writer is at least as reprehensible as the bore, yet less to blame than the public conscience, 'which is so lax and ill informed on the momentous bearings of authorship that it sanctions the total abstinence of scruple in undertaking and prosecuting what should be the best warranted of vocations'. Preliminary remarks in 'Diseases of Small Authorship' lead to a felicitous comment on the relationship between comedy and tragedy: 'Take a large enough area of human life and all comedy melts into tragedy, like the Fool's part by the side of Lear.' The essay is notable for the fictional satire of Vorticella, the most amusing of George Eliot's Theophrastian characters.

Her most outspoken criticism of Victorian hypocrisy occurs in 'Moral Swindlers'. Among the influences which militate against the establishment of right public values is the degradation of words in judging public behaviour. She notices that kings whose deeds have been base are described as 'religious' because they observed 'certain ritual and spiritual transactions with God', and is convinced that 'the augury is not good for the use of high ethical and theological disputation' when a man 'can be called moral because he comes home to dine with his wife and children and cherishes the happiness of his own hearth', even though he spends 'the solid part of every day' in unscrupulous business transactions which have 'every calculable chance of causing widespread injury and misery'. Until we have found another word than 'morality' for 'the duties of man to man', let us regard 'the contractor who enriches himself by using large machinery to make pasteboard soles pass as leather for the feet of unhappy conscripts fighting at miserable odds against invaders' as a miscreant, however exemplary his private life. The attack is continued against self-seeking political leaders who neglect their public responsibilities, and journalists who stimulate bad feeling, helping to create a 'hideous cancer in the commonwealth' by 'turning the channels of instruction into feeders of social and political disease'. The narrow meaning of 'moral' excludes 'half those actions of a man's life which tell momentously on the well-being of his fellow-citizens, and on the preparation of a future for the children growing up around him'.

What follows strikes an ominously significant note: 'Thoroughness of workmanship, care in the execution of every task undertaken, as if it were the acceptance of a trust which it would be a breach of faith not to discharge well, is a form of duty so momentous that if it were to die out from the feeling and practice of a people, all reforms of institutions would be helpless to create national prosperity and national happiness.' Pertinent remarks on priorities between political agitation and the quality of production, on educational requirements, and the vanity of pious hope, conclude with: 'meanwhile lax, make-shift work from the high conspicuous kind to the average and obscure, is allowed to pass unstamped with the disgrace of immorality, though there is not a member of society who is not daily suffering from it materially and spiritually, and though it is the fatal cause that must degrade our national rank and our commerce in spite of all open markets and discovery of available coal-seams'. Read 'North Sea oil' for 'coal-seams', and the passage is up-to-date.

The 'disfiguring work' created by industrial growth is at the root of the pessimism which forms the *point de départ* of 'Shadows of the Coming Race'; but this essay, following a contemporary evolutionary fantasy (found in Butler's *Erewhon*) raises the possibilities of human redundancy and degeneration in an age of technological progress. The optimist foresees a period when automation will have freed human energies for lofty purposes; but fear is expressed that the machines, instead of being man's slaves, will develop until they can reproduce themselves, and the human race is superseded by a process of 'natural selection'.

The last essay of the series is the most impassioned; it marks a return to the Zionism which George Eliot may appear to have championed in *Daniel Deronda*. A passage in the novel (xxxiii) sheds lurid light on the title:

. . . imaginatively transported to the borders of the Rhine at the end of the eleventh century, when in the ears listening for the signals of the Messiah, the Hep! Hep! Hep! of the Crusaders came like the bay of bloodhounds; and in the presence of those devilish missionaries with sword and firebrand the crouching figure of the reviled Jew turned round erect, heroic, flashing with sublime constancy in the face of torture and death.

We are reminded that the English obtained their homeland by force, and have an imperialistic history. Colonizers and punishers, not a despised and punished race, we have supported liberation movements in Greece and Italy, not from admiration of contemporary Greeks and Italians but from a sense of their past glories. National pride and loyalty are human characteristics. 'Affection, intelligence, duty, radiate from a centre, and nature has decided that for us English folk that centre can be neither China nor Peru.' There is no good reason why the Jews should be made an exception. The passionate hold of the religion which originated with them, and which inspires us, 'as possessors of the most truth and the most tonnage', to carry it to all nations, shows affinities between our race and them. As we honour the ancestors who won or rescued our civil and religious liberties, we should admire the steadfastness of the Jews in the face of foreign tyranny, and their preservation of 'the nationality which was the very hearth of our own religion'. They have suffered many pogroms and dispersions. George Eliot's sympathies do not blind her to Jewish vices; they give her understanding. It is no wonder that Jews reacted cunningly against oppression and persecution. It was the Christians — 'alien men whom cross, creed, and baptism had left cruel, rapacious, and debauched' — who made Christianity a curse to them. 'It is more reverent to Christ to believe that He must have approved the Jewish martyrs who deliberately chose to be burned or massacred rather than be guilty of a blaspheming lie, more than He approved the rabble of Crusaders who robbed and murdered them in His name.' Having been exposed to alienism more than any other race, the Jews have undoubtedly suffered moral degradation; but they have survived with great virtues, and this is due to their historic memories and their family affection. George Eliot was clearly alarmed at the threat of excessive immigration. Zionism is recommended as a more acceptable alternative, to counteract the 'dominant mode', which is to disown the origin of Christianity and revive anti-semitism, mainly from jealousy of Jewish talents and success. Liberty means the preservation of idiosyncrasies, national as well as individual. The 'effective bond of human action is feeling', and it is natural for the Jews to feel kinship in the glories and the tribulations of their race, as well as in its possible renovation.

Throughout her essays, George Eliot shows unusual powers of sustained reasoning, and apt illustration; she can be light, witty, and epigrammatic. She is rarely humorous, and any relief she provides from earnestness is incidental. One can admire her perceptiveness, integrity, and occasional irony and satire. Though direction and precision may sometimes seem dimmed at first by over-reliance on abstract generalities, her arguments are well organized. The patient reader will find they rarely fail to reach a high level of excellence in expression. Yet, though an imaginative glow of felt experience is often communicated, their general tone verges on the impersonal. As exercises in disciplined reflection, they show admirable judgment, but their idiosyncratic stamp is hardly remarkable.

*   *   *

A selection of notes made by George Eliot during her later years was made by Charles Lewes and added to the 1884 edition of her essays under the title of 'Leaves from a Note-Book'. They were probably written anticipatively, for inclusion or elaboration in later writings; four passages were omitted by Charles Lewes because they had already appeared in *Impressions of Theophrastus Such*. Most of the notes are brief, the longest being on authors and authorship.

George Eliot believes that the author should be guided by high ideals, for publishing makes him a teacher or 'influencer of the public mind'; 'he can no more escape influencing the moral taste, and with it the action of the intelligence, than a setter of fashions in furniture and dress can fill the shops with his designs and leave the garniture of persons and houses unaffected by his industry'. Authors who write easily to make profit 'as long as the market is open' are like the manufacturer of calico who 'buys a new invention of some light kind likely to attract the public fancy, is successful in finding a multitude who will give their testers for the transiently desirable commodity', and colours it with harmful arsenic green. His principle of authorship is that of the gin-palace.

To judge an author who does not write for the market, we have to consider 'his individual contribution to the spiritual wealth of mankind'. 'Did he impregnate any ideas with a fresh store of emotion, and in this way enlarge the area of moral sentiment?' Reputable critics who are more susceptible to 'their own reputation for passing a right judgment' than to 'qualities in the object of judgment' are strongly censured:

> Who learns to discriminate shades of colour by considering what is expected of him? The habit of expressing borrowed judgments stupefies the sensibilities, which are the only foundation of genuine judgments, just as the constant reading and retailing of results from other men's observations through the microscope, without ever looking through the lens oneself, is an instruction in some truths and some prejudices, but is no instruction in observant susceptibility; on the contrary, it breeds a habit of inward seeing according to verbal statement, which dulls the power of outward seeing according to visual evidence.

In her notes on 'the best way of telling a story', George Eliot stresses 'the superior mastery of images and pictures in grasping the attention', and dwells at some length on the advantage of creating curiosity about some person before proceeding with 'a retrospective narration' (as in *Felix Holt* and *Daniel Deronda*). She can see advantages also in opening a story 'with a date and necessary account of places and people, passing on quietly towards the more rousing elements of narrative and dramatic composition, without need of retrospect' (in the manner of Scott, *Adam Bede*, and *The Mill on the Floss*). Spirited narrative with an occasional touch of dialogue can be made 'eminently interesting'; she finds it supremely in French novelettes, though the opening chapters of *The Vicar of Wakefield* are 'as fine as anything that can be done in this way'. There is no reason why a story should not be told 'in the most irregular fashion', according to the author's idiosyncrasy, as in Sterne's *Tristram Shandy*.

Turning to history, she observes how easy it is to misinterpret movements and change through lack of 'veracious imagination' or 'real, minute vision'.

> I want something different from the abstract treatment which belongs to grave history from a doctrinal point of view, and something different from the schemed picturesqueness of ordinary historical fiction. I want brief, severely conscientious reproductions, in their concrete incidents, of pregnant movements in the past.

On the value of religion George Eliot asserts that no deity can be 'impotent or neutral' if it is really believed in, for 'every object of thought reacts on the mind that conceives it, still more on that which habitually contemplates it'. Looking at the question from her own philosophical angle, she concludes that 'we may be said to solicit help from a generalisation or abstraction', as Wordsworth implies when he describes general truths as 'a sort/Of Elements and Agents, Under-Powers,/Subordinate helpers of the living mind'.

In the present stage of thinking, she concludes, one cannot insist too much on 'the efficacy of feeling in stimulating to ardent co-operation' for good causes:

> No doubt the passionate inspiration which prompts and sustains a course of self-sacrificing labour in the light of soberly estimated results gathers the highest title to our veneration, and makes the supreme heroism. But the generous leap of impulse is needed too to swell the flood of sympathy in us beholders, that we may not fall completely under the mastery of calculation, which in its turn may fail of ends for want of energy got from ardour. We have need to keep the sluices open for possible influxes of the rarer sort.

Postscript

In recent years George Eliot's greatness has been recognised more than at any time since she reached the peak of her contemporary fame; even so, the masterly presentation of most of her Gwendolen Harleth–Grandcourt scenes prompts the question whether she achieved all she might have done as a novelist. Diffidence led too often to over-inclusiveness, and to the kind of problems which she solved by compression in the final phase of *The Mill on the Floss* and by expansion in *Middlemarch*. Over-conscientiousness led to massive research, particularly for *Romola*, and sometimes, as in *Felix Holt* and *Daniel Deronda*, when she had exhausted all other possibilities, to consultation with experts on minutiae of relative insignificance to most readers. Such time-consuming insistence on exactitude led to recurrent periods of anxiety, depression, and illness; in the later years of her life, further tolls were self-inflicted by the writing of lengthy, elaborately-constructed works to comply with heavy serialization programmes. The success of *Silas Marner* suggests that she would have taxed her artistic energy less had she enjoyed the confidence to undertake less demanding plots than she usually set herself. The tragedy of Lydgate and Rosamond is worthy of full-scale presentation; and the 'Miss Brooke' story is not, one feels, adequately developed in its later stages. Greater imaginative concentration in the tragic Gwendolen–Grandcourt story marks the continuing emergence of creative powers which needed wider scope than could be given in *Felix Holt* and *Middlemarch*. By seeking too many safeguards, George Eliot had repeatedly checked and hampered the unfolding of her genius.

As a novelist she had always recognised 'the high responsibilities of literature that undertakes to represent life' (30.iii.61). Sharing Feuerbach's view that 'the idea of God, so far as it has been a high spiritual influence, is the ideal of a goodness entirely human' (10.xii.74), and believing in the 'one comprehensive Church whose fellowship consists in the desire to purify and ennoble human life' (11.xi.74), she regarded herself as a 'religious' writer. Her creed was humanitarian; she had realized early in life that religious differences were ineradicable, and that 'the only universal bond of union' depends on 'truth of feeling'. For this reason she sympathized with any faith in which human sorrow and longing for purity expressed themselves (6.xii.59). However men disagree speculatively, they should be 'of one mind' in 'the desire to do an honest part towards the general well-being' (17.x.77). She described her writing as 'a set of experiments in life — an endeavour to see what our thought and emotion may be capable of — what stores of motive, actual or hinted as possible, give promise of a better after which we may strive — what gains from past revelations and discipline we must strive to keep hold of as something more sure than shifting theory' (25.i.76).

This scientific metaphor implies nothing unusual in narrative or dramatic art; the question is how, 'under the varying experiments of Time' (M. Prelude), people of certain character will behave in particular circumstances, and to what extent their actions are blameworthy or admirable. It was the habit of George Eliot's imagination 'to strive after as full a vision of the medium in which a character moves as of the character itself' (8.viii.63). Defending Maggie Tulliver's behaviour, after Sir Edward Lytton's criticism, she speaks of the circumstances in which she 'deliberately placed' her heroine (9.viii.60). The critical test is one of probability, and not of convention; George Eliot passes it uncommonly well, as may be gauged by the number of living characters she has created, and by the convincing changes they undergo as a result of their experiences. Nowhere is such a transformation greater or more striking than in Gwendolen Grandcourt.

Serious literature, conveying the artist's impression of life, is inevitably moral; and George Eliot, enlarging on the general intention of her 'experiments', is quite explicit. Her criticism of life is positive; she believed, as she indicated in her notes on *The Spanish Gypsy*, that art 'which leaves the soul in despair is laming to the soul, and is denounced by the healthy sentiment of an active community'. The story of *Silas Marner* is enriched and universalized by its moral implications. Only when a writer breaks the illusion of life, by interposing to stress or dilate on his ulterior aims, or by attempting to further them by making his characters speak or act implausibly, will readers object as Keats did to the egotistical didacticism of Wordsworth; 'We hate poetry that has a palpable design upon us', he wrote. George Eliot made the mistake of obtruding her views unnecessarily, and the hortatory role of characters such as Adam Bede, Dinah Morris, the Garths (and occasionally Daniel Deronda) is sometimes very thinly disguised. By and large, however, she appeals to the emotions in a non-prescriptive way, through the imagination. 'My function', she claims, 'is that of the *aesthetic*, not the doctrinal teacher – the rousing of the nobler emotions, which make mankind desire the social right, not the prescribing of special measures, concerning which the artistic mind, however strongly moved by social sympathy, is often not the best judge' (18.vii.78). Much as she admired the Jews, it cannot be said that she advocates the cause of Zionism in *Daniel Deronda* any more than she does that of the Zincali in *The Spanish Gypsy*. It differs only in being topically controversial; equally it serves to dramatize the assertion of something greater than self-interest, a call which is not arbitrary or quixotic but rooted in Daniel's racial kinship.

The design of a novel inspired by idealism may appear too obvious, as it sometimes does in *Romola*, or in *Daniel Deronda*, where it supplies the counterbalancing theme. What matters most, however, is whether it is presented in a convincing action which holds the reader through its appeal to his sympathy and imagination, or whether, as Lawrence says, the novelist commits the immorality of putting 'his thumb in the scale, to pull down the balance' of his delicately-adjusted human relationships 'to his own predilection'. George Eliot's awareness of the problem is clear in her reply to the suggestion prompted by Frederic Harrison's admiration of *Felix Holt* that it might be her destiny to produce a Positivist poem in dramatic form but without doctrine. She told him (15.viii.66) that she had 'gone through again and again the severe effort of trying to make certain ideas thoroughly incarnate, as if they had revealed themselves . . . first in the flesh and not in the spirit'. Her conclusion that 'aesthetic teaching' is the highest of all, but that 'if it ceases to be purely aesthetic – if it lapses anywhere from the picture to the diagram – it becomes the most offensive of all teaching' happens to be a distillation of views which Philip Sidney had convincingly argued in *An Apologie for Poetrie*. The religious or moral purpose of serious literature is evident in Greek tragedy, *Macbeth*, Jane Austen, *Lyrical Ballads*, *Wuthering Heights*, or in *Tess of the d'Urbervilles*, which seemed like a Positivist allegory to Harrison. The critical factor is the manner in which it is conveyed; it must be intrinsic, inseparable from the imaginative whole. *King Lear* has greater inherent probability and ennobling power than parts of the Deronda story, though its conception is further removed from probability in the ordinary sense. Godfrey Cass's childless marriage may appear right in terms of artistic probability, but an arbitrary judgment in terms of everyday life.

The crucial test for George Eliot is the emergence of the higher self, or the transcending of egoism. The realization of this virtue seems to have been the fruit of refractory experience and bitter irreconciliations in the author's youth, as earlier episodes in *The Mill on the Floss* repeatedly suggest. Confirmation of this comes in a letter to Mrs Charles Bray (19.v.54):

> When we are young we think our troubles a mighty business — that the world is spread out expressly as a stage for the particular drama of our lives and that we have a right to rant and foam at the mouth if we are crossed. I have done enough of that in my time. But we begin at last to understand that these things are important only to one's own consciousness, which is but as a globule of dew on a rose-leaf that at mid-day there will be no trace of. This is no high-flown sentimentality, but a simple reflection which I find useful to me every day.

This maturing and civilizing vision, with '*Caritas*, the highest love or fellowship' (29.xii.62) as the positive corollary of the rejection of 'miserable aims that end with self', is inherent in all her fiction. There was no change from *Scenes of Clerical Life* onwards, she wrote; the principles 'at the root of my effort to paint Dinah Morris are equally at the root of my effort to paint Mordecai' (16.xii.76).

Altruism assumes a variety of forms in George Eliot's fiction; in antithetical juxtaposition or proximity of one kind or another to self-centredness, it is expressed in the love of distance and large prospects. While Hetty gazes at herself in the mirror, Dinah Morris looks at the beautiful fields as the moon rises, and thinks of all the people out there whom she has learned to care for. Mrs Transome, proud, withdrawn, and self-pitying, looks out on the black boundary of the trees and the long line of the river, two images which reflect the utter loneliness and dreariness of her life; Esther Lyon gazes at the identical scene, and sees 'the lines of the for-ever flowing river', the 'bending movement of the black trees', and 'veiled glimmerings of moonlight'. Life (the river) goes on; she yearns for change, which is implicit in the 'bending movement' of the trees; and the moonlight suggests hope. It is like the pearly dawn when Dorothea recovers her better, humanitarian self, after seeing Ladislaw compromised with Rosamond. 'The dominant spirit of justice within her' returns; she draws the curtains, and sees, on the road and in the fields beyond, a man with a bundle on his back, a woman carrying her baby, and a shepherd with his dog; the pearly light makes her feel 'the largeness of the world and the manifold wakings of men to labour and endurance'; she can neither remain a spectator nor 'hide her eyes in selfish complaining'. Mordecai's love of sunrise or sunset is shared by Deronda, the leader whom he awaits for their people, as is shown *ab initio* when, just before rescuing Mirah, Deronda reclines in his boat, watching the sunset and emerging stars, and forgets everything else in 'a half-speculative, half-involuntary identification of himself with the objects' in view.

By such pictorial means George Eliot communicates appraisal of character and life. It has been said that she is the most important character in her novels (and few authors take us more into their confidence), but the remark is misleading, for novelists with vision generally express themselves more intensely and incisively through imaginative creation than by overt comment. George Eliot's ability to impart a universalizing dimension to situation and character by sharing her thoughts and feelings with subtle unobtrusiveness is equalled by few writers; yet, at times, even in her later novels, despite the outlet of her sententious epigraphs, she jolts the reader with adventitious philosophical reflections. D. H. Lawrence was 'very fond of her', but wished 'she'd take her specs off, and come down off the public platform'. Reacting also to the psychological analysis which deepens our awareness, Trollope concluded that 'in studying her latter writings, one feels oneself to be in company with some philosopher rather than with a novelist'; and Hardy described her as 'a moral essayist who had mistaken her vocation', an outdated over-emphasis which does not appear to be substantiated by *Impressions of Theophrastus Such*.

Although George Eliot shrank from any form of sectarianism, there is no basic difference between her humanitarian beliefs and the main principles of Positivism. Rejecting trust in a hypothetical Providence, and founding its hope on human effort and enlightenment, it insisted that the progress of civilization depends on the promotion of altruism above self-interest, with science and education as its means. The stress was on compassion; without its motivating force there could be little social justice and amelioration. Its main import is expressed by Hardy in 'A Plaint to Man':

> The truth should be told, and the fact be faced
> That had best been faced in earlier years:
>
> The fact of life with dependence placed
> On the human heart's resource alone,
> In brotherhood bonded close and graced
>
> With loving-kindness fully blown,
> And visioned help unsought, unknown.

George Eliot summed up its practical purport when she wrote in 'Stradivarius': 'I say, not God Himself can make man's best/ Without best men to help Him.' Hers was 'emphatically a religious mind', as J. W. Cross wrote:

> My own impression is that her whole soul was so imbued with, and her imagination was so fired by, the scientific spirit of the age . . . that she could not conceive that there was, as yet, any religious formula sufficient nor any known political system likely to be final. She had great hope, for the future, in the improvement of human nature by the gradual development of the affections and the sympathetic emotions, and 'by the slow stupendous teaching of the world's events' — rather than by means of legislative enactments.

Her radicalism ran deeper than that of the typical politician, and it did not change; she belonged, William Hale White thought, to 'the great and noble church . . . of the Insurgents'. It seemed to her that pity and fairness, 'two little words which, carried out, would embrace the utmost delicacies of the moral life', rested on 'facts quite as irreversible as the perception that a pyramid will not stand on its apex' (17.x.77). Commenting on Geraldine Jewsbury's *Constance Herbert*, she insists that the only motive to true moral action is 'the immediate impulse of love and justice'. Her faith was sustained by the Wordsworthian conviction 'That we have all of us one human heart.'

This spirit informs her fiction from first to last, and is particularly evident in characters such as Dinah Morris, Dolly Winthrop, Romola, Felix Holt, and Dorothea Brooke. In *Adam Bede* (xxvii) she states simply, 'We are children of a large family, and must learn . . . to be content with little nurture and caressing, and help each other the more.' Writing of Rufus Lyon's love of Esther's mother, she slyly observes that this passion 'induced a more thorough renunciation than he had ever known in the time of his complete devotion to his ministerial career' (FH.vi). She knew that the individual is determined by heredity and environment, and that the 'fatal meshes' are woven within and without (DD.liv; cf. M.ep.iv and her comments on the questionable aphorism of Novalis, with reference to Hamlet, MF.VI.vi), but she wisely emphasizes the importance of the human corollary to the natural law of consequences throughout the universe, that 'Our deeds determine us, as much as we determine our deeds' (cf. FH.ep.xlviii); and she illustrates this in victims as diverse as Arthur Donnithorne, Mr Tulliver, and Tito Melema. Gambling with chance is a recurrent subject; and the consequences are seen not only with these three but also with Godfrey Cass, Mrs Transome, Bulstrode, Lydgate, and Gwendolen Grandcourt. The effect of social environment is a special feature of *Middlemarch*; *Felix Holt* reflects the danger of political explosiveness rather than the likelihood of a well-ordered process of reform when the masses are uneducated. No sudden amelioration is likely: 'What has grown up historically can only die out historically, by the gradual operation of necessary laws', George Eliot writes in her essay on Riehl.

Believing that man has choice and moral responsibility, she did not lose faith in human progress; she was not a determinist. 'The contaminating effect of deeds often lies less in the commission than in the consequent adjustment of our desires − the enlistment of our self-interest on the side of falsity', she writes (R.ix) with reference to a choice which Tito would have been ashamed to avow. Again (xxiii), 'Tito was experiencing that inexorable law of human souls, that we prepare for sudden deeds by the reiterated choice of good or evil which gradually determines character.' She takes up the question in letters to Mrs Ponsonby: progress happens only by 'the modified action of the individual beings who compose the world', and the fact that we can keep certain considerations in mind, 'so that they may continually be the prompters of certain feelings and actions', seems undeniable (10.xii.74); 'I shall not be

satisfied with your philosophy till you have conciliated neces-
sitarianism — I hate the ugly word — with the practice of willing
strongly, willing to will strongly, and so on, that being what you
certainly can do and have done about a great many things in life',
she tells her (19.viii.75). One of the most poignant moments in
Felix Holt comes when Mrs Transome, weighed down with
anxiety, is about to reproach Jermyn, but is checked by the inner
voice which retorts, 'You brought it on yourself' (ix).

George Eliot's outlook was complex but integrated; it was both
humanistic and scientific. Her use of scientific terms and analogies
was criticized by contemporary reviewers, but found a champion
in Edward Dowden, who argued that they reflect 'the chief intellectual movement of her time'. They indicate her scrupulous
regard for truth, extend our awareness, and serve sometimes to
stress the relativity of individual lives in nature at large. Objections
to them usually derive from a unilateral education. With the
spread of knowledge, much of their strangeness or apparent in-
congruity has been eroded, but occasionally they are pursued too
far; one example relates to the 'thought and speech vortices' which
bring food to Mrs Cadwallader's match-making mind (M.vi).
George Eliot's similes show her interest in biology, nature, and
literature, very strikingly sometimes in music, but even more
memorably in the freshness and accuracy of non-specialized observations: Bulstrode's past comes 'between him and everything else,
as obstinately as when we look through the window from a lighted
room', and 'the objects we turn our backs on are still before us,
instead of the grass and the trees' (M.lxi; cf. ep.lxxii). Never
hackneyed or otiose, her comparisons are incidental reminders of
her integrity, drawing continually from observed, recollected, or
re-created experience. Sometimes they are rather too elaborate to
be fully assimilated at first reading. Some of the more effective are
imagined or invented: Adam could no more stir love in Hetty 'than
the mere picture of a sun can stir the spring sap in the subtle fibres
of the plant'; the thought of Mrs Glasher and her children makes
the brilliant prospects of Gwendolen's engagement to Grandcourt
'come to her hunger like food with the taint of sacrilege upon it';
she sets no store on Deronda's 'reading Hebrew' with Mordecai,
and the phrase 'fleeted unimpressively across her sense of hearing,
as a stray stork might have made its peculiar flight across her
landscape without raising any surprised reflection on its natural
history'.

Epic associations characterize an interesting feature of George Eliot's imaginative thinking. Homeric parallels occur in *Scenes of Clerical Life*, and Dempster's premature triumph over the Tryanites recalls the pre-campaign braggadocio of Xerxes. Usually such aggrandizement of presentation has deeper effects: by accentuating 'the universal heart' it enlarges our sympathy for the sufferings and hopes of people like ourselves. 'Deronda had as reverential an interest in Mordecai and Mirah as he could have had in the offspring of Agamemnon; but he was caring for destinies still moving in the dim streets of our earthly life, not yet lifted among the constellations'; his cause is given Promethean overtones in two epigraphs (xvi, xxviii). Like Oedipus, Mr Tulliver has his destiny. The struggles of Maggie and Tom recall the days of Hecuba and Hector, when women inside the gates filled 'long, empty days with memories and fears' while men outside lost 'the sense of dread and even of wounds in the hurrying ardour of action'. Every marriage, like that of Adam and Eve, is 'still the beginning of the home epic'; 'some set out, like Crusaders of old, with a glorious equipment of hope and enthusiasm'. The opportunity may be there for a Lydgate; for the modern Theresa there is 'no epic life' with 'a constant unfolding of far-resonant action', though George Eliot holds that 'we insignificant people' may do something to help many Dorotheas whose idealism will promote 'the growing good of the world'. In her later novels sympathy is enlarged through evocations of classical tragedy. In *Daniel Deronda* (as in *Felix Holt*) references to Dante also play a similar role, as may be seen in the comment on Gwendolen's guilt-ridden distress at Genoa, after her release from Grandcourt: 'For what place, though it were the flowery vale of Enna, may not the inward sense turn into a circle of punishment where the flowers are no better than a crop of flame-tongues burning the souls of our feet?'

George Eliot's remarks on Miss Mulock, authoress of *John Halifax, Gentleman*, 'a writer who is read only by novel readers, pure and simple, never by people of high culture' (7.vi.60), are more discriminatory than condescending; the two authors belong to 'entirely different' orders. The popular novel provides escape from life in sensation and exciting narrative, whereas George Eliot's main interest is less in the story than in people and 'the growing good of the world'. She is a religious writer in the sense that her ulterior motive is the progress of civilization, yet it would be wrong to conclude that she is narrow and puritanical. She is

humanitarian; Jane Austen would not have presented Arthur
Donnithorne with the sympathetic understanding he receives in
Adam Bede. Occasionally there are events in George Eliot's novels
which are exciting by popular standards, but they soon fade into
dim outline. Most imaginatively alive by contrast are situations
which convey pictorially or dramatically crises or turning-points in
the lives of particular characters. Dickens may have a greater
creative imagination, but it is peculiar to his own world and less
true to life than George Eliot's. She can use the outer scene to
reflect the inner world, notably in Maggie's drifting down the river
with Stephen Guest; particularly in her later novels she explores
this inner world with impressive insight and consistency. Her
ironical treatment of the inexperienced Dorothea Brooke is not
nearly as characteristic as her sympathetic presentation of
Gwendolen Grandcourt. Like Jane Austen, she sometimes combines the expression of a character's feeling or view of things with
narrative detachment; and the interweaving of mediated and
direct experience creates a quickening and immediacy which may
energize paragraphs, or produce a dramatic effect even in a few
words, as is illustrated within the sentence which introduces
Dorothea's burning reproaches when 'the bright creature whom
she had trusted' falls from grace. Here the inner voice of despair is
momentarily stilled by a sudden surge of feeling: 'persistently with
her . . . was the Will Ladislaw who was a changed belief exhausted
of hope, a detected illusion — no, a living man towards whom
there could not yet struggle any wail of regretful pity, from the
midst of scorn and indignation and jealous wounded pride'.

Wrong choice is inevitably subject to chance; it may involve
being false to one's true self as well as to others. Such is the tragedy
of Maggie Tulliver, who suffers the condemnation of society as
well as remorse. She is far more the victim of circumstances than
Gwendolen Harleth, who (unlike Esther Lyon) chooses to risk
marriage for the sake of grandeur. More and more in the later
novels, where characters rise progressively in stature, consequences reach their peak in tense dramatic confrontations, some
of which are imaginatively heightened by association with recurring images of quasi-symbolic significance, the triptych and
crucifix of *Romola*, for example, or Gwendolen's turquoise
necklace and diamonds, the insignia respectively of her dependence on Deronda and of the tyrannical mastery which she cedes to
Grandcourt when she accepts a guilty alliance with him. Few

novelists have equalled George Eliot in the imaginative intensity of dramatic peaks, or her cogency in the analysis of character through the inner life and excitement of thought and feeling. Her progress towards greater power and control is offset somewhat by a diminution of colour, spontaneity, and humour; the movement is from a type of fiction rather in the Fielding tradition to one more Richardsonian and (influenced by Greek tragedy) more dramatic in its organization. The emphasis is on character and motivation from the first.

Although capable of coping with narrative intricacies, as the sub-plot of *Felix Holt* shows, George Eliot seems deliberately to have avoided finesse in ending her novels. Her problem was to combine probability with neatness or effect. Though well aware that marriage was conventionally 'the bourne of so many narratives', she uses it to round off four of her novels. Most of her endings take the form of commendably brief epilogues. That of *Felix Holt* seems rather perfunctory. Charismatically radiant in *Silas Marner*, it is artistically congruent with the main narrative. The sobriety of the epilogue in *Middlemarch* is equally convincing, with mixed fortunes ranging from failure through compromise to hard-won success. In *Romola* the epilogue is homiletic, and little above the level of anticlimax. That of *Adam Bede* is a postscript to a happy ending which appears more contrived than probable. The conclusion of *The Mill on the Floss* is George Eliot's most ambitious; it was ordained from the first, but it is abruptly introduced, is imaginatively out of key, and seems neither convincing nor necessary. A new beginning, as for Gwendolen Grandcourt, would have been more appropriate for a girl like Maggie Tulliver, more sinned against than sinning. The short-lived reconciliation between her and Tom which comes from the threat of death by water brings emotional relief to the reader. Yet the finale, with the memorial 'In their death they were not divided', however satisfying to Victorian readers, must savour of fictional pretence from the author of 'O May I Join the Choir Invisible'.

The winds of critical change are rich in ironies. George Eliot's fame rose rapidly during her lifetime and declined almost as suddenly after her death. With the extension of higher education it has risen again during the last thirty years. In *Corrected Impressions* (1895) George Saintsbury wrote:

for some years past George Eliot, though she may still be read, has more or less passed out of contemporary critical appreciation. There are, of course, a few obstinate and 'know-nothing' worshippers; perhaps there are some who kept their heads even in the heyday, and who can now say *sunt lachrymae rerum*, as they contemplate a fame once so great, in part so solidly founded, and yet now to a greater extent than strict justice can approve almost utterly vanished away.

Accepting the common view that George Eliot was at her best in the rural scenes and humour of her early novels, Edmund Gosse (in *Aspects and Impressions*, 1922) found *Middlemarch* mechanical and unimaginative, 'a very remarkable instance of elaborate mental resources misapplied, and genius revolving, with tremendous machinery, like some great water-wheel, while no water is flowing underneath it'; he could say nothing ('not a word') in favour of *Daniel Deronda*. Three years later, in *The Common Reader*, Virginia Woolf showed freshness of perception; *Middlemarch* to her was adult and magnificent. In *Early Victorian Novelists* (1934) Lord David Cecil pronounced George Eliot 'the first modern novelist', but hedged his enthusiasm with many qualifications. He seems to have missed the greatness of her achievement in *Felix Holt* and *Daniel Deronda*, precisely where F. R. Leavis located and analysed her mature genius. It is mainly to his challenging essays in *The Great Tradition* (1948) that George Eliot's revival is due. 'For us in these days, it seems to me,' he writes, 'she is a peculiarly fortifying and wholesome author, and a suggestive one: she might well be pondered by those who tend to prescribe simple recourses . . . in face of the demoralizations and discouragements of an age that isn't one of "enthusiastic assent to old articles of faith".' With increasing secularization, our major problem is basically the same; it is still moral and religious, though it has moved very largely into the political area of socio-economics. George Eliot was a novelist with a historical sense who anticipated the problems of a secular age, and affirmed values which cannot be disregarded if civilization is to prosper. A country which breeds divisiveness at the expense of humanitarianism may learn from experience some of the wisdom which is implicit in her faith. It is expressed in *Scenes of Clerical Life* and all her novels; the inhumanity of its negative counterpart is the ultimate theme of that minor, far-sighted masterpiece 'The Lifted Veil'. George Eliot, like Deronda, cared for 'destinies still moving in the dim streets of our earthly life'.

Appendixes

GEORGE ELIOT AND THOMAS HARDY

The influence of literature on Hardy's novels is great, and a study of the evidence suggests that his indebtedness to George Eliot, especially in his early writing, was not inconsiderable. One must allow for coincidences, even more for what can be retained by the subconscious memory; but there can be little doubt that Hardy took hints from George Eliot's fiction, and developed them for his own artistic ends.

Perhaps this explains his apprehension when the opening chapters of *Far from the Madding Crowd*, published anonymously in the January 1874 number of *The Cornhill Magazine*, reminded a reviewer of George Eliot. A year later, when the novel appeared as a whole, attention was drawn to similarities with *Adam Bede* by one critic; another began with Hardy's pastoral vein, and described *Under the Greenwood Tree* as 'a series of rustic sketches — Dutch paintings . . . after the manner of *Silas Marner*'. The result was that Hardy decided to set aside the rural subject he had intended for his next novel, and to experiment with *The Hand of Ethelberta*, showing that 'he did not mean to imitate anybody'.

So he wrote nearly half a century later when preparing his *Life*. At the time he seems to have forgotten what George Eliot had meant to him, and to subscribe to the current view (represented by his friend Edmund Gosse) that George Eliot was a philosopher rather than a novelist. He is on safe ground in expressing surprise that the reviewer had detected her pen in the opening chapters of *Far from the Madding Crowd*, just as he is in asserting that 'she had never touched the life of the fields', but the remainder of his comments are less reliable. The reviews of 1875 were nearer the mark, and it was for that reason that Hardy decided to postpone *The Woodlanders* story. His assessment of George Eliot's rustics and their speech is less convincing than that of a reviewer who in 1872 referred to 'the wonderful village talk which the author of "Adam Bede" has evolved out of her consciousness, and which sounds as good as if she had waited in taprooms all her life'. George Eliot's rich evocations of farm-life in that novel came from her imaginative memory; Hardy's, mainly from direct impressions. *Adam Bede* shows that rustic speech came more readily to her; Hardy's is more selective, more artfully fashioned, at times comparable to Shakespeare's. His conjecture that Positivist expressions must have been responsible for the reviewer's judgment in January 1874 is surprising; they are not noticeable in the opening chapters of *Far from the Madding Crowd*, or in the work as a whole as much as in some of his later novels; near the end (1) there is a reference to the subjective view of immortality which could have been prompted by 'O May I Join the Choir Invisible' (published in May 1874).

Adam Bede, one of the greatest immediate successes of all time, was the kind of novel Hardy's mother would have enjoyed, and one cannot imagine that he was not familiar with it long before he became anxious to succeed as a writer of fiction. This did not happen until after the rejection of *The Poor Man and the Lady* in 1869, when (following Meredith's advice) he began to consider a novel with a more complicated plot. For *Desperate Remedies* Hardy took hints from more popular writers such as Miss Braddon and Wilkie Collins, but it would have been most unlike him to neglect the works of George Eliot, the most eminent English novelist of the period. *Felix Holt* had been published in 1866. It is one of those rare novels which have tragic scenes as awe-inspiring as anything in classical drama, and Hardy could not fail to respond to the Transome story, or to such chapter epigraphs as this from the *Agamemnon* of Aeschylus: ''Tis law as stedfast as the throne of Zeus/Our days are heritors of days gone by.' *Felix Holt* may have given Hardy greater assurance in adopting a complicated criminal plot. He was probably emboldened further by George Eliot's example in rooting her tragedy in a lady's affair which leads to the anguish of concealment (and extreme bitterness of grief when her illegitimate son hardens his heart against her), for he turns a similar but more romantic complication into the mingled tragedy and villainy of Miss Aldclyffe and her illegitimate son Manston. Cognisant of hardships in the youth of his paternal grandmother, he would have been particularly susceptible to a passage on *Felix Holt* in *The Saturday Review* (which he read regularly) on 'the evil usage which women receive at the hands of men'. Miss Aldclyffe's tragedy comes to the fore in the bedroom scene at Knapwater House (VI.i), and it is here, particularly in detail, that the similarity to *Felix Holt* (xlix–l) is most remarkable, though Hardy's adaptation is more psychologically complex. Mrs Transome is a proud woman who yearns for affection; Miss Aldclyffe is a haughty, impatient woman who is overcome by long-checked feelings, and wishes to love as well as be loved. Her passion shows no lesbian propensity, but the sudden reawakening of the love she had felt for Cytherea's feather, the thwarting of which in her youth had gradually warped her nature.

The possibilities of the old village instrumental choir in Hardy's second surviving novel *Under the Greenwood Tree* may have been suggested by George Eliot's humorous reminiscence at the opening of 'Amos Barton'. Three of the choir, the wheelwright leader, the bassoon, and one of the key-bugles, appear at the Rainbow in *Silas Marner*, in a scene which had an immense influence on the development of Hardy's rustic chorus. *Silas Marner* recalls Christmas carols and the Christmas service in the country, but the great social event of the season is the dance at Squire Cass's on New Year's Eve. With Solomon the fiddler leading the procession into the White Parlour (after some preliminary flourishing and 'Sir Roger de Coverley') and social priorities being observed in the dance, we are reminded of the Christmas party at the tranter's in *Under the Greenwood Tree*. Humorous comments from observers, and details of dress, supply other parallels. Ben Winthrop's description of Mrs Osgood, tripping along with little steps as if she had wheels on her feet, recalls Hardy's Mrs Crumpler, who 'moved so smoothly through the figure that her feet were never seen', making the imaginative think that 'she rolled on castors'. John Morley's approval of the Christmas Eve pictures at the tranter's in *The Poor Man and the Lady* and high praise of his rustic humour in a review of *Desperate Remedies* had not been forgotten by Hardy. He revised the first for *Under the Greenwood Tree*, and planned his story in accordance with the reviewer's recommendation that he should give himself greater scope to present more 'consequential village worthies, and gaping village rustics', figures reminiscent of Wilkie's paintings and 'still more perhaps of those of Teniers'. This advice lent weight to the views expressed by George Eliot in *Adam Bede* (xvii), and the first effect of both may be seen in the subtitle of *Under the Greenwood Tree*, 'A Rural Painting of the Dutch School'. George Eliot's long digression on Dutch paintings continued to support Hardy in his novels, in tragic as in humorous scenes, long after he had ceased to give it conscious heed.

Would Hardy have chosen 'Far from the Madding Crowd' for the title of his fourth novel but for George Eliot? His interest in Greek drama must have made him dwell on the penultimate paragraph of her introduction to *Felix Holt*. The 'pain that is quite noiseless', 'unknown to the world' and remote from 'the roar of hurrying existence', recalls Gray's lines: 'Far from the madding crowd's ignoble strife . . . They kept the noiseless tenor of their way.' Hardy expresses George Eliot's thought when he writes in *The Woodlanders* of 'dramas of a grandeur and unity truly Sophoclean' which are enacted in 'sequestered spots outside the gates of the world'.

Other brief literary passages kindled Hardy's imagination. In the introduction to *Felix Holt* he read, about the shepherd: 'his solar system was the parish; the master's temper and the casualties of lambing-time were his region of storms'. There are events of the latter kind in Gabriel Oak's life, on Norcombe Hill and with Bathsheba at Weatherbury. Although its dimension is spatial, 'his solar system was his parish' is reminiscent of those seemingly changeless times when the uprooting of a great cider-bearing tree or the demolition of Dicky Hill's cider-house was a major event to the frequenters of Warren's malthouse; reminiscent too of a visual harmony between the shearers and the great barn that had scarcely changed for centuries. The introductory words, 'To-day the large side doors were thrown open', echo with less rousing resonance 'For the great barn-doors are thrown wide open' in *Adam Bede*, where the scene within (unlike Hardy's) is given only passing notice. The same novel presents a great harvest supper, with songs, which is altogether more realistic, though less imaginatively fused with the story, than Hardy's shearing-supper. There, as the evening wears on, the rustics grow as merry as the gods in Homer's heaven, a comparison as felicitous as bold, anticipated in *Scenes of Clerical Life* with the oak table in the housekeeper's room at Cheverel Manor, high enough for Homer's gods, and Mr Bates a latter-day Bacchus from Olympus. Passing over the harvest supper in *Far from the Madding Crowd*, Hardy presents the revels which follow, thereby confirming the realization of disaster which comes premonitorily to Bathsheba as she helps Gabriel to save her corn. A pregnant metaphor in *Adam Bede* may have sown the seed for this remarkably imaginative scene: 'and yet the time of harvest and ingathering is not come, and we tremble at the possible storms that may ruin the precious fruit in the moment of its ripeness'. The picture here is of the corn before it is harvested, but Hardy's mind was as imaginatively fertile as it was imaginatively receptive.

Tragic seduction in *Adam Bede* may obviously have helped to initiate Hardy's plot, but correspondences between the Hetty–Arthur Donnithorne–Adam Bede and the Fanny Robin–Sergeant Troy–Gabriel Oak relationships do not go far. Donnithorne is an army man like Troy, but more important is the similarity between Adam Bede and Gabriel Oak. The quality they share is epitomized in Gabriel's surname, and suggested in a description of a glimpse of the chase, the scene of Arthur and Hetty's seduction: 'Those beeches and smooth limes – there was something enervating in the very sight of them; but the strong knotted old oaks had no bending languor in them – the sight of them would give a man some energy.' 'But it is with men as with trees', George Eliot had written at the end of 'Mr Gilfil's Love-Story'. Alone, in his old age, Mr Gilfil was like a 'poor lopped oak', but he had been 'sketched out by nature as a noble tree. The heart of him was sound, the grain was of the finest'; the main trunk of his nature remained loyal to 'a first and only love'.

Perhaps nothing in George Eliot created more artistic emulation in Hardy than the Rainbow scene in *Silas Marner*. *The Saturday Review* thought it worthy of Shakespeare, and its resemblance to the Warren malthouse scenes is significant. Some of the worthies who meet at the Rainbow are closely connected with the Church, and their communicative example contributed to Hardy's inspiration in *Under the Greenwood Tree*. In *Far from the Madding Crowd* and *The Return of the Native* the role of the rustic group is extended. They are an unfailing source of humour, and help signally to create a sense of parish background. In their comments on the course of the main action, they also function more like the Greek chorus, the drift of their conversation being artfully contrived to reveal relevant portions of the past or hint at developments to come. Hardy's style and presentation are crisper and livelier than George Eliot's; he has a greater fund of humour. He was more indebted to Shakespeare, but technically, in all respects (see p. 139), he was influenced chiefly by the manner in which she introduced light relief in the Rainbow scene, and even more by her method of relating it closely to the story. The way in which her dialogue leads to its climax, with the ghostlike appearance of Silas after his loss of gold, has its nearest parallel in Hardy when Boldwood unexpectedly enters the malthouse with the letter announcing Fanny Robin's sudden departure in the hope of marrying Troy; and the artistic comparison is here much in George Eliot's favour.

This brings us to early 1875, when Hardy chose to write *The Hand of Ethelberta*, and prove that 'he did not mean to imitate anybody'. Further experimentation followed until he found his strength in *The Mayor of Casterbridge*. Hardy's novel benefited, as *The Return of the Native* had done, from his taking time to read, relax, and study artistic presentation. There seems to be little doubt that he read *The Mill on the Floss* during this period, for he quotes Novalis in words much nearer George Eliot's than the original (cf. xvii and MF.VI.vi). The maxim 'Character is Fate' applies as much to Mr Tulliver as to Henchard. A man of strong feeling, kind-hearted but rashly impulsive and rather superstitious, Tulliver is temperamentally akin to the mayor. Like him he belongs to the old rule-of-thumb world of provincial business; 'if the world had been left as God made it', he says, he could have seen his way and held his own. He trusts to luck, and takes great risks when things go wrong. *Vis-à-vis* the Dodsons he recalls the Henchard–Farfrae polarity. His natural lack of foresight, particularly when he borrows money from his enemy's client, means that he has 'a destiny as well as Oedipus', and that 'he might plead, like Oedipus, that his deed was inflicted on him rather than committed by him'; these words apply even more to Henchard. Tulliver's dependence on his 'little wench' Maggie, at the time of his downfall, is more touching than Henchard's on Elizabeth–Jane; and his curse on Wakem reminds us of the terrible imprecation dramatically produced by the unwitting choir on Farfrae. Tulliver's thirst for revenge drives him to sadistic rage; Henchard is on the brink of murder when he saves himself.

It has already been suggested that the extent and importance of a literary influence bears no relation to the magnitude of the original; a phrase may communicate a whole scene. The following notes present brief passages or incidental detail which may have influenced Hardy:

1. 'Mr Gilfil's Love-Story', iii. The image of Caterina as a bird

beating against the iron bars of the inevitable, recalling Carlyle's 'The Soul of Man . . . lacerates itself, like a captive bird, against the iron limits which Necessity has drawn round it', occurs in connection with the suffering heroine, notably in *Desperate Remedies* and *Tess of the d'Urbervilles*; see also Florence Hardy, *The Life of Thomas Hardy*, 1962, p. 171.

2. *The Mill on the Floss*, II.i. Maggie's 'I suppose it's all astronomers: because, you know, they live up in high towers, and if the women came there, they might talk and hinder them from looking at the stars' could have been the germ for the story of *Two on a Tower*.

3. *Silas Marner*, x. '. . . perhaps there was hardly a person in the parish who would not have held that to go to church every Sunday in the calendar would have shown a greedy desire to stand well with Heaven, and get an undue advantage over their neighbours'; cf. Coggan on Church and chapel people, *Far from the Madding Crowd*, xlii.

4. *Romola*, lxi. Compare the image of a whole scene presenting the heroine deprived of all hope with that of Tess, after she had sacrificed herself to Alec; Angel returns and has 'a vague consciousness . . . that his original Tess had spiritually ceased to recognize the body before him as hers — allowing it to drift, like a corpse upon the current, in a direction dissociated from its living will' (lv). See *Desperate Remedies*, XII.vi, for the creative link.

5. *Felix Holt*, ep.iii. Compare the description of Casterbridge in *The Mayor of Casterbridge*, iv and ix (opening paragraph).

6. *Middlemarch*, xxviii. The snow and low-hanging uniformity of cloud create a 'white vapour-walled landscape', and an image of almost extinguished hope; cf. *Far from the Madding Crowd*, xi, where the image is intensified.

7. ibid, xxxi, 'the crystallizing feather-touch' which 'shook flirtation into love'; cf. 'At the Word "Farewell"' (*Moments of Vision*).

8. ibid, liii, the sinister Raffles, 'an ugly black spot on the landscape' to Bulstrode; cf. Alec d'Urberville's first appearance, a 'black speck' in the distance, at Flintcomb-Ash (*Tess*, xlvi).

9. *Daniel Deronda*, xvii, girl-tragedies and dying birds in copse or hedgerow; cf. *Tess*, xli.

10. ibid, end xlv: 'If these are the sort of lovers' vows at which Jove laughs, he must have a merry time of it'; cf. the conclusion of *Tess*, 'the President of the Immortals . . . had ended his sport . . .'.

11. ibid, lvi: Gwendolen's temptation to let her loathed and dreaded husband drown, and her hesitation before she leaps into the sea in an attempt to save him; cf. 'A Tragedy of Two Ambitions' (*Life's Little Ironies*). Both stories are concerned with mercenary marriages.

12. ibid, end lvi: 'the thorn-pressure which must come with the crowning of the sorrowful Better, suffering because of the Worse'; cf. the second 'In Tenebris' poem, 'if way to the Better there be, it exacts a full look at the Worst'.

A further possibility is to be seen in J. W. Cross, *George Eliot's Life* (1885). George Eliot writes (29.xii.62): '*Caritas*, the highest love or fellowship, which I am happy to believe that no philosophy will expel from the world'; cf. *Jude the Obscure*, VI.iv, where the hero expresses his belief that the verses on charity (I. Corinthians xiii 1–13) will 'stand fast' when all that Sue calls religion has passed away.

Daniel Deronda appeared in 1876, and it seems unlikely that Hardy, who wished above all to succeed as a poet, would miss two of George Eliot's comments. Most conspicuously, in the opening paragraph of the third book, she wrote:

And perhaps poetry and romance are as plentiful as ever in the world except for those phlegmatic natures who I suspect would in any age have regarded them as a dull form of erroneous thinking. They exist very easily in the same room with the microscope and even in railway carriages: what banishes them is the vacuum in gentlemen and lady passengers.

She repeated the idea in the following book: 'Here undoubtedly lies the chief poetic energy:— in the force of imagination that pierces or exalts the solid fact, instead of floating among cloud-pictures'. In June 1877 Hardy wrote: 'There is enough poetry in what is left, after all the false romance has been abstracted, to make a sweet pattern.' The following April he cited Hobbema's method of 'infusing emotion into the baldest external objects'. His next novel was *A Laodicean*. How far, one must ask, was he stimulated by George Eliot's remark on the poetry of the microscope and railways to link his new romance with technology, including the telegraph system and such engineering triumphs as a railway tunnel? In the poem 'After a Romantic Day' he finds enough poetry of place in a railway cutting; the poetry is in the mind of the beholder, he says, as George Eliot does with reference to railway carriages. In *A Laodicean*, prefacing a romantic moment near the entrance of a railway tunnel, he writes, 'The popular commonplace that science, steam, and travel must always be unromantic and hideous, was not proven.' Many of his poems, including a number on railway subjects, illustrate what Wilkie Collins called 'the poetry of every-day truth'.

Hardy regarded George Eliot as one of the greatest thinkers of her time. They were both Positivist in sympathy, believing that the welfare of mankind depended on an enlightened altruism. Their philosophical positions were similar; each had a scientific outlook, assuming that life on earth is the only life of which one can be assured. People are too much subject to the chance of birth and circumstances. The higher aim therefore is to do everything possible for the less fortunate, for the general good, and for the generations to come. Hardy was less optimistic. In his fiction he puts the emphasis on chance (including heredity), whereas George Eliot stresses the importance of moral choice; in his later years he concluded that mankind was swayed too much by 'unreason'. Inspired by greater resolution, and in no way blinded to human shortcomings and dangers, George Eliot believed in 'the slow stupendous teaching of the world's events' and did not doubt 'the efficacy of feeling in stimulating to ardent co-operation' for humanitarian ends.

GEORGE ELIOT'S NOTES ON
'THE SPANISH GYPSY' AND TRAGEDY

The subject of 'The Spanish Gypsy' was originally suggested to me by a picture which hangs in the Scuola di San Rocco at Venice, over the door of the large Sala containing Tintoretto's frescoes. It is an Annunciation, said to be by Titian. Of course I had seen numerous pictures of this subject before, and the subject had always attracted me. But in this my second visit to the Scuola di San Rocco, this small picture of Titian's, pointed out to me for the first time, brought a new train of thought. It occurred to me that here was a great dramatic motive of the same class as those used by the Greek dramatists, yet specifically differing from them. A young maiden, believing herself to be on the eve of the chief event of her life — marriage — about to share in the ordinary lot of womanhood, full of young hope, has suddenly announced to her that she is chosen to fulfil a great destiny, entailing a terribly different experience from that of ordinary womanhood. She is chosen, not by any momentary arbitrariness, but as a result of foregoing hereditary conditions: she obeys. 'Behold the handmaid of the Lord.' Here, I thought, is a subject grander than that of Iphigenia, and it has never been used. I came home with this in my mind, meaning to give the motive a clothing in some suitable set of historical and local conditions. My reflections brought me nothing that would serve me except that moment in Spanish history when the struggle with the Moors was attaining its climax, and when there was the gypsy race present under such conditions as would enable me to get my heroine and the hereditary claim on her among the gypsies. I required the opposition of race to give the need for renouncing the expectation of marriage. I could not use the Jews or the Moors, because the facts of their history were too conspicuously opposed to the working out of my catastrophe. Meanwhile the subject had become more and more pregnant to me. I saw it might be taken as a symbol of the part which is played in the general human lot by hereditary conditions in the largest sense, and of the fact that what we call duty is entirely made up of such conditions; for even in cases of just antagonism to the narrow view of hereditary claims, the whole background of the particular struggle is made up of our inherited nature. Suppose for a moment that our conduct at great epochs was determined entirely by reflection, without the immediate intervention of feeling which supersedes reflection, our determination as to the right would consist in an adjustment of our individual needs to the dire necessities of our lot, partly as to our natural constitution, partly as sharers of life with our fellow-beings. Tragedy consists in the terrible difficulty of this adjustment –

> 'The dire strife
> Of poor Humanity's afflicted will,
> Struggling in vain with ruthless destiny.'

Looking at individual lots, I seemed to see in each the same story, wrought out with more or less of tragedy, and I determined the elements of my drama under the influence of these ideas.

In order to judge properly of the dramatic structure, it must not be considered first in the light of doctrinal symbolism, but in the light of a tragedy representing some grand collision in the human lot. And it must be judged accordingly. A good tragic subject must represent a possible, sufficiently probable, not a common action; and to be really tragic, it must represent irreparable collision between the individual and the general (in differing degrees of generality). It is the individual with whom we sympathise, and the general of which we recognise the irrestible power. The truth of this test will be seen by applying it to the greatest tragedies. The collision of Greek tragedy is often that between hereditary, entailed Nemesis, and the peculiar individual lot, awakening our sympathy, of the particular man or woman whom the Nemesis is shown to grasp with terrific force. Sometimes, as in the 'Oresteia', there is the clashing of two irreconcilable requirements – two duties, as we should say in these times. The murder of the father must be avenged by the murder of the mother, which must again be avenged. These two tragic relations of the individual and general, and of two irreconcilable 'oughts', may be – will be – seen to be almost always combined. The Greeks were not taking an artificial, entirely erroneous standpoint in their art – a standpoint which disappeared altogether with their religion and their art. They had the same essential elements of life presented to them as we have, and their art symbolised these in grand schematic forms. The Prometheus represents the ineffectual struggle to redeem the small and miserable race of man, against the stronger adverse ordinances that govern the frame of things with a triumphant power. Coming to modern tragedies, what is it that makes

'Othello' a great tragic subject? A story simply of a jealous husband is elevated into a most pathetic tragedy by the hereditary conditions of Othello's lot, which give him a subjective ground for distrust. Faust, Rigoletto ('Le Roi s'Amuse'), Brutus. It might be a reasonable ground of objection against the whole structure of 'The Spanish Gypsy' if it were shown that the action is outrageously improbable — lying outside all that can be congruously conceived of human actions. It is *not* a reasonable ground of objection that they would have done better to act otherwise, any more than it is a reasonable objection against the 'Iphigenia' that Agamemnon would have done better not to sacrifice his daughter.

As renunciations coming under the same great class, take the renunciation of marriage, where marriage cannot take place without entailing misery on the children.

A tragedy has not to expound why the individual must give way to the general: it has to show that it is compelled to give way, the tragedy consisting in the struggle involved, and often in the entirely calamitous issue in spite of a grand submission. Silva presents the tragedy of entire rebellion: Fedalma of a grand submission, which is rendered vain by the effects of Silva's rebellion: Zarca, the struggle for a great end, rendered vain by the surrounding conditions of life.

Now, what is the fact about our individual lots? A woman, say, finds herself on the earth with an inherited organisation: she may be lame, she may inherit a disease, or what is tantamount to a disease: she may be a negress, or have other marks of race repulsive in the community where she is born, &c., &c. One may go on for a long while without reaching the limits of the commonest inherited misfortunes. It is almost a mockery to say to such human beings, 'Seek your own happiness.' The utmost approach to well-being that can be made in such a case is through large resignation and acceptance of the inevitable, with as much effort to overcome any disadvantage as good sense will show to be attended with a likelihood of success. Any one may say, that is the dictate of mere rational reflection. But calm can, in hardly any human organism, be attained by rational reflection. Happily we are not left to that. Love, pity, constituting sympathy, and generous joy with regard to the lot of our fellowmen, comes in — has been growing since the beginning — enormously enhanced by wider vision of results — by an imagination actively interested in the lot of mankind generally; and these feelings become piety — i.e., loving, willing submission, and heroic Promethean effort towards high possibilities, which may result from our individual life.

There is really no moral 'sanction' but this inward impulse. The will of God is the same thing as the will of other men, compelling us to work and avoid what they have seen to be harmful to social existence. Disjoined from any perceived good, the divine will is simply so much as we have ascertained of the facts of existence which compel obedience at our peril. Any other notion comes from the supposition of arbitrary revelation.

That favourite view, expressed so often in Clough's poems, of doing duty in blindness as to the result, is likely to deepen the substitution of egoistic yearnings for really moral impulses. We cannot be utterly blind to the results of duty, since that cannot be duty which is not already judged to be for human good. To say the contrary, is to say that mankind have reached no inductions as to what is for their good or evil.

The art which leaves the soul in despair is laming to the soul, and is denounced by the healthy sentiment of an active community. The consolatory elements in 'The Spanish Gypsy' are derived from two convictions or sentiments which so conspicuously pervade it, that they may be said to be its very warp on which the whole action is woven. These are − (1) The importance of individual deeds; (2) The all-sufficiency of the soul's passions in determining sympathetic action.

In Silva is presented the claim of fidelity to social pledges; in Fedalma, the claim constituted by an hereditary lot less consciously shared.

With regard to the supremacy of Love: it it were a fact without exception that man or woman never did renounce the joys of love, there could never have sprung up a notion that such renunciation could present itself as a duty. If no parents had ever cared for their children, how could parental affection have been reckoned among the elements of life? But what are the facts in relation to this matter? Will any one say that faithfulness to the marriage tie has never been regarded as a duty, in spite of the presence of the profoundest passion experienced after marriage? Is Guinevere's conduct the type of duty?

(from J. W. Cross, *George Eliot's Life*)

A KEY TO PEOPLE AND PLACES
IN GEORGE ELIOT'S FICTION

It should not be assumed that identifications are precise, although people in and near Nuneaton had no difficulty in recognising characters in *Scenes of Clerical Life* from their positions, if not from other characteristics. George Eliot was an imaginative writer, and anything she drew from reality was partial rather than photographic. She admitted that there were two modified portraits in *Scenes from Clerical Life* (see BARTON and DEMPSTER), but her general principles are indicated in what she says about *Adam Bede*, after stating that it could never have been written had she not known something about her father's early life: 'There is not a single portrait in the book, nor will there be in any future book of mine' (27.vi.59). 'The whole course of the story . . . the descriptions of scenery or houses – the characters . . . *everything* is a combination from widely sundered elements of experience' (19.ix.59).

Charles S. Olcott in *George Eliot, Scenes and People in her Novels*, London, 1911, gives local and contemporary identifications which he discovered in copies of *Scenes of Clerical Life*. Only the most consistent of these have been included.

ABBOT'S TOPPING = MONK'S TOPPING = TOPPING ABBEY (DD): partly from Lacock Abbey, Wiltshire, which GE visited in 1874.

ASSHER, Lady (SCL2): Lady Anstruther, mother of Jane who married Charles Parker (BEATRICE ASSHER and CAPTAIN WYBROW).

BAIRD, Mr (SCL1): Revd G. W. Sanford, Weddington, near Nuneaton.

BARTON, Amos (SCL1): Revd John Gwyther, Chilvers Coton; m. Emma (original of MILLY BARTON), who died at Chilvers Coton in 1836, leaving seven children. Amos 'is made a much better man than he really was, and far more unimpeachable in conduct', GE wrote (19.ix.59).

BATES, Mr (SCL2): Mr Baines, gardener at Arbury Hall. His cottage stood in a part of the grounds known as the MOSSLANDS: Swanlands.

BEDE, Adam: Robert Evans, GE's father.

BEDE, Seth: Samuel Evans, GE's uncle.

BINTON HILLS (AB): Weaver Hills, north of Ellastone, Staffs.

BRASSING (M): Birmingham.

BRIDMAIN, Mr (SCL1): half-brother of the Countess CZERLASKI. In a letter to the editor of *Blackwood's Magazine* (13.vi.59), the Revd J. Gwyther (see BARTON) refers to the Countess and her 'professed Father' (*sic*), the Revd Sir John Waldron. This identification is confirmed by Olcott.

BROOKE, Celia (M): Christiana, GE's sister.

BROOKE, Dorothea (M): Mary A. Evans (GE). Her plan for building workers' cottages was suggested by Harriet Martineau's Building Society scheme at Ambleside (see p. 22).

BROOKE, Mr (M): Professor Haight identifies him with Charles H. Bracebridge, a magistrate of Atherstone who dabbled in many things, and took up the cause of Liggins (p. 29), after annoying his wife's friend Florence Nightingale by the tactless ineptitude of his remarks on the Army in the Crimea during a lecture given at Coventry; see Cecil Woodham-Smith, *Florence Nightingale*, London, 1951, pp. 230–1.

BROXTON (AB): named after Roston, near Ellastone.

BUDD, Mr, the churchwarden (SCL3): Mr Burton (Olcott).

CARPE, Mr (SCL1): Revd George Hake, vicar of Chilvers Coton (1829–44), who held livings at Rocester and Ellastone, Staffs. (all Newdigate appointments).

CASAUBON, Revd Edward (M): Dr Brabant (see p. 17). For the name, see p. 219. The Yew-Tree Walk, the summer-house at the end of it, and the stone table at which he died were all remembered from the Griff House garden.

CATERINA (SCL2): See SARTI.

CHEVEREL, Sir Anthony (SCL2): Sir Richard Newdigate, 1st Bart.

CHEVEREL, Sir Christopher (SCL2): Sir Roger Newdigate (1719–1806. Lady HENRIETTA: his second wife, Hester Margaretta, Lady Newdigate.

CHEVEREL MANOR (SCL2): Arbury Hall, rebuilt in Gothic style by Sir Roger Newdigate. The motto over the fireplace in the house-keeper's room runs, 'Truste in God, and feare him with al thy harte.'

CLEVES, Revd Martin (SCL1): Revd J. Fisher, rector of Calde-cote and Higham, near Nuneaton.

CREWE, Mr (SCL3): Revd Hugh Hughes (d. 1830), curate of Nuneaton and head of the Grammar School.

CZERLASKI, Countess (SCL1): 'The affair of the "Countess" was never fully known to me: so far as it *was* known, it is varied from my knowledge of the alleged fact', GE wrote (19.ix.59). Olcott gives 'Countess Isabel'. See BRIDMAIN.

DEANE, Lucy (MF): Christiana, GE's sister.

DEANE, Mrs Susan (MF): Ann, GE's maternal aunt, wife of George Garner of Sole End.

DEMPSTER, Mrs Janet (SCL3): the wife of J. W. Buchanan, a lawyer of Nuneaton. The lived in Church Street, opposite where the public library now stands. GE stated that 'the real Dempster was far more disgusting than mine'. Mrs Buchanan was the daughter of Mrs Wallington (p. 9). See also p. 13.

DERONDA, Daniel: thought to be drawn from Edmund Gurney, whom GE met at Trinity College, Cambridge, in 1873.

DONNITHORNE ARMS (AB): originally the Bromley Davenport Arms, Ellastone, kept by an Evans, a cousin of GE.

DONNITHORNE CHASE (AB): Wootton Hall (now demolished) just north of Ellastone, the estate of Francis Parker Newdigate, who employed Robert Evans first as forester and then as bailiff. GE depended on her father's reminiscences, but the woodland scenes owe much to her recollections of the Arbury Hall estate.

DORLCOTE MILL (MF): based on GE's childhood memories of Arbury Mill, though imagined on the Idle near its confluence with the Trent north of Gainsborough. The attics were remembered from Griff House.

EAGLEDALE (AB): Dovedale, though the distance from Hayslope which is given (xx) is misleading.

ELY, Mr (SCL1): Revd W. H. King, who succeeded the Revd H. Hughes (CREWE) as curate of Nuneaton.

FARQUHAR, Mr (SCL1): Squire Harpur of Caldwell Hall, Nuneaton.

FELLOWES, Mr (SCL1): Revd H. Bellairs, Bedworth.

FITCHETT, Mr (SCL1): Mr Baker, the verger (Olcott).

FURNESS, Mr (SCL1) has been identified with the Revd W. S. Bucknill, vicar of Burton Hastings, near Nuneaton, though he is represented as unbeneficed.

GARTH, Caleb (M): Robert Evans, GE's father.

GARUM FIRS (MF): Marston Hall, Bulkington, where GE's aunt Elizabeth (Mrs Richard Johnson) lived.

GILFIL, Revd Maynard (SCL2): Revd Bernard Gilpin Ebdell, vicar of Chilvers Coton, 1786–1828, incumbent of Astley, 1789–1828, and chaplain at Arbury Hall. He married GE's parents at Astley.

GLEGG, Mrs Jane (MF): Mary, GE's maternal aunt, wife of John Evarard of Attleborough.

GUEST, Stephen (MF): from John Chapman (?).

HACKIT, Mr and Mrs (SCL1, SCL2): Mr and Mrs Robert Evans, GE's parents.

HALL FARM (AB): largely from recollections of Griff House, though the stone lionesses surmounting the entrance pillars were suggested by the griffins at the entrance to Corley Hall.

HALM-EBERSTEIN, Princess (DD): Her dislike of her race and lack of affection for her son may be drawn from Benjamin Disraeli's grandmother; see the memoir which he wrote for the 1849 edition of his father Isaac's *Curiosities of Literature*.

HAYSLOPE (AB): Ellastone, Staffs. See pp. 4–5.

JAKIN, Bob (MF): William Jaques, who attended the dame school at Griff with Mary Evans (GE).

JEROME, Mr (SCL3): Mr John Evarard of Attleborough, GE's uncle.

KLESMER, Herr Julius (DD): Mainly imaginary. The general impression is that he is drawn from Liszt (see p. 25), although GE writes (xxii): 'Klesmer was not yet a Liszt, understood to be adored by ladies of all European countries with the exception of Lapland.' Professor Haight suggests Anton Rubinstein; Marghanita Laski, Joseph Joachim.

KNEBLEY (SCL1, SCL2): Astley. KNEBLEY ABBEY (SCL2): Astley Castle, near the church.

LACEHAM (MF): Nottingham, noted for its lace.

LANDOR, Ben (SCL3): William Craddock.

LADISLAW (M): There seems to be no evidence for the common assumption that he is based on G. H. Lewes.

LINNET, Mrs (SCL3): Mrs Hill. MARY and REBECCA: Mrs Hill's daughters.

LOAMFORD (FH) is an imaginary Midland town.

LOAMSHIRE (AB): Staffordshire; (M.i) a fertile region in the Midlands.

LOWME, Mr (SCL3): Mr Towle (Olcott).

LYON, Revd Rufus (FH): Revd F. Franklin, Coventry (pp. 9–10). Like Rufus Lyon, he had 'little legs and a large head'; like Esther Lyon, his daughter Rebecca had spent a year in Paris. The Independent Chapel was suggested by his Baptist Chapel in Cow Lane.

MASSEY, Bartle (AB): Bartle Massey, who kept the night-school near Norbury which Robert Evans attended.

MIDDLEMARCH: Coventry to some extent. See pp. 182–3.

MILBY (SCL): Nuneaton; the name alludes to the flour-mill which stood near the centre of the town. The Bear and Ragged Staff takes its name from the coat of arms of the Earl of Warwick. The Red Lion is the Bull Hotel. Orchard Street is Church Street.

MORDECAI (DD): His only resemblance to the watchmater Cohn or Kohn whom G. H. Lewes met at the Philosophers Club in Red Lion Square (cf. xlii) is that he consumptive.

MORRIS, Dinah (AB): Elizabeth Evans, GE's aunt. See pp. 13 and 92.

NELLO (R): from Domenico Burchiello, barber and poet, half a century before the period of the novel. The description of his shop is taken from a picture in the Medici Gallery (Olcott).

NORBURNE (AB): named after Norbury, near Ellastone.

OAKBOURNE (AB): GE's place-names for the area around HAYSLOPE are deliberately misleading. Occasionally Ashbourne, Derbyshire, is intended. See TREDDLESTON.

OLDINPORT, Mr (SCL1): Charles Newdigate Newdegate, who succeeded at Arbury Hall in 1835 and died unmarried in 1887. The Newdigates have long been patrons of Chilvers Coton Church. (SCL2): Francis Parker Newdigate, who succeeded to the Arbury estate in 1806. 'Oldinport' partly from the French usage of *porte* = gate.

OLDINPORT ARMS (SCL2): Newdegate Arms, Nuneaton.

PADDIFORD COMMON (SCL3): Stockingford, near Nuneaton.

PATTEN, Mrs (SCL1, SCL2): Mrs Hutchings or Hutchins.

PETTIFER, Mrs (SCL3): Mrs John Robinson.

PHIPPS, Mr and Mrs (SCL3): Mr and Mrs Bull.

PILGRIM, Mr (SCL): Mr Bucknill, a Nuneaton surgeon, who attended GE's father, and 'blooded' him several times, and set 'six or seven dozen of leeches' about his kidneys on 3 January 1836. See p. 10.

PITTMAN, Mr, an old lawyer (SCL3): Mr Greenway (Olcott).

POYSER, Mrs Rachel (AB): to some extent from GE's mother.

PRATT, Mr Richard, a Milby doctor (SCL3): Mr Bond (Olcott).

PRENDERGAST, the Hon. and Revd Mr (SCL3): the Hon. and Revd R. B. Stopford, non-resident vicar of Nuneaton.

PULLET, Mrs Sophy (MF): Elizabeth, GE's aunt, wife of Richard Johnson of Marston Jabbett. See GARUM FIRS.

RAVELOE (SM): GE informed Walter Skeat that the district 'imagined' was in north Warwickshire. Bulkington, south-east of Nuneaton, has been suggested. The Rainbow was named after an inn at Allesley, near Coventry.

RED DEEPS (MF): Griff Hollows (transferred to Lincolnshire).

ROSSETER (AB): named after Rocester near Ellastone, Staffs.

ROTHERBY (SCL) = ROTHEBY (SCL2): Coventry.

ST OGG'S (MF): Gainsborough on the Trent (the 'Floss'). The tidal wave, or 'eagre', reaches the town. George Eliot had no time to examine the Old Hall, most of the features of which are taken from St Mary's Guildhall, Coventry.

SARTI, Caterina (SCL2): Sarah Shilton, a local miner's daughter with a beautiful voice, who was trained at Arbury Hall by Dominico Motta, the music tutor of Hester, Lady Newdigate (see CHEVEREL). In 1801 she married the Revd B. G. Ebdell (see GILFIL), with whom she lived many years.

SHEPPERTON (SCL1): Chilvers Coton. GE attended the church and was baptized there. The choir instrumentalists will be found at Hayslope (AB.xviii) and, with the leading singer, at Raveloe (SM.vi). The workhouse called 'the College' had been provided by Sir Roger Newdigate and built by French prisoners-of-war. 'The Jolly Colliers' was the name of an inn in the neighbourhood. 'Shepperton' is referred to by GE in *Adam Bede* (xvii).

SNOWFIELD (AB): Wirksworth, Derbyshire, where GE's aunt Elizabeth Evans lived. As a result of the ban imposed on women preachers, she left Derby with her husband Samuel in 1814, and founded an Arminian Methodist church at Wirksworth.

SORREL, Hetty (AB): See p. 13 and pp. 96–7.

SPRATT, Mr (SCL1): Mr Hackett (Olcott).

SPROXTON (FH): the Griff–Chilvers Coton area; see p. 50.

STONITON (AB): Derby, the county town of STONYSHIRE. The Court Room (xliii) suggests a recollection of St Mary's Guildhall, Coventry.

TOMLINSON, Mr, a rich miller (SCL3): Mr Hinks (Olcott).

TREBY MAGNA (FH): largely typical and imaginary. The surroundings (see p. 51) suggest Coventry; see Rufus LYON. The election riot was based on one GE remembered at Nuneaton in December 1832, when the Scots Greys were called in, and one man died of injuries. See SPROXTON.

TREDDLESTON (AB): Suggests Ashbourne, if any particular place; see OAKBOURNE. GE denied that it was Ellastone (19.ix.59).

TRIPPLEGATE (SCL1): Higham, near Nuneaton (Olcott).

TRYAN, Revd Edgar (SCL3): Though an idealized character, and 'not a portrait' (GE), his story is based on the work of the Revd J. E. Jones of Stockingford, Nuneaton. He was 'persecuted', especially in 1829, for his Evangelical zeal, and died in 1831, after a long illness, at the age of 34.

TULLIVER, Edward (MF): His affection for Maggie recalls that of Robert Evans for the author in her early years. It has been claimed that his irascible temper and litigious proneness were drawn from Tom Hollick, a farmer and miller of Nuneaton.

TULLIVER, Maggie (MF): Though some of the events in her childhood, and the influence of Thomas à Kempis, are based on GE's recollections, it is misleading to hold, as many do, that she is autobiographical.

TULLIVER, Tom (MF): Some incidents in his childhood, and his relationship with Maggie, are based on GE's recollections of her brother Isaac. Tom's unrelenting intransigence towards her (when compromised in love) reflects Isaac's rejection of GE and his refusal to recognise her as the wife of G. H. Lewes.

WAKEM, Philip (MF): Francois D'Albert Durade, 'not more than 4 feet high with a deformed spine' (GE). Cultured like Philip, and a painter; see p. 20.

WHARF, the (SCL2): probably the Wharf Inn in Chilvers Coton, by the bridge over the Coventry Canal.

WYBROW, Captain Anthony (SCL2): He resembles Charles Parker, nephew and heir of Sir Roger Newdigate, only in his appearance and sudden death.

GLOSSARY

adust, in a dusty state
allays, always
along of, because of
arter, after
as, who
atween, between
avised, reflected, considered

bandy, game similar to hockey
bang, Indian hemp
bashaw, grandee
baste, soak, smear (culinary)
bents, grassland *or* grass stalks
blackleg, sharper
(put o') board, (reduced to) subsistence level, enough to pay for board and lodging
Bösewicht, scoundrel
brinin', burning (probably the weeds before sowing)
briny, brainy
Brummagem, counterfeit
by, bye, boy

cade, (of the young of animals) brought up by hand
calender, mendicant dervish
call, reason
chany, china
cheapen, bargain over
chop in, thrust, cut across
Chuppa, velvet canopy held over bride and bridegroom in the Jewish marriage ceremony
clemmed, starved
cochon de lait, sucking-pig
colly, blacken
come over, dupe, outwit
comparse, supernumerary
confetti, sweets, sweetmeats
contadina, country woman
coxy, cocky, impudent
crack, boast, brag
creachy, creechy, feeble, sickly
cunning, wits, comprehension

da capo, over again

dagged, wet, muddied, bedraggled
dee'd, d − d, damned
démangeaison, itch
ding, strike
do, cheat
done, defeated
doubt, fear
douse, extinguish
dratchell, slattern
dredged, sprinkled
drench, administer a draught of medicine (to animal)
duree, tureen

ear'n, ears
emissary, foreign agent or spy
energumen, one possessed by the devil, fanatic
enow, enough
estimate, esteem

fain an', very ('fine and')
a fain sight, much, far ('a fine sight')
fancy, boxing, the ring
fast, quite
fat, fop, puppy
fawst enough, readily
feckins, i' faith, truly (i' faikins)
fence, defence, self-justification
fend, make shift, manage
finger-poasses, handposts (giving road directions)
flat, simpleton
flush, liberal, lavish
follyer, man who courts a maidservant (follower)
for all, although
forrard, bring forward, make earlier
franzy, passion, temper; bad-tempered, difficult to manage
friggling, trifling, fiddling, tiresome

gallowsness, wickedness
gammon, nonsense
geck, simpleton
Geistlicher, clergyman
gen, gev, gave, given

gird at, scold
go, single measure
gun-cases, trousers (jocular)

haft, handle
happen, perhaps
hile, oil
hing, hang
hobble, awkward situation, fix

ill-favoured, ugly
indifferent, neutral, disinterested
istid, instead

jack (run down like a), topple, plummet
jaw, talk to
jockey, horse-dealer

Kaddish, the Jewish daily prayer
kettle-cake, cake baked under a pot or 'kettle'
kittle cattle, difficult person(s) to manage

laches, negligence
leather, beat
leggio, reading-desk
lief, lieve, willingly, gladly
loobies, louts, bumpkins
low, common, vulgar
lucco, robe, gown
lungeous, rough-mannered

makdom, form, figure
marl, marble
marranos, term of contempt used by Spanish Jews for Jews who had become Christians
mawkin, scarecrow
mazarine, deep blue
meat, food
megrims, whims
modus, a form of payment in lieu of tithe
moithered, bothered, worried
mummy, pulpy mass
mun, must
mushed, crushed, depressed

nash, see nesh
natter, nag
natty, neat, spruce
nécessaire, lady's dressing-case
nesh, soft, delicate
nodus, tricky problem
nor, than
nor common, than usual
notomize, (anatomy), skeleton
nullifidian, sceptic

offal, disreputable, worthless
opodeldoc, kind of soap liniment
ouzel, blackbird
overrun, run away from, desert

paletot, short overcoat
palio, prize for the race
passill, lot, load (parcel)
patrigno, father-in-law
pazzarella, little madcap
peaky, sharp, thin
perkises, tips, extras
person, figure
pfuscherei, a mess
piert, lively
platter, plate
pluck, fail (a person) in an examination
plumper, a vote given to only one candidate when one has two or more votes
point device, quite perfect, just so
poke, poke-bonnet
porte cochère, gateway, carriage entrance
puck, picked
pull up, stop

Quaresima, Lent
quarter, drive to the side of the road to let a vehicle pass
queechy, weak
quiz, make fun of

raff, rubbish
ragazza, girl
raker, large lump of coal for keeping the fire in all night

rare, fine, splendid
receipt, recipe
rigattiere, second-hand dealer
roll, impose on, 'push round'
runt, undersized horse or cow

sachem, leader, chief
sallet, salad
san-benito, garment worn by a confessed and penitent heretic (Spanish Inquisition)
sawder, see soft sawder
sawney, fool
sbirro, policeman
scarsella, purse
scatheless, unharmed
score, reckon what is owed
scrat, cultivate lightly, struggle to make money, 'scrape'
scratter, scratcher
scratchins, residue of pork fat after rendering lard
scraze, scratch or graze (a surface)
set-down, scolding
shear-hog, lamb after the first shearing, yearling
Shool, synagogue
shophar, curved ram's horn used as a musical instrument by the Jews to express God's power
shying, hurling a missile
slack-baked, underdone, doughy
snap, snack
sniff, snaff, to answer 'snaff' to 'sniff' = to consent (especially in courting)
soft sawder, blarney
souse, use for dashing, or bathing with, water
spooney, foolish, simple
springe, nimble
stattits, statutes, hiring fairs

statty, statue
stirring-cup, parting drink
stockinger, stocking-weaver
stret, straitened, badly off
sweltered, overcome with the heat (sometimes fatally)

tackled, hitched, married
take, holding (of land)
tale, amount
tatchy, touchy, irritable, peevish
taters, potatoes
tea-board, tea-tray
tentin', watching, looking after
thack, thatch
a that'n, in that way
thralls, stands or frames for milk-pans
thrums, waste ends from weaving
tight, neat
toodlin', singing
torpedo, cramp-fish
tracking, delivering religious tracts
trimming, turning this way or that according to self-interest (politics)

underhung, having a projecting under-jaw
unstring, open one's purse
urchin, hedgehog

vally, value

waternixie, water nymph
weeds, clothes (generally for mourning)
well-favoured, handsome
welly, well-nigh
withe, withy, willow
working-day, workaday, ordinary

yarbs, herbs

SELECT BIBLIOGRAPHY

Works

Cabinet Edition (20 vols.), Edinburgh and London, 1877–80.

Fiction, with introductions and notes: some in the Riverside Editions, more in the Penguin English Library. Standard texts are being prepared for the Oxford University Press; the first two volumes (*The Mill on the Floss*, ed. Gordon S. Haight, and *Felix Holt*, ed. F. C. Thomson) are expected in 1980.

Thomas Pinney (ed.), *Essays of George Eliot*, London, 1963. Contains the most important of the early essays and reviews, with 'Address to Working Men, by Felix Holt', and 'Leaves from a Note-Book'.

Letters

Gordon S. Haight (ed.), *The George Eliot Letters*, New Haven and Oxford, vols. I–III, 1954; IV–VII, 1957; VIII–IX supplementary), New Haven and London, 1978.

Biography

J. W. Cross, *George Eliot's Life*, London, Edinburgh, New York, 1885. Whatever its omissions, it has the great virtue of including most of the important passages from GE's letters and journals, and of making them readily accessible.

Gordon S. Haight, *George Eliot, A Biography*, New York and Oxford, 1968. The most authoritative and informed of GE biographies. Now available in paperback.

Rosemary Sprague, *George Eliot, A Biography*, Philadelphia, New York, London, 1968. More general and introductory.

Marghanita Laski, *George Eliot and her World*, London, 1973. Pictorial summary.

Major Critical Studies

Gerald Bullett, *George Eliot: Her Life and Books*, London, 1947.

Joan Bennett, *George Eliot: Her Mind and Art*, Cambridge, 1948.
Barbara Hardy, *The Novels of George Eliot: A Study in Form*, London, 1959.
Jerome Thale, *The Novels of George Eliot*, New York, 1959.
W. J. Harvey, *The Art of George Eliot*, London, 1961.
T. A. Noble, *George Eliot's 'Scenes of Clerical Life'*, New Haven and London, 1965.
Bernard J. Paris, *Experiments in Life: George Eliot's Quest for Values*, Detroit, 1965.
Henry Auster, *Local Habitations: Regionalism in the Early Novels of George Eliot*, Cambridge, Mass., 1970.
Neil Roberts, *George Eliot: Her Beliefs and Art*, London, 1975.
Hugh Witemeyer, *George Eliot and the Visual Arts*, New Haven and London, 1979. A specialized but revealing study.

See also:

F. R. Leavis, *The Great Tradition*, London and New York, 1948; Pelican, 1972.
Basil Willey, *Nineteenth Century Studies*, London, 1955. On the thought and influence of Hennell, Strauss, and Feuerbach.
David Daiches, *George Eliot: Middlemarch*, London, 1963.
Patricia Beer, *Reader, I Married Him*, London, 1974.
T. B. Tomlinson, *The English Middle-Class Novel*, London, 1976.

Critical Essays

Edward Dowden, '*Middlemarch* and *Daniel Deronda*', *The Contemporary Review*, February, 1877.
Quentin Anderson, 'George Eliot in *Middlemarch*', *The Pelican Guide to English Literature*, vol. 6, 1958.
George Levine, 'Determinism and Responsibility in the Works of George Eliot', *PMLA*, June 1962.
David R. Carroll, '*Silas Marner*: Reversing the Oracles of Religion'. This essay and the next in E. Rothstein and T. K. Dunseath (edd.), *Literary Monographs*, vol. 1, Madison, Milwaukee, London, 1967.
Albert R. Cirillo, 'Salvation in *Daniel Deronda*: The Fortunate Overthrow of Gwendolen Harleth' (see above).

Derek Oldfield, 'The Language of the Novel: The Character of Dorothea', *Middlemarch: Critical Approaches to the Novel* (ed. Barbara Hardy), London, 1967.

U. C. Knoepflmacher, '*Middlemarch*: Affirmation through Compromise', in his *Laughter and Despair: Readings in Ten Novels of the Victorian Era*, Berkeley, Los Angeles, London, 1971.

Collections:

Gordon S. Haight (ed.), *A Century of George Eliot Criticism*, New York, 1965; London, 1966.

Barbara Hardy (ed.), *Critical Essays on George Eliot*, London, 1970.

David R. Carroll (ed.), *George Eliot: The Critical Heritage*, London, 1971.

William Baker (ed.), *Critics on George Eliot*, London, 1973.

Index

Index